LYNCHBURG COLLEGE LIBRARY

WITHDRAWN

STUDIES IN HISTORY, ECONOMICS, AND PUBLIC LAW

EDITED BY THE FACULTY OF POLITICAL SCIENCE
OF COLUMBIA UNIVERSITY

Number 380

SHORTER HOURS

A Study of the Movement
Since the Civil War

SHORTER HOURS

A STUDY OF THE MOVEMENT SINCE THE CIVIL WAR

BY

MARION COTTER CAHILL

AMS PRESS
NEW YORK

COLUMBIA UNIVERSITY
STUDIES IN THE
SOCIAL SCIENCES
380

The series was formerly known as *Studies in History, Economics and Public Law.*

Reprinted with the permission of Columbia University Press
From the edition of 1932, New York
First AMS EDITION published 1968
Manufactured in the United States of America

Library of Congress Catalog Number: 68-54258
International Standard Book Number:
  Complete Set. . . . 0-404-51000-0
  Number 380 0-404-51380-8

AMS PRESS, INC.
New York, N.Y. 10003

PREFACE

THE object of this study is to present a historical survey of the methods by which hours have been shortened in the United States since the Civil War. The writer had long been interested in the problem resulting from the combination of rapid and tremendous increase in the productivity of labor, and great inequalities of distribution of income. Conservative labor had two solutions: shorter hours and restriction of output—the one preached openly, the other practiced only covertly. The attention which the depression of 1929 onwards focused on the former solution, the presentation on the one hand of the ineffectual but insistent demands of labor for a radical reduction of working hours, and on the other hand of publicized statements of prominent industrial leaders urging a shorter-hour standard, created a desire to know what was the background of the situation. As the period of depression lengthened, and the amount of action in the direction of establishing a new standard became ever more negligible, this desire crystallized into the determination to find out how hours had been lessened in the past, when the viewpoints of the two antagonists were even further apart than during the present impasse. With this knowledge it should be possible to estimate the chances for a reduction of hours in the present if labor, the intellectuals, and a few leading industrialists—providing their publicized statements are sincere—are correct in interpreting one need of the times.

The historical approach is used in this study. The more direct means of decreasing hours have been legislative action, trade-union action, and voluntary action initiated by the employer. Hours have been shortened, also, as a result of more general influences, economic and social conditions having played an important part. Conditions favoring the adoption of shorter hours for labor not directly affected by the above three means have been: business prosperity, improved machinery, more efficient management, and a new attitude toward leisure. These indirect influences, however, are so general and so interrelated that it is impossible to trace their effect in detail. This study, therefore, is limited to the three immediate means by which hours have been shortened. A chronological account of the reduction of hours by each of these methods is given. Naturally they overlap, and interact on each other. No one method was used at any one time to the exclusion of the other two, but at times any one was subject to greater emphasis, and its failure or success determined the swing of the pendulum away from or toward this method. Of course, in surveying the methods by which hours were reduced in the past, it is obviously necessary to mention the number of hours toward which the work-day or work-week was declining. Consequently tables of hours as fixed by law and by trade unions and in unorganized trades have been placed in appendices and references in the text are made to them. The study, however, has been concentrated on the means which gained the reduction, rather than on the amount of the reduction itself.

The scope of the study has been limited as to time, and as to the inclusiveness of the term "the shorter-hour movement." The period covered extends from the Civil War to the present. The former date is a logical starting point, because the return of the soldiers to civilian status, by raising the spectre of unemployment, caused an active revival of the shorter-hour movement which, after the moderately successful struggle of the mechanics for the ten-hour day in the forties, had dragged on in the pre-war period in an undramatic manner. The term "shorter-hour movement" has been limited to mean the movement for a smaller number of daily or weekly hours for laborers, although in its broadest aspects the term includes as distinct and separate tendencies: the movement for one day of rest in seven, the Saturday half-holiday struggle, the effort to eliminate over-time, and the growing custom of vacations with pay. Insofar as any of these bear directly on a standard of reduced daily or weekly hours, they have been included: beyond that, they are left for a further study. To speak of the eight-hour movement as has been done since 1865, or the five-day week or six-hour movement as is done at present, is confusing inasmuch as it puts undue emphasis on the hopes of the organized few, rather than on a rational expectation for the great majority.

TABLE OF CONTENTS

PAGE

PREFACE 5

CHAPTER I
SUMMARY AND CONCLUSIONS 11

PART I
REDUCTION OF HOURS BY LEGISLATION

CHAPTER II
ATTITUDE OF LABOR AND EMPLOYERS

Labor. 31
    Early Labor Associations 31
    Knights of Labor 40
    American Federation of Labor. 48
Employers 58

CHAPTER III
NATIONAL LEGISLATION

Government Work 68
Railroad Employees. 82
Seamen. 91
Summary. 93

CHAPTER IV
STATE LEGISLATION

Early General Laws. 95
Laws for Special Classes. 98
    Government Work 98
    Women. 106
    Hazardous Work 116
Late General Laws 128

PART II
REDUCTION OF HOURS BY TRADE UNIONS

CHAPTER V
DIRECT ACTION

Early Efforts, 1865-1886. 138
American Federation of Labor. 152

CHAPTER VI
DIRECT ACTION: TYPE CASES

A Trade Union—International Typographical Union 172
An Industrial Union—Amalgamated Clothing Workers. 189
An Unorganized Industry—Steel 206
Summary. 216

PART III
REDUCTION OF HOURS BY EMPLOYERS

CHAPTER VII
VOLUNTARY ACTION OF EMPLOYERS 221

APPENDICES A-I. 261
BIBLIOGRAPHY 289
INDEX 295

CHAPTER I

SUMMARY AND CONCLUSIONS

REDUCTION of hours has been one of the two major demands of labor in the United States. It might have been expected, perhaps, that the struggle to shorten hours would have passed through distinct phases, characterized by special attributes, and by moments of tremendous dramatic appeal. This, however, has not been the case. The movement has been, instead, a constant, dogged, frequently hopeless insistence by one great part of society on the need for a shorter day in the face of an equally determined resistance by a smaller part to every suggestion for immediate change. While the greatest success has been achieved in periods of business prosperity, when labor has been in a strong bargaining position, Appendix H shows that there has been a steady annual decrease. This can be explained in part by the enactment of new or improved laws by States, stimulated by the example of pioneer States, and in part by less direct forces, as favoring conditions in certain industries or the influence of example on progressive employers.

The magnetic influence which the demand for shorter hours exerted on the labor movement in the post-Civil War period of the nineteenth century is evident. In the first place, it was the demand for the eight-hour day which led to the formation of the first national labor organization in America, the National Labor Union, which, founded in 1866, shortly attained the astonishingly large membership of 640,000. Likewise, shorter hours were an important factor in the growth of the American Federation of Labor in its early period. In the words of the Report of the Industrial Commission, made at the close of the nineteenth century, "The general drift of opinion among American trade unionists is strongly in the direction of emphasizing the importance of a shorter work-day. The most progressive leaders . . . are constantly urging their associates to put the shorter work-day in the forefront of their demands."

The titanic proportions that strikes which were predominantly for shorter hours—on the part of the Machinists in 1901, the Printers in 1906, the New England Textile Workers in 1922, to mention only a few—attained in the twentieth century attest the continued importance of this question.

That labor is intensely aware of the greater need for shorter hours today as the result of the tremendous pace of technological improvements is conclusively proved by an examination of the publications of organized labor. Their contention is supported by such surveys as that of the President's Committee on Recent Economic Changes which concluded (p. 451) that in the four main divisions of industry—farms, factories, mines and railroads—"production per capita of population is now [1927] nearly 60% greater than it was in the final years of the nineteenth century." In manufacturing alone, this Committee pointed out that "the increase . . . for the 16-year period from 1909 to 1925 was 33%, as compared with 10% from 1899 to 1909. The average annual rate of increase for the later period is twice the annual increment during the first decade." The report showed, however, that during the latter period hours decreased only seven per week from 57.3 to 49.9. While this lag may not have been regarded as of great consequence in economic theory, in the world of reality it has meant a steadily mounting fear of unemployment which may or may not be followed by reabsorption in the field of production. It is this rapidly accelerating tempo of the rate of improvement in production

SUMMARY AND CONCLUSIONS

that makes the hours' question one of primary importance today.

Although both statistical methods and the collection of data have advanced tremendously in the period under survey, the last thirty years offer practically no more scientific data on the hours' question than the period immediately after the Civil War. There is little conclusive material on the effect of hours on health, or the relation of hours to output. There is no valid material on the question of the number of working hours which might establish equilibrium between consumption and production. Because of this lack of scientific data the question has not advanced from the plane of opinion, prejudice and self-interest to that of verifiable fact. The result is that the arguments for and against a reduction of hours are the same today as those used at the beginning of the period, though subject to difference in emphasis and implication.

The fundamental causes of labor's demands for shorter hours have been the desire for leisure, and, more important still, the fear of unemployment. When gigantic strides in technological improvements made possible one or the other eventuality—and they are, after all, merely two opposed views of the same phenomenon—labor pressed its demand for shorter hours more vigorously. The fundamental cause of the employer's hostility to reducing hours has been a desire to keep profits of his own particular plant at a maximum. With no means available to test what hours are most productive of profits, employers have, on the whole, held fast to the concept that the existing standard, or even that of a former time, if they have been coerced into adopting the newer one, is the best one for attaining their end. The arguments which the two antagonists have developed are attempts to rationalize these fundamental instincts in order to convert the opponent, or, since that is a rare possibility, to attract public opinion by justifying the position taken. These arguments cover a wide field, and are very often closely interrelated.

Labor has predicated its demand for leisure as a means to the creation of a better social order. To produce intelligent citizens, essential to the existence of a democracy, everybody should have sufficient leisure to permit attendance at night schools, time for reading, discussion, and attendance at political meetings. This phase of the question was stressed more in the early period of excessive hours, and in the struggle against the twelve-hour day in continuous industries, than it is at present. But the second argument that leisure provided health has been made to bear on citizenship by stressing the need of a strong race for defensive purposes. In the earlier part of the period, shorter hours were demanded to preserve health, endangered by the physical strain of industry; with the growing mechanization and speeding up of work, requests for further reductions came to be based on the need for relief from nervous strain. The growth of cities, necessitating a longer period of time in travel to and from work, the belief in the increased health and the more natural course of life in the suburbs, the recognition of the social as well as individual gain from a fuller home life, have all buttressed this argument for additional leisure. To this defense of shorter hours on social grounds, the usual reply of employers throughout the period has been the unsupported statement that the hours are not long enough to cause undue strain, and the assertion that the laboring class through inability to use leisure well would endanger the social fabric if hours were reduced.[1]

[1] Surveys and international conferences on this subject show a real recognition of the problem in the last five years, not as a result of shorter hours alone, but of the limitations of city life combined with those

SUMMARY AND CONCLUSIONS

The second ground to which the debate is carried is the effect on production of more leisure. By far the greater part of the employers have taken the attitude that a reduction in hours necessarily causes a decreased output per worker; some even state as a positive outcome that the decrease in output will be in exact proportion to the reduction in hours. On the basis of the assumed decrease in output, many dire results from lessening hours are prophesied. These are: first, that the increased burden of cost will be placed on the consumer; second, that labor will suffer from the necessary decrease in wages; third, that capital will flee the district, profits having decreased due to the cost of the change; and last, that foreign competitors will invade the home market, and in addition we will lose our ability to compete in foreign markets. The fact that the first result would necessarily exclude the second or the third, and so on through the list, has not prevented the use of the imposing mass of calamities as a negative argument at any one time. Labor's answer has been that past experience proves that decreased hours cause increased output per worker. In the early period, the results of the English nine-hour law in textile mills, and later examples from the experience of the United States, were cited. This paradox of increased output with decreased hours, they pointed out, was the result of the improved health and spirit of the worker which lessened the amount of absenteeism and increased his interest in the job, and the improvements in machinery and organization which the change in hours encouraged the management to make. On the ques-

of automatic work. See: Conference on Christian Politics, Economics and Citizenship, *Report on Leisure,* London, 1924; Cutten, G. B., *The Threat of Leisure,* New Haven, 1926; May, H. L., and Petgen, D., *Leisure and Its Use,* New York, 1928; Alger, G. W., "Leisure for What," *Atlantic Monthly,* April, 1925.

tion of wages in relation to changes in hours, labor's attitude has not remained consistent throughout the period. Organized labor's original position was to accept a cut in wages to obtain the shorter day because the latter, having the effect of decreasing the supply of labor, would cause an eventual increase in wages. Past examples of decreased hours resulting in higher wages helped confirm this reasoning. In the latter part of the period, however, organized labor adopted the position that the shorter hours, which they contend are necessitated by the tremendous increase in productivity, must be accompanied by no decrease in earnings per worker. Even in face of the wage cuts which the depression has caused, organized labor's insistence on the absolute necessity of a shorter work-week has been accompanied by a demand for maintenance of the former standard of wages.

Leisure for consumption is the third ground on which employers and labor have tilted on the question of reduced hours; it is the one field in which, so far as admission of the theory and some action by advanced industrialists are concerned, labor has been awarded the victory. Ira Steward, a Boston mechanic, who was so ardent a shorter-hours' advocate that his epithet was the "eight-hour monomaniac," in the 1860's preached the doctrine that decreased hours, through giving the worker time to observe the mode of living of other people, and to carry on a social life, would increase wants. The result of these increased wants would be a successful demand for higher wages; therefore, Steward posited that the first step away from poverty must come by a reduction of hours. Danryid, who wrote the "History and Philosophy of the Eight-Hour Movement" for the American Federation of Labor's campaign in 1886, added the next link in this chain of reasoning that based the need for shorter hours on stimulating consumption. He envisaged the hours' question not as a problem of production,

SUMMARY AND CONCLUSIONS 17

but as one of distribution, the old one stated by Carlyle of "30,000 idle needlewomen in London and 100,000 shirtless backs." His argument was that the growth of labor-saving machinery had resulted in a supply of goods far greater than the demand for them, and that the only remedy was to increase consumption through increasing the leisure time of workers. George Gunton, in *Gunton's Magazine,* and by his other publications, continued to elaborate the need to shorten hours because of labor's importance as a consumer, incorporating in his argument the Steward doctrine that wages depend on the standard of living. Therefore, shorter hours through increasing the workers' wants would raise their standard of living and so raise wages, thereby enlarging the market for our rapidly increasing productivity. The American Federation of Labor, although placing far greater emphasis on the more practical argument of unemployment, constantly stressed this need for shorter hours to balance consumption and production.

Until comparatively recent times, the employers have disregarded this argument, as unworthy of answer. Then Ford announced in 1926 as his contribution to practical economics, that mass production necessitated mass consumption, and led the way in shortening hours to allow this force to work. His doctrine of shorter hours was accompanied by a declaration of faith in the principle of high wages, so that labor had both the time and the money to purchase goods. Despite the immediate reaction of mistrust to his announcement, industrialists began to adopt the theory, and one of the slogans of America's prosperity was high wages and shorter hours to permit the laborer to function as a consumer. After the lapse of fifty years, the theory of a worker, consistently urged by workers, had been adopted as a practical business method by a few of the leading industrialists of America. The great majority of them have yet to be convinced sufficiently of its validity to put it into practice.

The other basic cause of labor's demand for reduced hours has been fear of unemployment. On this ground, employers have rarely met the workers in argument, except for an occasional statement that a reduction of hours offers no solution for this problem, in which position they have had the support of the deductive reasoning of the theoretical economists. Labor has instinctively reasoned that to shorten hours would spread the work among a larger number, thereby decreasing the number enduring unemployment. There has been slight effort to present real proof, and no conscious attempt to break the question into a discussion of the effect of reduced hours as a remedy for the different kinds of unemployment—cyclical, technological and seasonal. Labor has always unconsciously distinguished between the first two, while comparatively recently certain unions and some employers in highly seasonal trades have studied the effect of decreased hours and punitive overtime as a means of ironing out excessive fluctuations.

Labor very evidently, if unconsciously, recognized technological unemployment as a distinct phenomenon which must be remedied by a decrease in hours. From the very beginning of the period, their demand for reduction has been posited on the results of the rapid introduction of machinery. Of recent years, organized labor has differentiated this type of unemployment by name, has advanced figures to prove the urgency of the problem, and has taken the position that for economic equilibrium hours and wages must be changed in proportion to the changes in productivity. The employers have answered with the arguments of the classical economists that in the long run labor is benefitted by the introduction of machinery. The reasoning is almost too well-known to repeat: that productivity, increased by machinery, decreases price, thereby making

SUMMARY AND CONCLUSIONS

possible a bigger demand for the goods which will absorb that part of the unemployed which has not found work in the trades which make the new machinery, or in the luxury and service trades which have been steadily growing, due to the release of man-power.[2] Labor answers these deductive conclusions as to future eventualities in a perfectly functioning system by figures showing an annual increment of unemployed, which make essential the consideration of the immediate result of the introduction of machinery. Labor's view is not yet openly accepted by employers, but some economists buttress the former's stand today. A recent Fabian syllabus briefly states: "The deflation we need is one of working hours";[3] while Stuart Chase, at greater length, concludes: " The logical, sensible and only final answer to technological unemployment is to shorten working hours. Under present conditions as the machine advances, fewer men work equally long [or approximately so]. Why not put the entire force on the payroll but work them less? Thus the whole nation would share in technological advances; the worker by a steady job with fewer hours, the owner by steady markets and profits."[4]

Labor's differentiation between cyclical and technological unemployment in the past has not been clear cut. During depressions labor has tended to argue that a decrease in

[2] Miss Perkins, New York State Commissioner of Labor, stressed the urgency of this problem when she pointed to the relatively low rate of unemployment in the machine trades as evidence that employers are improving the equipment of their plants which will increase technological unemployment when the upturn of business occurs. United States, *Hearings before Senate Committee on a Bill to Establish a National Economic Council*, 1931. Wm. Green, President of the American Federation of Labor, makes the same point in "Benefits of Five-Day Week," *New York Times*, August 9, 1931.

[3] *Fabian Syllabus*, London, 1931.

[4] Stuart Chase, *Nemesis of American Business*, New York, 1931, p. 21.

hours, through establishing a better equilibrium between production and consumption, would have prevented business stagnation, and the consequent unemployment. In the depression of 1921, just as today, labor made efforts through individual unions, and through co-operation with employers, to decrease the number of days of work per week of each individual, as a means of spreading available work among a larger number. This is recognized by labor, however, as an adjustment to a temporary situation, and is quite distinct from the long and continuous struggle to establish a standard of shorter hours as a means of lessening the more or less constant unemployment caused by the improved technique of industry. Just as few employers have recognized the problem of unemployment as one that industry must solve, so the relation of hours to this problem has not been investigated. In times of depression, employers merely alleviate some of the evils of cyclical unemployment by sharing work among a larger group, and in times of prosperity forget that this problem will again arise.

Some employers and labor have been keenly interested in finding solutions for the problem of seasonal unemployment. A decrease in hours, as a sole remedy, can accomplish nothing. Attacks on the problem in individual plants, however, by research which enables a better control of demand, by diversifying output, by scientific sales planning, etc., have had considerable success in ironing out excessive seasonal fluctuations, thereby providing a shorter work-week for a longer period of employment, in place of excessive hours for a short season, followed by a long period of unemployment.[5] In the past decade, the more

[5] Cf. Feldman, H., *The Regularization of Employment*, New York, 1925, passim.

SUMMARY AND CONCLUSIONS 21

liberal group of employers concentrated attention on this problem, and are giving great publicity to successful methods in an effort to spread this knowledge throughout industry. Labor has been able in certain strongly organized seasonal trades to negotiate contracts providing for fewer hours than the accepted standard and punitive overtime in an effort to spread production somewhat more evenly through the year.

Reduction of hours, so keenly desired by labor, can be accomplished by three methods: legislative action, trade union action, and voluntary action of employers. Each has its advantages and distinct limitations. No one method has been used in the period, which this study covers, to the exclusion of the other two. At times or in certain specific cases, however, one method offers more obvious advantages and, insofar as the choice rests with labor, that means is used.

In the post-Civil War period, labor pinned its faith principally to the legislative method, both nationally and in the several States. The powers of the Federal Government to legislate on the question of hours are distinctly limited by the Constitution. Unless changed in this respect —and an amendment has frequently been proposed to give Congress power to control hours of labor—the field of national action is limited to workers directly or indirectly employed by the Federal Government, and to those engaged in foreign or interstate commerce. Labor's immediate demand was the passage of an Eight-Hour Law for all employed on Federal Government jobs. Labor's purpose was wider than the gain of a shorter work-day for the large group of government workers: it was felt that the change by the government would serve both as example and proof of the feasibility and desirability of the eight-hour day. Pressure on Congress exerted by labor groups resulted in the enactment in 1868 of an Eight-Hour Law for all employees on Federal Government work. While as a consequence of the failure of this law, due both to its inherent weaknesses and lack of enforcement, labor adopted the method of direct action, it did not abandon the legislative method. Continued pressure by organized labor brought about the enactment in 1892 and in 1912 of improved Eight-Hour Laws for employees on government work. Laws were passed in 1907 and 1916 which regulated the length of the work-day of railroad employees engaged in interstate commerce, and one in 1915 established the hours of labor of seamen.

The enactment of these federal statutes has served to reveal some of the advantages and the weaknesses of the legislative method. Of the two advantages, the first and more important is that by legal enactment only can the hours of the unorganized be effectively decreased. The American Federation of Labor, admitting the impossibility of adequately organizing government employees, strongly advocates the legislative method of reducing hours for these workers. The second and less important advantage is that the legislative enactment of the shorter day for government employees sets not only a standard for all labor to work towards, but also a model for all employers to emulate. The first weakness of the legislative method is that the field which it can cover is narrowly limited by constitutional provisions. A general federal hours' statute is a Utopian hope. In the second place, the work of agitating, lobbying and securing the enactment of hours' laws is tremendous, not to mention the immeasurably greater difficulty of achieving a clearly worded law which eliminates loopholes for evasion. And, finally, there is the question of enforcement, which depends but little on the penalties in the law, but greatly on the spirit and adequacy of the body responsible for its administration, supplemented by the watchfulness and strength which organized labor can exert.

The parallel movement for shorter hours by State enactment revealed further limitations of the legislative method. Decisions of the courts that hours' legislation was an unjustifiable interference with freedom of contract, guaranteed by State Constitutions and by that of the United States, hampered the development of this means of control for many years. The philosophy of our courts has gradually broadened, and they now recognize the need and justifiability of general legislative regulation of hours. Professor Frankfurter points out that the turning point in the judicial interpretation of the Constitution in regard to legislation on hours was the case of Muller *v.* Oregon in 1908, in which the Supreme Court of the United States sustained the constitutionality of the Oregon Ten-Hour Law for women. With this case, the early tendency of the courts to show an "unmistakable dread" of hours' legislation, and to decide such measures on theories of economic and political philosophy, only sustaining hours' laws as an exceptional protection to the weak, shifted to one which dealt with these statutes in the light of a realistic study of industrial conditions and from the viewpoint of community interests. As a result of this change in judicial attitude, the constitutionality of hours' legislation has been sustained by the Supreme Court of the United States, not only for women employees and for laborers on State and city jobs and in specially designated industries, but also for all workers under the terms of a general law. Insofar as precedents established by the highest court of the country guide the decisions of the inferior courts, it can be stated that the question of constitutionality is no longer of primary importance.

The enactment, however, of State legislation has been hampered by difficulties which do not exist in the case of national hours' statutes. The first, lack of uniformity in the hours adopted by the forty-eight States, results in the telling argument that such laws will place the State at a competitive disadvantage, and has continued to be one of the biggest stumbling blocks to the adoption of improved hours' standards. The second is the active hostility of the American Federation of Labor toward general hours' legislation, which is in strong contrast to its leadership in efforts to have hour laws enacted for women, for workers on State and city jobs, and for those in hazardous industries. The evidence is convincing that a broadcast of the Federation's opposition was used to defeat general eight-hour laws which had been initiated prior to the war in the liberal States of the Pacific slope as a result of strong agitation by local labor organizations. How much restraining influence the Federation's antagonism had outside these States cannot be as definitely stated. The fact that general hour laws exist only in two States, whereas legal regulation of hours is not unusual in the fields in which the Federation has approved, offers evidence that the hostile position of the American Federation of Labor has been an important factor. On the other hand, an examination of the roster of States reveals the large number which fail to regulate hours in the sanctioned fields, and leads to the conclusion that the absolute lack of general hours' legislation, as well as the comparative deficiency of special hours' statutes, is due in greater part to the grip of laissez-faire philosophy in the field of labor legislation.

This resumé of the hindrances which beset the enactment of State hours' legislation makes it pertinent to inquire how much has, nevertheless, been accomplished. Fourteen States still have the general hour statutes—eight establish

SUMMARY AND CONCLUSIONS 25

the eight-hour day, and six the ten-hour day—which are absolutely ineffectual on account of the provision which permits a contract for longer hours. Nineteen States have enacted Eight-Hour Laws for laborers on State and city jobs, five additional States make this provision for workers on State jobs only, and two for laborers engaged on work for the principal city of the respective States. Special provisions in hours' legislation for women to allow for one short day a week, differences within a State in the hours established for certain work, and differences in the inclusiveness of the laws of the separate States, make a summary of this legislation of no real value. It can be said, however, that five States place no special restrictions on the hours of women workers, thirteen States and the District of Columbia establish an average eight-hour day, although only half this number make provision for a forty-eight-hour week, and the larger proportion of the remaining States establish an average nine-hour day. A summary of hours' legislation for men in specified industries has little value for much the same reasons. It can, however, be pointed out that most of the western mining States have passed Eight-Hour Laws for workers in mines and smelters, scattered States have provided for a ten or twelve-hour day for employees of transit lines, three eastern States have placed restrictions on hours of compressed air workers, one western and one eastern State have limited the hours of employees in drug stores to nine and ten hours per day, respectively, and two southern States have statutes which establish the ten-hour day for operatives in cotton and woolen factories. General hour laws, not nullified by permission to contract differently, exist in two States only: Mississippi and Oregon have established a ten-hour day, but the latter State permits three hours over-time each day at time-and-a-half rate.

Under the guidance of the American Federation of Labor, complete dependence has been placed on the method of direct action to establish shorter hours for men except in the case of government employees and hazardous work. Although strikes were used in the late sixties and early seventies to enforce legislative enactment of shorter hours, direct action has, with this exception, meant the use of collective bargaining to establish the shorter day. Early attempts were weak, scattered and produced short-lived success even for the most strongly organized trades. The unplanned but concerted strike of New York laborers in 1872 demonstrated the potential strength of a general demand for a reduction in hours backed by the strike, and the idea was adopted in 1884 by the young and belligerent Federation of Organized Trades and Labor Unions, which shortly reorganized as the American Federation of Labor. This organization's original acceptance of the general strike as the most effective weapon of direct action for reducing hours shifted in a short time to a plan for successive strikes by chosen trades, which were to have the support of all organized labor. When this plan, too, proved a failure, the American Federation of Labor followed the line of least resistance, and left the entire question of tactics to the individual unions. They have used all the weapons and strategy of collective bargaining to decrease hours; in times of great strength, as during the World War, peaceful negotiations have been successful, in other periods strikes have been protracted and have reached staggering financial costs.

It is an accepted fact that collective bargaining has established a better standard of hours for trade unionists, and this has been confirmed by statistics, which are available since 1914, and which show that the average hours of the organized tend to be from four to six per week less than those of the unorganized. This difference, however, cannot be taken as the full measure of the effectiveness of trade-union activity, since the hours of unorganized workers are not independent of those established by the organized, insofar as the latter set up a standard toward which legislative enactment tends and the unorganized struggle.

Proof of the comparatively greater efficacy of direct action must be accompanied by a statement of its limitations. The first of these, the folly of depending on direct action to reduce the hours of the unorganized, was clearly demonstrated in the steel strike; its potency must be limited to the organized group which in the United States has always been a distinct minority. Even at the height of trade-union membership in 1920, only one fifth of the wage earners were organized. Conditions in the last decade give no promise of a growth of trade unionism, and confirm the belief that this valuable means of reducing hours is restricted to the small number of workers that the American labor movement is able to organize. But, even for the organized, the financial cost of this method is so grave a disadvantage that strong unions, insistent on the need for a reduction of hours, discuss, hesitate and postpone the day of action.

Voluntary reduction of hours by employers is the third possible method of establishing the shorter work-day. It is presumably this means to which employers and employers' associations refer in their constantly repeated aspirations for a "natural evolution" of the shorter day. The available evidence, however, shows clearly that reduction of hours by pioneer employers has been less common than that brought about by legislative or trade-union action. The apparently widespread acceptance of the Ford philosophy of higher wages and shorter hours might have been expected to produce a marked change in the past decade. Little is discernible. In fact, the conclusion seems justified that even liberal employers, who admit the need for reduction—and that, by voluntary action—continue to place the date at which such action will be wise in the future. The advantages of the method are obvious; it is peaceful and entails no cost to those agitating for reduction or to industry, according to the general testimony of employers who have voluntarily reduced hours. While voluntary reduction, initiated by pioneer employers as a matter of conscious policy has not been common in the past, and indications do not warrant the assumption that it will be in the near future, it should be remembered that general conditions have played a part in the spread of the reduction of hours and will continue to do so.

Labor's intuitive and insistent statements supplemented by the reasoning of an intellectual such as J. M. Keynes,[6] have brought prominently before the public the question of shorter hours as an important factor in the solution of the present economic situation. Accordingly, this survey of methods by which hours have been reduced in the United States was undertaken as a means of estimating the possibilities of further reduction in the near future. The answer to that question is, to the writer, at least, disappointingly trite. Unless an unforeseeable change occurs, there is every prospect that history will repeat itself, and that the period to come will be a steady, dogged, frequently hopeless insistence by one great part of society on the need for shorter hours, which will bring about a further but gradual reduction through a combination of legislative, direct and voluntary action.

[6] Keynes, J. M., *Essays in Persuasion*, London, 1931, pp. 368, 369.

PART I
REDUCTION OF HOURS BY LEGISLATION

CHAPTER II

ATTITUDE OF LABOR AND EMPLOYERS

LABOR organizations in the United States have not maintained a consistent attitude in favor of or in opposition to the legislative method as a means of shortening the work-day. The early and naive confidence of organized labor, in the period immediately following the Civil War, in the complete efficacy of legislative action, gave way under the Knights of Labor to a vacillating and uncertain attitude on the question of method, and changed with the American Federation of Labor to an absolute denial of the adequacy of legal enactment to reduce hours for men.

LABOR

Early Labor Associations

To legislate an eight-hour day into existence was the objective of many labor organizations in the period immediately following the Civil War. Pressure for shorter hours was strong due to a number of reasons. In the first place, the return of the soldiers to civilian occupations, roused the fear of job scarcity.[1] Secondly, national unions, which grew at a rapid pace after the war,[2] made labor more articulate on its grievances. Furthermore, the growth of cities lengthened the effective work-day by involving additional time to go to and from the job. Lastly, a growing sense of the

[1] Commons, J. R., and Associates, *History of Labor in the United States,* New York, 1918, Vol. 2, p. 94.

[2] Ely, R. T., *The Labor Movement,* New York, 1886, p. 62; Commons and Associates, *op. cit.,* pp, 45-48.

injustice of an economic system which made for very great extremes of wealth and poverty, of excessive hours for the many and leisure for the few, stirred not only the laborers but those idealists who had led the attack against slavery, to demand reform. The panacea on which all efforts concentrated was the eight-hour day.

The choice of the legislative method was to be expected. On the one hand, voluntary grant was most unlikely as the American entrepreneur had not reached the enlightened stage of recognizing its advantages; on the other hand, the unions had not yet attained sufficient power to consider it advisable to stage a struggle on this question. Furthermore, precedent pointed to this method: the reform element of American labor had long pinned its faith to the ballot. Indeed, specific precedents existed for the use of legislation to bring about hours' reform. There were: first, Van Buren's Ten-Hour Executive Order of April 10, 1840, which was promulgated after determined use of the ballot by laborers[3]; second, Pennsylvania's law of 1849, establishing a ten-hour day in cotton, woolen, silk, paper, bagging and flax factories;[4] and, last, the example of England's legislation.

In the first days of the movement, there is no evidence of any doubt as to the entire adequacy of this method. Labor apparently had complete confidence in the power of the ballot to control representatives, naive reliance on the legislature's ability to pass an effective law, and hopeful dependence on the good-will of the executive to enforce the law. But, by 1867, William Sylvis, President of the Iron Molders' Union, a most ardent advocate of education, agitation and legislation to establish the eight-hour day,

[3] Ely, op. cit., p. 55.
[4] U. S. Commissioner of Labor, *First Annual Report*, 1886, p. 481.

ATTITUDE OF LABOR AND EMPLOYERS 33

commented regretfully on the difficulties of arousing labor to use the ballot for this end, and of framing a law which could not be evaded. Yet, despite recognition of the weakness of the legislative method, he continued to advocate it as the only means of inaugurating the eight-hour day.[5]

Eight-hour leagues of laborers were formed in numerous places to agitate and plan for the establishment of the shorter day. Many were organized in Boston and adjacent towns, and "spread rapidly to the Middle West, and even to New Orleans and San Francisco."[6] Some of these scattered organizations united for more effective action. The Grand Eight-Hour League of Illinois, for example, was formed by some twenty-two subordinate eight-hour leagues of that State.[7] Leagues of the same name were established in Massachusetts, Indiana, Michigan and Iowa.[8]

The Grand Eight-Hour League of Massachusetts, under the leadership of Phillips, Steward and McNeill, was very active. Wendell Phillips, having successfully used his powers of oratory to stir New England on the Abolition question, transferred his abilities to the labor problem, in which, he stated, long hours were the root of the evil. At a meeting in Faneuil Hall in November, 1865, he demanded the eight-hour day to establish justice and equality of opportunity, by giving the worker time to develop his intellect. He urged the use of the ballot to get this reform,

---

[5] Sylvis, W. H., *Life, Speeches, Labors and Essays,* edited by J. C. Sylvis, Philadelphia, 1872, pp. 206, 210.

[6] Commons, J. R., and others, *A Documentary History of American Industrial Society,* Cleveland, 1910-1911, Vol. 9, p. 277.

[7] Commons and Associates, *op. cit.,* Vol. 2, p. 91.

[8] *Ibid.,* pp. 95, 96 n.

both because it was the best means to right wrongs, and because it would give the movement the publicity which it needed.[9] At the same meeting, Ira Steward, the "workingman philosopher" of the movement, introduced a resolution which outlined a program of legal enactments to establish the eight-hour day. This program supplemented the request for a general law making eight hours the legal day's work by demands for an eight-hour law for all Massachusetts corporations and for all city work. To secure enforcement, he called for the creation of a commission with powers of investigation and prosecution.[10] Like Phillips, he emphasized the need for developing public opinion to bring about this legislative reform.

Supplementing the work of these leagues was the active agitation of trades' assemblies and central trades unions. The New York State Workingmen's Assembly invited a national convention to meet in New York in July, 1865, to make plans to secure a legal eight-hour day.[11] The State Trades' Association's meeting in Albany in September, 1865, decided to carry on an eight-hour campaign to educate public opinion, and to follow this up by a demand for legislation.[12] The State Labor Convention of Connecticut passed a resolution favoring an eight-hour day by law.[13]

While these local organizations continued to function, and to increase their effectiveness through state-wide combination, a movement toward greater unity of action was

---

[9] Phillips, W., *Speeches, Lectures and Letters*, Boston, 1894, p. 142.

[10] Documentary History, Vol. 9, pp. 302, 303.

[11] Ware, N. J., *The Labor Movement in the United States, 1860-1895*, New York, 1929, p. 5.

[12] *Nation* (N. Y.), October 5, 1865, p. 419.

[13] *New York Times*, February 24, 1867.

developing. The idea of a General National Convention, recommended at the first meeting of the Indiana Grand Eight-Hour League,[14] met with the approval of the National Unions. The leaders of the Coachmakers' International Union and the Iron Molders' Union co-operated with the Baltimore Trades' Assembly to issue a call to a national convention to meet in Baltimore in August, 1866. It read: " The agitation of the question of eight hours as a day's labor has assumed an importance requiring concerted and harmonious action upon all matters appertaining to the inauguration of labor reforms." [15] The *Workingman's Advocate,* which became the official newspaper of the movement, reported that the most important business of the convention would be the consideration of "the most effective manner of obtaining a reduction of the hours of labor to eight per day."[16]

The convention, attended by seventy-seven delegates from thirteen States and the District of Columbia, met as planned. The first plank in the platform adopted by the congress ratified the legislative method for establishing shorter hours. The resolution declared: "That the first and grand desideratum of the hour, in order to deliver the labor of this country from thralldom, is the enactment of a law whereby eight hours shall be made to constitute a legal day's work in every State of the American Union." The movement was short-lived and the causes of its eventual collapse were evident at the first convention. These were, first, failure to concentrate on one reform—besides the eight-hour demand, the convention discussed the land question, co-operation, prison labor, and women in industry—

[14] Commons and Associates, *op. cit.,* Vol. 2, p. 95.
[15] Sylvis, *op. cit.,* p. 65.
[16] *Workingman's Advocate,* August 11, 1866.

and, second, loss of energy through an attempt to form an independent political party. Heated argument on the adequacy of an established party as a vehicle for reform resulted in a resolution to form a National Labor Party "as soon as possible." Until the National Labor Union petered out in 1872, this attempt was the primary aim of the organization.[17]

At the convention of 1867, at which the name the National Labor Union was adopted, the Committee on Political Action reported at length on the need for a labor party "to secure by proper legislation the labor reforms necessary to the prosperity of the nation," and expressed great faith in monetary reform by which "the natural rights of labor will be secured."[18] The report by the Eight-Hour Committee on the cure-all which the last convention had adopted offered a sharp contrast to the optimism with which this new panacea was introduced. The report characterized the State eight-hour laws which had been passed as "frauds on the working class."[19] However, it recommended further effort for legislative action, such as the appointment of a lobbyist to secure an eight-hour law for Federal Government employees, and the election of laborers to State and National Legislatures to work primarily for eight-hour laws.[18]

Plainly, the fine fervor for the eight-hour day as the most pressing problem was dying down. This was more obviously true at the next convention in 1868.[18a] Mention of the eight-hour legislative efforts was confined to the

[17] Commons and Associates, *op. cit.*, pp. 96-102.

[18] *Documentary History,* Vol. 9, pp. 175-185.

[19] *Cf. infra*, pp. 96, 97.

[18a] Professor Ely says that the membership was reported to be 640,000 at this time, *op. cit.*, p. 69.

reports of the President and Vice-President. The former commented on the situation of the federal eight-hour bill, and on the fact that the petition for the New York Eight-Hour Law had been signed by five thousand; the latter reported enthusiastically on the enactment of the California Eight-Hour Law. The discussion of the meeting centered on the panacea suggested at the preceding convention—cheap money and low interest rates.[20] William Sylvis, who was elected President, issued a circular on October 18 which promised to undertake the foundation of an independent labor party, and urged the slogan: "Down with a moneyed aristocracy, and up with the people." A second circular of November 16 stressed the need for a monetary system which would "give to the people a cheap, secure and abundant currency."[21] Both the discussion and the circulars show that the eight-hour reform had been relegated to the background.

The most important work of the convention of 1869 was the adoption of the platform of the Labor Reform Party. Not until the twelfth plank was the hours' question mentioned. This urged all workers to secure the eight-hour day, and exhorted the State Legislatures to follow the example of the National Government by passing eight-hour laws. Just as the position of this plank showed the lack of importance which had come to be attached to legislation for hours' reform, so a resolution recommending a concerted strike to bring about the enforcement of the Eight-Hour Law, introduced by a New York laborer, presaged a change in attitude on the method of attaining shorter hours.[22] An editorial in the *Workingman's Advocate*

[20] *Ibid.*, pp. 195-227.
[21] Sylvis, *op. cit.*, p. 80.
[22] *Documentary History*, Vol. 9, pp. 233-238.

stated that the success of trade unions in reducing hours was limited to periods of prosperity: their efforts had to be supplemented by a labor reform party to establish permanent gains.[23]

The real work of the 1870 convention was to make arrangements to call a convention to complete the organization of the Labor Reform Party, and to modify the constitution of the National Labor Union so as to make it a purely industrial body with no political interests. Despite this limitation of interests, the 1871 convention did not plan action for the eight-hour day. Mention of it was confined to the President's report on violations of the Federal Eight-Hour Law, and to his statement of the importance of more correct knowledge of wages, hours and unemployment.[24]

The Political Congress, held in February 1872, failed in its attempt to nominate a national ticket. The Industrial Congress, held in September, was attended by only seven members. They appointed a committee to consider the expediency of calling a congress for the discussion of non-political questions. The first question suggested was: "How to secure the adoption and enforcement of the eight-hour system."[25] Six years earlier, the National Labor Union had been organized with this same optimistic objective. As we have seen, however, the objective was soon lost sight of, partly because of an attempt to organize, as a means to this end, an independent labor party; and partly through the acquisition of other aims which seemed to promise greater and quicker gains. The leaders had learned one lesson: that was, to eliminate interest in independent political action. Beyond this, the question

[23] *Workingman's Advocate*, May 14, 1870.
[24] *Documentary History*, Vol. 9, pp. 257-271.
[25] *Ibid*, pp. 272-274.

showed they still considered reduction of hours of primary importance, but were uncertain as to the best means of attaining this end.

Like the National Labor Union, the New England Labor Reform League under the leadership of Wendell Phillips had substituted an independent labor party and monetary reform for the earlier faith in shorter hours. The Boston Eight-Hour League, on the other hand, under Steward and McNeill, stressed concentration on the eight-hour day as the solution of all labor's ills. The short-lived success of the former organization in electing members of the State Legislature had vanished by 1872. In the same year the convention of the Boston Eight-Hour League reiterated its original position that reduction in hours must be the first step in labor reform. The program which they mapped out, while it showed a recognition of the futility of general eight-hour laws, still depended on the legislative method. In detail, it called, first, for an amended patent law, by which the patent would be forfeited if an employee of the concern manufacturing the patented article worked more than eight hours; second, for an eight-hour law for all workers on State and municipal jobs, whether employed directly or by contractors; third, for an eight-hour law for all under twenty-one; and last, for a general eight-hour law in the absence of any contract.[26]

The Industrial Brotherhood, another attempt at national organization in 1873, did not emphasize the need for reduction in hours. It is mentioned here only because the Knights of Labor later adopted its declaration of principles almost without change. The eighteenth resolution, which was devoted to the hours' question, stated that the Brotherhood aimed: "to secure the reduction of the hours of labor to eight per day, so that the laborers may have more time

[26] McNeill, G. E., *The Labor Movement*, Boston, 1887, pp. 139-144.

Knights of Labor

Unlike the National Labor Union, the Knights of Labor was not organized with the hours' question as a dominant interest. That it ever became a leading one with them was due to pressure from outside and from some of the members, rather than to any vital interest among the leaders. They gave lip service to it, and since their interest in the question was not very real, so their attitude as to the best method of obtaining it was vague and subject to change.[28]

At the first meeting of 1876, hours were not mentioned, but the preamble, adopted in 1878, stated a resolve to secure " more of the leisure that rightfully belongs to them [the laborers]." At the next convention, a resolution was unanimously adopted "urging upon the members of the order the necessity of reducing the hours of labor to eight per day." No discussion was reported, and evidently the question of the method of attaining this objective was not considered.[29] However, the address of Stephens, the Grand Master Workman, to the convention in September, 1879, suggested a stand in favor of legislative action. He pointed out the need for agitation to create a public sentiment to get eight hours "firmly established by statute law in the various States, backed as such laws will have to be by penal enactments, in order to make them efficient."[30]

At the 1880 convention, Powderly, who was then enter-

---

[27] Ibid., pp. 149-153.

[28] Powderly, T. V., Thirty Years of Labor, Columbus, O., 1889, p. 225.

[29] Knights of Labor, Proceedings of General Association, January, 1879, p. 74.

[30] Ibid., September, 1879, p. 103.

ing on his long career as Grand Master Workman was not clear as to the best method of attaining shorter hours, due either to his delight in florid language, or to the fact that he had not thoroughly grasped the problem. He said: "Men must be compelled to help themselves, and a law should be passed at this General Assembly requiring of each member to assist by voice and pen, by petition and means, every honest effort looking towards the amelioration of the condition of the wage slave, by reducing his hours of labor." Whether he would classify the attempt to get shorter hours by law as an "honest effort," he does not say. Lichtman, the General Secretary, however, promised the aid of the officers to secure eight-hour laws. He urged the collection of funds for lobbying to compel the enforcement of the Federal Eight-Hour Law. This accomplishment would be an example to the States and private entrepreneurs to reduce hours, so that labor might be compensated "for the introduction of labor-saving machinery." [31] Lichtman continued his efforts in Washington without pay until 1886 when he retired, convinced Congress would not act until the voters showed a real interest.[32]

While the officials failed to mention hours at the convention of 1881, a concrete plan to combine legislative and direct action was introduced by Representative Elliott of Maryland. He suggested that the local assemblies agitate and organize in preparation for a concerted demand for eight-hour legislation on the first Monday of September, 1882. The Committee on Resolutions reported the plan to be "inexpedient on account of numerical weakness." [33] At the 1882 convention, Representative Elliott introduced a

[31] *Ibid.*, September, 1880, pp. 174, 177.
[32] Powderly, *op. cit.*, p. 478.
[33] Knights of Labor, *Proceedings*, September, 1881, pp. 269, 309.

resolution which slightly modified his earlier one by providing that labor proclaim eight-hours the legal work-day as of the first Monday of May, 1883. While no action was reported on this motion, a resolution asking members to buy between 6 A. M. and 7 P. M., to get shorter hours for store clerks, was approved.[34] Peaceful direct action appealed to the Knights' philosophy.

Still another resolution, offered at the convention of 1883, fixing May 1, 1884, as the date for proclaiming the eight-hour day, was reported on unfavorably and failed to pass. Yet at this convention, the Statistician of the Order cited many cases of excessive hours, and the comment of the Brooklyn Statistician on the occurrence of fifteen-hour days was: "at one time they drive us like slaves, and at other times we have to beg for work." [35]

The Statistician's report to the 1884 convention, stating that further agitation would establish the eight-hour day, is typical of the lack of realization on the part of the Order's officers of the need for a definite plan of action: so was the adoption of the eight-hour day for the employees of the Order on recommendation of the Grand Master Workman. The Knights had not learned that hours could not be effectively diminished by agitation without concentration, by boycott without central direction, or by the occasional example of a model employer.

Nevertheless, at this convention, the Knights apparently decided to take real action to establish the eight-hour day. The Committee on Laws submitted a new constitution, which was adopted after it had been acted on section by section. While the preamble definitely declared for legislative measures to obtain objectives, the statement on hours

[34] *Ibid.*, September, 1882, pp. 312, 356.
[35] *Ibid.*, September, 1883, pp. 40, 503, 428.

ATTITUDE OF LABOR AND EMPLOYERS 43

pointed to direct action. This, the twenty-first aim, was "to shorten the hours of labor by a general refusal to work more than eight hours." [36] This change of attitude was not the fruit of the rejected Maryland resolutions. Its cause is obscure unless Powderly's explanation of a later date is accepted. He said that it was in part the result of hasty action, in part the result of the prevalent idea that the "preamble was only intended to be a list of glittering generalities, and that it mattered little what it contained." [37] This definite statement of the preamble, combined with the Federated Trades' choice of May 1, 1886, for the inauguration of the eight-hour day, caused much confusion. Newspaper accounts fostered the opinion that the Knights of Labor supported the movement for mass action to achieve the shorter day. Powderly issued a secret circular discountenancing the plan for a general strike on the grounds that the date was not suitable, and that its proposers were incapable of understanding the situation. As a substitute for it, he outlined a plan for discussion and agitation at the local assemblies, which was to culminate in the publication of prize-winning essays on Washington's Birthday, 1885. Powderly expressed great faith that the publicity given to these essays "would cause public opinion to establish the eight-hour day." [38] Puerile as the plan was, it was at least an attempt at concentration of effort, and as such is noteworthy in a movement which met the hours' question with nothing that could be termed a policy.

At the 1885 convention, Powderly insisted that a general strike for reduced hours "must prove abortive," but he offered no more effective alternative, legislative or other-

---

[36] *Ibid.*, September, 1884, pp. 590, 768.
[37] Powderly, *op. cit.*, p. 482.
[38] *Ibid.*, pp. 483, 484.

wise. The Secretary's report emphasized the need for an eight-hour day to bring employment to the "immense army of idle toilers." When the invitation of the Federation of Trades for assistance in direct action to establish the eight-hour day was read, the convention passed so general and obscurely worded a resolution that it cannot be told whether they subscribed to direct action or not. The only other resolution on this subject was a repetition of the demand that the National Eight-Hour Law be enforced.[39]

From this time, confusion prevailed as to the Knights' stand on the general strike for eight ours. Powderly blamed the newspapers for grossly exaggerating the numerical strength and power of the Order.[40] He blamed the organizers who made capital of this false publicity to enroll hastily large numbers who passed resolutions in favor of the strike for eight hours on May 1. He blamed the Federation of Trades for creating the impression that the Knights of Labor were behind the movement. A secret circular, issued in March, 1886, decried any participation by the Order in the movement, and insisted that the first need was to "learn why our hours should be reduced and then teach others."[41] At the fall convention, held in the year of the strike, Powderly denied that he opposed the eight-hour day, but pointed out that, while craft organizations could work for their own interests, a labor organization such as the Knights must consider the many who had not yet obtained the ten-hour day.[42] Unfortunately this

[39] Knights of Labor, *Proceedings*, September, 1885, pp. 15, 135, 117, 163.

[40] Powderly, *op. cit.*, p. 494, quotes an article on the Knights of Labor, from the *New York Sun*, which began: "Five men in this country control the chief interests of 500,000 workingmen, . . ."

[41] *Ibid., op. cit.*, pp. 494-498.

[42] Knights of Labor, *Proceedings*, September, 1886, pp. 39, 40.

well-taken point did not lead at any later date to plans for legislative or other action.

No action on hours was taken by the convention of 1887, but faith was expressed, first, in the legislative method by recommending the passage of State laws to reduce hours; and second, in the boycott by demanding that one be instituted against the firm of Browning King, which had established a ten-hour day, despite the fact that eighty-four firms belonging to the Manufacturers' Association had nine and one-half hours.[43]

The convention of 1888 heard Powderly bitterly denounce those who "attempt to inaugurate a new system with a hurrah." In place of this thoughtless action, he offered a plan which had been presented at the special Cleveland convention immediately following the May 1, 1886, debacle,[43a] but which had not received adequate consideration due to the tension at that time. This plan proposed by Mr. Norton, a Chicago manufacturer, suggested the organization of a national association of manufacturers to negotiate with the Knights as representing the nation's labor force. The object of the negotiation was to arrange to scale down the hours by one-half hour a day each year, so that at the end of the fourth year the eight-hour day would be inaugurated.[44] The obvious advantages were more than outweighed by the fact that it was only a paper plan, and hours of discussion by the Knights would not bring a majority of manufacturers to this way of thinking. It was characteristic of Powderly that this theoretical, rational plan appeared to him as practical, whereas that of the Federation of Trades, which was at least founded on a

[43] *Ibid.*, September, 1887, pp. 1761, 1304.
[43a] *Cf. infra*, pp. 154-159.
[44] Powderly, *op. cit.*, pp. 515-525.

step in which labor took the initiative was denounced by him as impractical. A second request from the American Federation of Labor [45] for co-operation in a renewal of the plan of 1886 for establishing the eight-hour day by a strike on May 1, 1890, was read to the convention of 1889. Although the committee reporting on the proposal substituted a wordy but meaningless resolution urging an aggressive campaign to educate the workers on the need for shorter hours, which was to be followed by a gradual reduction to nine and one-half, nine hours, etc., the convention passed a resolution that, while the Knights would not support the American Federation of Labor in a general strike, the Order would give "moral support to the movement in favor of such trade or trades" as the Federation held were in condition to strike.[46] The Knights were numerically so weak at this time, that according to Professor Ware, moral support was the only kind left to offer.[47]

This account shows how difficult it is to arrive at any conclusions as to the attitude of the Knights of Labor toward the use of the legislative method of attaining a reduction of hours. Certainly, Stephens, the first Grand Master Workman, declared definitely for it. Lichtman, the General Secretary, favored it, and advocated lobbying as a means of getting this legislative action. The attitude of Powderly, the second Grand Master Workman, who ruled through a long period which included that of the Order's greatest power, is obscure. Professor Ware says that the explanation of Powderly's attitude is to be found in his allegiance to the older American point of view that hour

[45] Successor to the Federation of Organized Trades and Labor Unions.
[46] Knights of Labor, *Proceedings*, September, 1889, pp. 51, 52.
[47] Ware, *op. cit.*, p. 319.

reduction should be secured by legislation. It would seem, however, that he was also influenced by his lack of faith in the possibility of attaining shorter hours by any method. Throughout his addresses as Grand Master Workman, his insistence was on education and agitation to prepare for the eight-hour day for the future. Yet, his statement that " Hours of labor will be reduced in vain where hundreds of thousands seek for employment as a result of unjust taxation and speculative landholding," [48] betrays a conviction that under the existing system a program for shorter hours was useless. He reasoned that since poverty forced workmen to accept over-time work with avidity, to shorten hours under a system which allowed poverty was an impossibility. His panacea "was co-operation, by which machine will be made the slave of man, not man kept in attendance on the machine."[49] With this wider objective rather hazily in view, the hours' question was relatively unimportant. When problems of method, legislative or otherwise, were forced to the front, his general attitude favored the peaceful legislative method.

The General Assembly reflected the attitude of the leaders. It gave apparent allegiance to the legislative method by passing resolutions to support lobbying committees, by demanding a fairer interpretation of the National Eight-Hour Law for Government employees, by asking State Legislatures and City Councils to pass eight-hour laws. On the other hand, some resolutions showed they relied on other methods of attaining a reduction. They endorsed, for instance, the use of the boycott, and favored voluntary reduction for their own employees as an example to other employers. Constant resolutions in favor of edu-

[48] Powderly, *op. cit.,* p. 361.
[49] Knights of Labor, *Proceedings,* September, 1886, p. 40.

cation and agitation are open to the interpretation that the result of this campaign might be the passage of hours' legislation, or the conversion of employers to a realization of the necessity of giving a reduction without the intervention of the Legislature. Meantime, the local assemblies of the Order were developing a faith in the use of direct action, and took part in the strikes demanding shorter hours.

American Federation of Labor

In contradistinction to the Knights of Labor, the American Federation of Labor took a definite stand in favor of shorter hours, and in opposition to the legislative method with certain exceptions. This unwillingness to use the legislative method has caused a strong group to dissent, but has not prevented the dominant party from adopting and presenting a clear-cut program to the public.

The first meeting of the Federation of Organized Trades and Labor Unions of the United States and Canada, which was the forerunner of the American Federation of Labor, evinced no great interest in hours. The fifth item of their declaration of principles, which called for the enforcement of the Federal Eight-Hour Law of 1868 "in the spirit of its designers," [50] showed both an acceptance of the legislative method for decreasing hours for government employees, and a recognition of the weakness which permitted evasion. By the next convention in 1882, demand for enforcement of this law was given first place in the Federation's platform. The President of the United States was called upon to give it "immediate and impartial enforcement" on the ground that this would "secure the adoption of similar provisions in nearly all the States of the Union." [51] Although

[50] Federation of Organized Trades and Labor Unions of the United States and Canada, *Proceedings, First Annual Convention,* 1881, p. 3.

[51] *Ibid,* 1882, pp. 3, 18.

approval was given to the legislative method for government employees, it was significant that the Federation's first resolution for a general eight-hour day, passed at this convention, did not specify any method of bringing about this end. While this might be interpreted as a failure to realize the need for a method, it was more probably the result, on the one hand, of unwillingness to endorse the legislative method which was too evidently functioning badly, and on the other hand, of inability to offer a feasible alternative.

As a supplement to the demand for enforcement of the Federal Eight-Hour Law, the 1883 convention directed the Secretary to interrogate both national conventions of the two major political parties as to their position on this question. Neither convention replied. This, combined with repeated failure to get the Executive to take action, led the Secretary to report in 1884: "This much has been determined by the National Eight-Hour Law—it is useless to wait for legislation in this matter. A united demand for a shorter working day, backed by thorough organization, will prove vastly more effective than the enactment of a thousand laws depending for enforcement upon the pleasure of aspiring politicians, of sycophantic department officials." To accomplish this, he urged that all organizations express by vote during the year their opinion on the feasibility of a universal strike for an eight or nine-hour day, to take effect by May, 1886. His plan was adopted, and the American Federation of Labor embarked on a policy of decreasing hours by direct action, which has continued to the present.[52] The hours' discussion of the convention from 1885 to 1890 was confined to adopting plans to make direct action an effective means of decreasing hours.[53]

[52] *Ibid.*, 1884, pp. 10, 11.
[53] *Ibid.*, 1885-1890, *passim*; *Cf. infra*, pp. 154-159.

The question of legislative action rose to a position of temporary importance when the 1893 convention passed a resolution to submit a political program to the constituent unions for consideration and instruction of delegates. This program stated that Great Britain's experiment with the principle of independent labor politics, as an auxiliary to economic action, was based on such measures as a legal eight-hour work-day; and called for an endorsement of Britain's policy, and its application to the United States. After the interval of a year for local consideration, the 1894 convention discussed this program at length. President Gompers and Secretary Evans earnestly opposed it on the grounds that union experience with politics had been productive of nothing but disruption. The vote, 1173 against endorsing the political platform and 735 in favor, showed that the adherents of the political method were not a small minority. Although the legislative method as a means of reducing hours in general was defeated by this vote, the President's report broadened the field which the American Federation of Labor recognized as coming within the scope of legal regulation by demanding: first, a law to compel the government to do all of its own work, and so prevent emasculation of the Federal Eight-Hour Law by letting out work on contracts; and second, "that national and State laws should be passed fixing eight hours as the maximum day for women and children." [54]

From 1894 to 1906, the proceedings, insofar as the hours' question is mentioned, were confined to reports on the attempts of individual unions to get the shorter day by direct action, and to the discouraging results of the earnest and repeated efforts of the Federation officials to get improvements in the National Eight-Hour Law. At the 1898 convention, Gompers reported very unfavorably on a

[54] *Ibid.*, 1894, pp. 4, 20, 36-40.

ATTITUDE OF LABOR AND EMPLOYERS   51

proposed constitutional amendment which gave Congress power to limit hours, expressing doubt of congressional will or ability to use this power effectively. Since one of the gravest obstacles to reducing hours in the United States had been lack of uniformity, hostility to this amendment showed how deeply imbedded was the Federation's opposition to the legislative method. Beginning in 1898, the Federation in giving valuable aid to the Utah Federation of Labor in its fight to uphold the constitutionality of the Eight-Hour Law for miners and smelters,[55] admitted that hazardous trades came within the scope of the legislative method to reduce hours.

The question of legislative action did not rise to a position of any importance again until, in 1906, the Bill of Grievances which labor presented to the President and Congress listed as its first demand the enforcement and improvement of the National Eight-Hour Law.[56] Since Congress took no action on the grievances, the Federation adopted the policy of pledging candidates. When even the very optimistic Samuel Gompers could only report in November, 1908, that "Several of those hostile to labor's interests were defeated," the small success of the attempt was evident.[57] In his report for 1910, when dealing directly with the question, he painted a vague but brighter picture of the political defeats "whereby many of our opponents have demonstrated beyond all quibble what element was responsible," yet the statement immediately following concluded: " That by far the greatest of its [labor's] benefits have come through the exercise of its economic power."[58]

[55] *Ibid.*, 1898, pp. 22, 23, 120.
[56] *Ibid.*, 1906, pp. 31-35; *American Federationist*, 1906, Vol. 13, pp. 294-296.
[57] American Federation of Labor, *Proceedings*, 1908, p. 31.
[58] *Ibid.*, 1910, pp. 44-47.

This tentative step in the direction of legislative action left the guiding hand of organized labor more firmly convinced that, in the last analysis, direct action was to be depended upon. And this idea dominated his policy in the shorter-hour movement.

Until 1913 there was no apparent development in the attitude of the American Federation of Labor concerning the desirability of attaining the eight-hour day by legislative act. Steady agitation and hard effort had resulted in 1912 in the passage of an improved National Eight-Hour Law. But in 1913, at the Seattle Convention, the scene was set for a battle on the relative merits of legislative action as compared with direct action. With little discussion, the report of the Committee on the Shorter Workday was adopted, that increased effort be made to secure eight-hour laws for women and children, and that "agitation should immediately begin for the enactment of general eight-hour laws."[59] In this manner, did the American Federation of Labor unexpectedly ratify the legislative method of securing shorter hours. Gompers, in his account of the proceedings in the *American Federationist,* reported this recommendation "for the enactment in all the States of general eight-hour laws."[60] Thus, it appeared that without a struggle the American Federation of Labor had renounced its opposition to reduction of hours by legal enactment.

This illusion was dispelled, however, at the next convention. Delegates from the California and Washington State Federations of Labor reported that petitions for general eight-hour laws in California, Oregon and Washington were voted down as a result of the circulation of statements

[59] *Ibid.,* 1913, p. 285.
[60] *American Federationist,* 1914, Vol. 21, p. 19.

ATTITUDE OF LABOR AND EMPLOYERS 53

that Samuel Gompers was opposed to and denounced eight-hour laws for men; in fact, "billboards were covered from one end of the State to the other with the warning of our distinguished President." This account precipitated a long and heated discussion,[60a] first, as to the meaning of "a general eight-hour law," and, second, on the relative merits of legislative action supplementary to direct action, as compared to direct action, pure and unalloyed. Gompers claimed that the point at issue was a question of definition. He and the officers of the American Federation of Labor held that "general eight-hour laws meant for the employees of the government only." As Vice-President Duncan stated: "The term 'general legislation' is accepted throughout the length and breadth of the land to refer to legislation by the Federal Government as far as the Federal Law can go, and by States where it can go." The quibble concerning the interpretation of the term "general eight-hour laws" was worthy of a court scene. In addition to this defense of the interpretation of the Seattle resolution on hours, Gompers claimed that when informed of this use of his statements, he had said "that in no sense were they to be used in connection with the pending matter."

When the discussion shifted from the immediate question at issue to the general one of the most effective means of obtaining shorter hours, four arguments were advanced against economic action unsupported by legal enactment. In the first place, it was not practical; it had been tried

[60a] The speakers in favor of legislative action were: John Mitchell and A. Germer, of the United Mine Workers; P. Scharrenberg, of the California State Federation of Labor; A. J. Gallagher, of the San Francisco Labor Council, and L. Goazion, of the Monongahela Valley Central Trades Council; J. A. Taylor, of the Machinists' Union; J. Brown, of the Timber Workers' Union. Those who spoke in opposition were: Samuel Gompers, James Duncan, First Vice-President, and J. P. Frey, of the Molders' Union.

and found wanting. The machinists reported that since 1910 they had spent $800,000 on direct action to reduce hours, with no success. The second claim was that direct action could not reduce hours for the unorganized; laws were needed for this—not only to benefit the unorganized, but to prevent their competition from hampering the efforts of the organized. The third argument based the feasibility of legislative means to reduce hours on labor's successful use of legislation for other reforms. And last, John Mitchell, of the United Mine Workers, maintaining that the method of getting eight hours was unimportant, pointed out that hour laws helped the union in organizing new territory. He attributed the success of his organization's efforts in Montana to that State's eight-hour law, which had prevented the non-union camps from driving the union employers out of business by making their laborers work more than eight hours. Throughout the discussion, the Western States were particularly insistent on the advantages of the legislative method, buttressed as it was in their States with the initiative, referendum and recall.

One minor and three major arguments were propounded against legislative action. The first, apparently a smoke screen which Gompers threw out to discredit the movement, suggested that the advocates of the legislative method had socialistic tendencies. Of the major arguments, the first was based on the fear of legal interference with the liberties of the worker which judicial interpretation might distort, and on the rigidity of the law. It was argued that a general eight-hour law might be interpreted as a minimum eight-hour law, thereby nullifying the successful effort of a trade union to establish shorter hours. The second argument advanced the claims that legislation for shorter hours would lead to a decreasing interest in unions, followed by declining membership and strength. Gompers said: "If we can get an eight-hour law for the working people, then you will find that the working people, themselves, will fail to have any interest in your economic organization, which even the advocates declare essential in order that such a law can be enforced." The last argument was a denial of the failure of direct action to attain shorter hours. Gompers cited as proof of the success of industrial tactics, the adoption of the eight-hour day of his own union, the Cigarmakers in 1886.

This last argument showed how far separated in viewpoint were the opponents. The one side envisaged the need of a method which would get shorter hours for the organized and the unorganizable. The other still thought only in terms of skilled labor, the hours attainable through organization, and the vital need of the hours' question as a spur to organization.

When the roll-call was taken on the committee's resolution, which affirmed the Federation's traditional stand, 11,237 votes were cast for it, 8,107 votes against it; 607 votes were not cast. Thus, after a lengthy discussion, the majority of the American Federation of Labor negatived the legislative method of getting shorter hours for men, maintaining that this benefit should be obtained through trade union activity, while the legislative method was reserved for regulating hours of women and children, for unhealthy or dangerous trades, and for government work. However, the minority had so forcibly expressed a preference for the legislative method as to expose the grave difference of opinion between the official group and, as one of the minority said, " the rank and file, the men in the shops, the mills, the factories, who would rise up if they had witnessed this farce comedy." [61]

[61] American Federation of Labor, *Proceedings*, 1914, pp. 421-444.

The interval between conventions witnessed a growth of agitation on this subject. Gompers enlarged on the socialist origin of the movement, contending that this party favored hours' legislation not as an end, but as a means to split the organization. The State Federations of Illinois and Minnesota joined those of the Pacific Coast in passing resolutions in favor of the enactment of eight-hour laws for men.[62]

When the 1915 convention opened, the Executive Council painted an optimistic picture of recent successful attempts at shorter hours by trade union activity. On the introduction by the Shorter Workday Committee of a resolution reaffirming this as the approved means, the storm broke. This time the advocates of legislative action included William Green, Chairman of the Committee, who was a representative of the United Mine Workers, an organization which almost unanimously favored the legislative method. The arguments were a repetition of those of the preceding convention, though the advocates of the legislative method placed even greater stress on the need for this method to reduce hours for the unorganized, estimated to be 98% of the labor force. The opponents supplemented their previous arguments by a discussion of the unconstitutionality of a general eight-hour law. They corrected—though their corrections scarcely altered the situation—the figures of the unorganized, placing the number at 80 or 82%. They summed up their argument by the sweeping statement that the decrease in hours of the past century for all workers, organized and unorganized, had been brought about "all through the activity of the trade union movement."

When the roll was called, the vote stood 8,500 for reaffirmation of direct action as the approved method, 6,396

[62] *Ibid.*, 1915, pp. 484-494.

against, while 4,061 refrained from voting. The large number in this last group is baffling. It renders insignificant the change in the vote, for while 56% voted against legislative action and 40% for it in 1914, and in 1915 44% voted against it and 33% for it, the proportion of the total vote cast against the use of the legislative method was approximately the same both years.[63]

By the 1916 convention, the Executive Council's rosy forecast of the efficacy of the trade union method for shorter hours had come true. War orders had begun to pour in, and labor had the opportunity to attain its end in this matter. So the struggle over methods, which had shown promise of continuing to a climax, subsided completely, not for the war period alone, but even subsequently. The cooperation in 1916 of the American Federation of Labor with the Brotherhoods, to secure the passage of the Adamson Eight-Hour Law for railroad employees, could be held to be in accord with its policy of favoring shorter hours by legislation, not in general, but in industries where health and safety demanded it.[64] This interpretation could not be placed on the action of the Executive Council in May, 1918, when it urged the President to establish by proclamation, as a war measure, the eight-hour day for all employees.[65] Apparently, when it appeared attainable, the Executive Council, opportunist that it was, willingly set aside its fears of the legal establishment of an eight-hour day.

But with the return of peace-time conditions, the Federation's mouthpiece, the convention, reaffirmed its faith in direct action as the vehicle to attain shorter hours for men,

[63] *Ibid.*, 1915, pp. 67-69, 484-504.
[64] *American Federationist*, 1916, Vol. 23, pp. 844-847.
[65] American Federation of Labor, *Proceedings*, 1918, p. 79.

while it continued to advocate improvements in hours' legislation for government employees, for women and children, and for unhealthy and dangerous trades. As if to cast doubt on the need for the legislative method, the Committee on the Shorter Workday in 1924 reviewed the effectiveness of trade union activity as a reform agent in the hours' field.[66] In 1928, and again in 1929, when the need for shorter hours for the unorganized compelled mention, because of the publicity given to the excessive hours in certain sections of the United States, the Executive Council renewed its expression of faith in the efficacy of direct action by urging the unorganized to join the American Federation of Labor to secure shorter hours.[67] That the ruling party of the Federation continued opposed to general legislation for hours was shown when in 1930, the Textile Workers' resolution, calling on the Federation to aid in the passage of forty-eight-hour legislation, was not passed until it was amended to read: "Forty-eight-hour legislation for women and children."[68] The opposition of the Executive Council to an amendment, proposed in the House of Representatives in 1931, which would give Congress the power to reduce the working hours in contracts,[69] may be cited as final proof that even the long drawn-out depression has not caused the Federation to incline more favorably to the legislative method.

EMPLOYERS

General recognition of the intense individualist philosophy of American employers makes it unnecessary to discuss at any length their hostile attitude to legislation to secure

[66] *Ibid.*, 1924, pp. 222, 223.
[67] *Ibid.*, 1928, p. 43; *ibid.*, 1929, p. 47.
[68] *Ibid.*, 1930, p. 261.
[69] *Ibid.*, 1931, p. 113.

ATTITUDE OF LABOR AND EMPLOYERS

shorter hours. As confirmed believers in the doctrine of laissez-faire on all labor questions, employers have, with no notable exceptions, opposed legal regulation of hours. The form, in which this opposition expressed itself, changed radically in the period under study. In the earlier years, it was a passive hostility which resulted in no preventive action. Later, it changed to informal cooperation among employers to hinder the enactment of such legislation, and finally to united action through State and national associations.

The available evidence shows that in the first movement for shorter hours by legislative enactment the employers took little overt action. This is apparent in the indifference encountered by the commissions appointed in Massachusetts to investigate the desirability of such a law. The first investigatory commission, appointed in 1866, received only eighty replies to the thousand printed circulars which it sent out. As approximately half of these were from towns and cities, it is plain that the employers, either did not wish to state their opinions, or did not consider it worth the effort. A like result attended the investigation of the commission which was appointed in 1867.[70] Later, in 1870, the Bureau of Statistics of Labor complained that no employers attended their advertised hearings on hour legislation.[71] In New York, too, it was reported that there was "not so much opposition as was expected" to the passage of the Eight-Hour Law in 1867.[72] While the

[70] Massachusetts Bureau of Statistics of Labor, *Seventh Annual Report*, 1876, p. 276.

[71] *Ibid.*, 1870, p. 111. Wm. Gray, Treasurer of the Atlantic Mills, which had voluntarily adopted the ten-hour day (*cf. infra*, p. 227), advocated this legislation. *Argument of Wm. Gray on Petitions for Ten-Hour Law*, Pamphlet, Boston, 1873.

[72] *New York Tribune*, March 22, 1867.

New York newspapers, and journals of the type which reflected the opinion of the employing class, devoted considerable space to denunciation of efforts to enact a federal eight-hour law, no reference was made to any special activity on the part of manufacturers to prevent its passage.

There are several possible explanations for this lack of exertion on the part of employers. Two seem most probable. The first and most obvious is that no credence was given to the likelihood of such statutes being enacted, either because of confidence in the laissez-faire policy of the legislative bodies, or because of covert means of controlling this policy. The second is that employers, as individuals, felt it was useless to endeavor to stem this tide. While the workers had organized into admittedly weak city, state, and even nation-wide associations which had hour legislation as a principal objective, the employers had not as yet developed either informal or formal means for united action.

This cooperative action against all protective labor legislation, including regulation of hours, evolved slowly within the separate States, and eventually on a national scale. The informal means naturally developed first, and resulted in the appointment of representatives by employers, in the same trade, to state the grounds for their hostility at legislative hearings. There is space here to cite only one national and one State example to illustrate such efforts. The Hearings of the House of Representatives, Committee on Labor in 1900 on a bill to improve the Federal Eight-Hour Law, was notable as being the last hearing at which representatives of individual employers endeavored to present their opposition without the aid of officials of national associations of employers. The arguments were not very original, and were distinctly repetitive. In addition to the general arguments,[73] the bill was opposed as an unconstitutional interference with freedom of contract, and as a measure which would cause an insurmountable difficulty of factory organization, inasmuch as it would be necessary for a plant with both government and private contracts to attempt to work an eight-hour day on the former, and a ten-hour day on the latter. Of particular interest was one employer's sweeping argument that it "would cause an immediate and disastrous industrial and social revolution. Hitherto relations between the employer and the employed have been adjusted by natural laws." [74] The bill failed of passage. Informal action by employers on the eight-hour bill in California has been selected as an example of this type of preventive effort within a State. So slight was the expectation of the passage of this measure, that not until it had passed the Lower House unanimously did the employers begin to take action. Then the business interests demanded and were granted a hearing to which the various industries united to send representatives. While the desirability of the principle of the eight-hour day was generally conceded, all opposed it on the ground that it would hurt the women of the State by causing unemployment and a reduction of wages.[75] Despite this attempt at preventive action, the statute was enacted.[76]

Far different from the informal, temporary cooperation of employers are the continuous lobbying efforts of employers' associations. These have been carried on within the several States and at Washington. For example, the

[73] *Cf. supra*, pp. 13-21.
[74] p. 50 *et seq.*
[75] U. S., *Bulletin of the Women's Bureau*, No. 66, p. 122.
[76] *Cf. infra*, pp. 113, 114.

Illinois Manufacturers' Association carried out a constant program to prevent the further shortening of women's hours. In 1913 this Association testified before the State Senate Labor Committee that the result of the proposed eight-hour law would be to drive the greater part of industry from the State, and to reduce women's wages to starvation levels.[77] The successful lobbying of this Association continued, and when in 1915 a nine-hour bill was defeated, a circular stating that "results to date have never before been so gratifying" was sent to all its members.[78] The maintenance of this continuous activity by associations of employers at the State Capitols is the common practice today, and every proposal to reduce the hours established by law is subjected to concerted efforts to prevent it, or at least postpone the time of its enactment.[79]

Associations of employers have been active opponents at Washington of federal hours' legislation since 1902. Although employers' associations on a national scale had come into existence in the last two decades of the nineteenth century, after national organizations of labor had begun to gain sufficient strength to force issues, these associations did not immediately institute active opposition to labor legislation. The National Association of Manufacturers is an outstanding example of this change of policy. From its establishment in 1895, until 1902, it concentrated its efforts on tariff reform, and on the promotion of foreign trade, but, in the latter year, the newly elected President, D. M. Parry, initiated a belligerent anti-labor

[77] *New York Times,* May 20, 1913.

[78] *New Republic,* June 5, 1915, July 10, 1915.

[79] For a brief account of opposition tactics, see *American Labor Legislation Review,* 1919, pp. 237, 238.

legislation policy.[80] This opposition policy centered in large part on the annual attempt to improve the National Eight-Hour Law of 1892, by providing that an eight-hour clause be incorporated in all contracts for the purchase of goods for the National Government.

The first steps, taken in 1902, were the sending of a resolution to Congress, and the deluging of individual Congressmen with telegrams. The Association claimed that these measures defeated the bill.[81] Their efforts in this direction continued in the form of educational pamphlets, and active opposition at all hearings. One pamphlet, written by the President, denounced the proposed improvement as a socialistic and artificial measure which contraverted the inalienable rights of the individual to use his time as he saw fit. The logical reasoning of the President led him to conclude that, if the majority worked ten hours, "it is an indication that it requires that number of hours of labor on the part of men in general in order to produce the commodities necessary to satisfy the needs and desires of the nation." [82]

This Association published a far more detailed criticism of the proposed improvement in the national Eight-Hour Law, in 1904, summarizing the arguments which their officials used at Congressional hearings. In the first place, the bill was discriminatory in that it militated against those employers who worked on government contracts. This discrimination was particularly unfair to the newly developing South "where at last the 'poor white' finds that the world has industrial use for him." The pamphlet

[80] Taylor, A. G., *Labor Policies of the National Association of Manufacturers*, Urbana, 1928, p. 13.

[81] *Ibid.*, p. 121.

[82] Parry, D. M., *Disastrous Effects of a National Eight-Hour Law*, Pamphlet, n. d.

stated further that the bill was unpatriotic and little "less than treason" because it restricted the rapidity of construction of the navy. It held that the bill was confiscatory inasmuch as its enactment would cause bankruptcy to those businesses which had made large investments in highly specialized capital, suited only for government contracts. To these sweeping statements was added criticism of the bill's ambiguity, and of the practical difficulties which its enforcement would involve.[83]

This Association has not only exerted great efforts to influence Congress, but has attempted to reach the public by propaganda. Its leaders have declared: "We must point out to the people that all this legislation that is going on affects them; shorter hours [a shorter workday] increases the cost of living, raises taxes, creates a condition for them that is really worse than it is for the manufacturers. We owe that to them. We must do it. That is the important thing for this organization to do." [84]

As was said above, these were the arguments advanced year after year against federal legislation. How successful it has been can be judged by the fact that Dr. Bonnett, who has made a comprehensive study of employers' associations, credits this organization and the League for Industrial Rights with having secured the defeat of all eight-hour measures from 1902 to 1912.[85]

The efforts of the National Association of Manufacturers to prevent improvements and extension of the Federal Government's hour legislation have been supplemented by those of many similar organizations. The

[83] National Association of Manufacturers, *Eight Hours by Act of Congress: Arbitrary, Needless, Destructive, Dangerous*, Pamphlet, 1904.

[84] Bonnett, C., *Employers' Associations of the United States*, New York, 1922, quoted p. 355.

[85] *Ibid.*, pp. 308, 456.

Citizens' Industrial Alliance of America, even at its organization meeting in 1903, found time to pass a resoluton which urged Congress to defeat the then pending eight-hour bill, on the ground that it would injure the public.[86] The National Metal Trades' Association and its branches have had officials in Washington to hinder the enactment of all such legislation, which it has condemned as vicious and pernicious.[87] And last, the League for Industrial Rights, which was mentioned above, since its establishment in 1902 has been represented in Washington in opposition to all legislation to decrease hours on government work, or to extend the inclusiveness of federal hours' legislation.[88]

[86] Citizens' Industrial Alliance, *Bulletin No. 1*, p. 18.
[87] Bonnett, *op. cit.*, p. 119.
[88] *Ibid.*, p. 456.

CHAPTER III

NATIONAL LEGISLATION

FROM the beginning of the movement, the demand for national legislation to establish the eight-hour day has suffered from misleading wording, and from a misconception of the scope of the Federal Government powers. This obscurity characterized alike the earliest demands of organized labor and those of a large group in the American Federation of Labor as late as 1913. It is still present, the writer believes, in the ideas of the layman today. Certainly the resolution of the National Labor Union in favor of organizing " the National Labor Party, the object of which shall be to secure the enactment of a law making eight hours a legal day's work," [1] seemed to assume the possibility of a national law establishing a general eight-hour day. Newspaper references to our successive National Eight-Hour Laws would lead the unthinking to conclude we had general legislation on this subject. Senator Copeland's statement that the six-hour day and five-day week by legislation are necessary at the present time is illustrative of lack of clarity on the subject today.[2] Newspapers and periodicals, as a result of the present unemployment, have constantly quoted misleading demands and suggestions for national legislation on hours in general. This, however, is not possible under our Constitution as it stands.

[1] *Workingman's Advocate,* March 5, 1870, quotes this resolution adopted August, 1866.
[2] *New York Times,* September 21, 1930.

Those laws regulating hours which the National Government has tried to enact, and has enacted, have had to come within the narrow limits of the constitutional powers of the Federal Government. A general eight-hour law, such as those passed by European countries, as a result of the Washington Hours' Convention of 1919, has been an absolute impossibility in the United States. Realization of this limitation ultimately caused labor to drop the sweeping demand for a universal eight-hour law. For example, by about 1870 the Boston Eight-Hour League had decided to concentrate on securing "the eight-hour system first for all labor employed at the public expense."[3] This narrower demand has been the basis for all national hours' legislation except in the case of workers engaged in interstate commerce; and is what is meant when our National Eight-Hour Laws are mentioned.

Other means of regulation within the constitutional limits have been sought. Among these may be mentioned a suggestion of the early labor associations that an eight-hour provision be attached to all patents granted,[4] and the introduction of bills in Congress prohibiting interstate trade for the products of women's labor where the hours exceeded eight. An effort to provide regulation for men, as well, was made when Senator Moses unsuccessfully sponsored a bill to establish an eight-hour day in all plants engaged in producing articles entering into interstate trade.[5] Congressmen have frequently proposed a constitutional amendment, and in 1913 the Massachusetts Legislature petitioned Congress to submit an amendment per-

[3] McNeill, *op. cit.*, p. 140.
[4] *Cf. supra*, p. 39.
[5] *New York Times*, May 24, 1919.

mitting the regulation of hours by the Federal Government "in the interests of justice and uniformity."[6] Defeat of the above mentioned bills was probably due in part to doubt as to their constitutionality. Repeated failure to amend the Constitution limits hours' regulation by the federal government to two classes of workers: those engaged on government work, and those employed in interstate or foreign commerce.

REGULATION OF HOURS ON GOVERNMENT WORK

The history of this type of regulation has been a repetitive cycle. There has been, first, the demand for legislation, accompanied by efforts to force its passage; second, questions of interpretation, followed in turn by disheartening struggles for enforcement of the law, emasculated by interpretation; and last, realization that a new law, remedying the flaws of interpretation and providing means of enforcement, must be sought.

Three National Eight-Hour Laws have been passed. The arguments presented have not changed with time. They include, besides those on the general principle of shorter hours,[7] others bearing only on federal enactment. Advocates of these measures have stressed two arguments: first, established precedent—since 1840 the National Government has regulated hours on government work; and second, the need for the government to serve as a model employer. Opponents of these measures have been loud and articulate in their objections. They have denounced them as placing an unnecessary expense upon the government, as a means of getting votes by the political party which sponsored them, and as the cause of increasing unemployment because the shorter day attracted more immigrants. So far as the laws

[6] *Congressional Record*, Vol. 49, p. 3624.
[7] *Cf. supra*, pp. 13-21.

applied to contractors on government work, they were opposed as an unjustifiable interference with the liberty of contract between employer and employee. It was also claimed that, inasmuch as contractors on government jobs also did private work, an insurmountable difficulty of organization, caused by these laws, would force an eight-hour day for the whole plant. Since this would make impossible competition with firms engaged only on private contracts, the outcome would be bankruptcy for those firms with sufficient patriotism to undertake government contracts.

Although the first eight-hour bill was introduced into Congress in 1865, it was not until June 25, 1868, that the law was enacted. The debate, at the time of its passage, showed that its advocates intended it to be very sweeping. It read, as follows: "Be it enacted (etc.) that eight hours shall constitute a day's work for all laborers, workmen and mechanics now employed or who may be hereafter employed by or on behalf of the Government of the United States." [8]

The first problem of interpreting the brief statute arose when some departments cut wages to correspond with the decrease in hours. The National Labor Congress passed a resolution asking the Attorney General to interpret the law in this respect, and agreed that, should he endorse this position of a one-fifth cut in pay, they would appeal to Congress to amend the law.[9] On November 25, 1868, Attorney General Evarts handed down an equivocal opinion "susceptible of being construed either way." [10] The Executive Departments, as might have been expected, read its meaning to be that the cut in wages

[8] 15 Stat. 77.
[9] *Workingman's Advocate*, October 10, 1868.
[10] *New York Times*, editorial, May 14, 1878.

was legal. Labor declared that the interpretation was a "patent violation of the intent of the law and destructive of its entity." [11] Senator Wilson, who had been active in the passage of the law, sustained labor's contention.[12] The outcome was President Grant's proclamation of May 19, 1869, directing that the standard of wages should be left unchanged when hours were reduced. Non-compliance by the Executive Offices caused the President to issue a second proclamation to the same effect on May 11, 1872. Congress supplemented the Presidential proclamations by appropriating funds on May 18, 1872, to pay the wages which labor had lost due to the improper interpretation of the law by the Executive Department officials.[13]

The second question of interpretation was the inclusiveness of the provisions of the law. Action was precipitated when the New York Workingmen's Union asked the Secretary of the Treasury to restrain the contractor on the construction of the New York Post Office from working his laborers ten hours a day. The Secretary replied that the law did not control contractors on government jobs.[14] He was sustained in this opinion by the Attorney General who ruled that "the act was not intended to extend to any others than the immediate employees of the government." [15] The decision of the Supreme Court of the United States in the case of United States *v.* Martin, in 1876, completely emasculated the law by ruling that the Act was "in the nature of a direction by the government to its agents," and that it did not "prevent the govern-

[11] *Workingman's Advocate,* April 24, 1869.
[12] *New York Times,* April 26, 1869.
[13] *American Federationist,* 1898, Vol. 5, p. 57.
[14] *New York Times,* November 12, 1869.
[15] 14 Op. A. G. 37, 1872.

ment from making agreements with them [its employees] by which their labor may be more or less than eight hours." [16] In other words, by this decision a government official could decide on the hours of work with no regard for "the direction" of the law.

This Act failed to accomplish its purpose, not only because of these adverse interpretations, but because of lack of enforcement. While there were no provisions for enforcement in the law itself, the two proclamations of the President were attempts in that direction. The continued failure of the Executive to make further efforts was a constant source of complaint and agitation. *The Workingman's Advocate* saw in the failure an attempt to prove that "the 'higher law' of supply and demand alone controlled the labor market, thus giving a semi-official rebuff to all future movements of like kind." [17] On the other hand, the *New York Times* offered the failure of the law, which it held to be non-enforceable, as proof "that all things will be best regulated when they are left to be freely regulated by the parties concerned." [18] A meeting of the Workingmen's Council of the United States passed the following resolution: "The Government of the United States in taking pains to enforce its financial and other laws made in favor of the rich, while deliberately and impudently violating the Eight-Hour Law made in the interest of labor, shows itself to be a tyrannous fraud, fit only to be despised by honest men." [19] General B. F. Butler expressed the same opinion. He wrote: "It is not creditable to the administration of justice and law in this country"

[16] 94 U. S. 400.
[17] *Workingman's Advocate,* March 12, 1870.
[18] *New York Times,* January 5, 1869.
[19] *Ibid.,* May 19, 1874.

that government officials should set aside the one law which had been passed for labor's benefit.[20] The insistent demands for the law's enforcement by the national labor organizations have been recounted in the preceding chapter.[21]

Agitation resulted in the passage in 1888 of improved eight-hour laws for the employees of two Federal Departments. The first of these, enacted March 30, provided: "The Public Printer is hereby directed to rigidly enforce the provisions of the eight-hour law in the department under his charge."[22] The second, passed on May 24, specifically fixed an eight-hour day with no reduction in pay for letter-carriers in all cities.[23] The Post Office Department did not reduce the hours, interpreting the eight-hour provision to apply only to time spent in carrying mail. The decision of the Supreme Court, in 1893, overthrew this interpretation, holding the eight-hour provision applied to all work done in and around the post office.[24]

In 1892, a congressional committee held a general investigation to determine the need for an improved hour law for all government work. As a result of the testimony of officials in charge of government construction, the committee reported unanimously in favor of a more specific law with provisions for enforcement. After lengthy discussion in both houses, the tenor of which showed that the eight-hour provision was to include not only those working directly for the government, but also those employed indirectly, and that careful consideration

[20] *Ibid.*, March 26, 1883.
[21] *Cf. supra*, pp. 38, 41, 48, 49, 51.
[22] 25 Stat. 57.
[23] 25 U. S. 157.
[24] United States *v.* Post, 148 U. S. 124, 1893.

NATIONAL LEGISLATION 73

had been given to provisions for enforcement, the Act became law August 1, 1892.[25] It read:

"Be it enacted, etc., That the service and employment of all laborers and mechanics who are now, or may hereafter be, employed by the Government of the United States, by the District of Columbia, or by any contractor or sub-contractor upon any of the public works of the United States, or of the said District, is hereby limited and restricted to eight hours in any one calendar day, and it shall be unlawful for any officer of the United States Government or the District of Columbia, or any such contractor, or sub-contractor, whose duty it shall be to employ, direct or control the services of such laborer or mechanic to work more than eight hours in any calendar day: except in cases of extraordinary emergency."

Section 2. "Any officer or agent of the Government of the United States or of the District of Columbia, or any contractor or sub-contractor, whose duty it shall be to employ, direct or control any laborer or mechanic employed upon any of the public works of the United States or of the District of Columbia, who shall intentionally violate any provision of this Act, shall be deemed guilty of a misdemeanor, and for each and every such offense, upon conviction, be punished by a fine not to exceed one thousand dollars, or by imprisonment for not more than six months, or by both such fine and imprisonment, in the discretion of the court having jurisdiction thereof."

Section 3. "The provisions of this Act shall not be construed as to in any manner apply to or affect contractors or sub-contractors, or to limit the hours of daily service of laborers or mechanics engaged upon the public works of the United States, or of the District of Columbia for which contracts have been entered into prior to the passage of this Act." [26]

Despite its length, the law is quoted in full as proof that Congress tried to eliminate those weaknesses for which the brevity of the Act of 1868 had been blamed. Yet, in its turn, the later law was greatly weakened by interpretation and lack of enforcement. The first limitation placed on the scope of the law was by the definition given to "public works." The committee report and the

[25] *Congressional Record,* Vol. 23, pp. 5723-5738.
[26] 27 Stat. 340.

debate at the passage of the law showed that its advocates used " public works " in a general and not in a technical sense, that is, to include all work done for the government. The Supreme Court, however, said that "the words 'upon' and 'any of the' and the plural 'works' import that the objects of labor referred to have some kind of permanent existence and structural unity, and are severally capable of being regarded as complete wholes." [27] Adopting this narrowed definition, the Attorney General ruled: "The Act . . . does not apply to vessels under construction for the Navy by contract with builders at private establishments." [28] So also contracts for post-office lock-boxes, lock drawers, etc., which were to be placed in their final position by the government were ruled not to be "public works;" [29] but "as a timber dry dock is intended to be a valuable and permanent improvement of real estate belonging to the United States, . . . it is . . . to be regarded as one of the 'public works' of the United States under this Eight-Hour Law." [30] In other words, by the definition the application of the law was limited to laborers on fixed works on property of the United States.

It was limited still more by the very loose interpretation of the term "emergency." A case in point was the construction of the government dam at McMechen, West Virginia, which Gompers said "served as a monument to the violation of the Eight-Hour Law." No official investigation was held to determine the necessity for the decision of a Major in the Engineering Corps and the contractor that conditions in the Ohio River were so

[27] Ellis v. U. S., 206 U. S. 246, 1907.
[28] 26 Op. A. G. 30, 1906.
[29] 20 Op. A. G. 454, 1892.
[30] 20 Op. A. G. 445, 1892.

peculiar that an emergency existed, which required the suspension of the eight-hour provision. Yet the American Federation of Labor had made repeated and continuous efforts to have action taken on this and similar cases.[31] It was not until 1911 that emasculation of the law, by means of such "permanent emergencies," was eliminated. In that year, the Supreme Court of the United States reversed the ruling of a circuit court that levee work on the Mississippi presented "at all times an extraordinary emergency." In this decision, the Supreme Court declared that the phrase "continuing extraordinary emergency" was self-contradictory.[32]

Not only was the statute of 1892 weakened by narrowing interpretations, but for a long time it also suffered the fate of the earlier law—lack of enforcement. Provision for punishment of violators, which in the congressional debates at its passage had loomed as an important improvement, was not used. The Committee on Labor, in its report to Congress in 1898, said: "That contractors and sub-contractors on government work continue to direct their men in violation of the plain terms of this Act is not denied," yet "the Committee has been unable to learn of any instance where an attempt has been made to enforce the law as against any contractor or sub-contractor."[33] Seven years after its enactment, the Bulletin of the New York State Bureau of Labor Statistics, after remarking that the law had "remained more or less of a dead letter so far as contract work was concerned," stated that an important precedent had been set when on November 21,

[31] *American Federationist,* 1906, Vol. 13, p. 298.
[32] U. S. v. Garbish, 222 U. S. 257, 1911.
[33] *Congressional Record,* Vol. 31, p. 3536, refers to Com. Report no. 957, p. 5.

1899, the United States District Court at Baltimore had fined a contractor five hundred dollars for requiring an employee to work more than eight hours.[34] The question of the applicability of the Law of 1892 to the construction of the Panama Canal caused great agitation and discussion. When Attorney General Moody ruled that the eight-hour provision covered all workers on the project, except the clerical force,[35] Secretary of War Taft protested his decision on the ground that it would cost millions, and delay the completion of the job.[36] The newspapers adopted Taft's view, and gave great publicity to the unwarranted expense which the shorter day would entail. The final outcome was, according to Labor's Bill of Grievances, that, "without hearing of any kind granted to those who are the advocates of the eight-hour law and principle, Congress passed, and the President signed an appropriation bill containing a rider nullifying the eight-hour law and principle in its application to the greatest public work ever undertaken by our government, the construction of the Panama Canal."[37]

The Bill of Grievances, however, did rouse the President to take action in regard to violations of the Eight-Hour Law for which the Federation had for years sought redress.[38] In September, 1908, an Executive order was issued commanding enforcement of the law, and prompt reports of all violations by the government representatives in charge of construction.[39] This order reversed the de-

[34] New York, *Bulletin of the Bureau of Labor Statistics*, 1899, p. 153.
[35] 25 Op. A. G. 441, 1905.
[36] *Philadelphia Press*, June 16, 1905.
[37] *American Federationist*, 1906, Vol. 13, p. 689.
[38] *Ibid.*, pp. 299-304.
[39] 20 Op. A. G. 500, 1892.

NATIONAL LEGISLATION

cision of the Attorney General, made in 1892 that: "The duty to employ, direct or control such laborers or mechanics, and the penalty for their wrongful employment, is with the contractor and not with the government or any of its officers or agents." To aid prompt enforcement, a deputy attorney general was appointed to handle exclusively violations of the Eight-Hour Law of 1892.[40] Throughout this period in which narrowing interpretations, lack of aggressiveness in enforcement, and finally direct act of Congress, emasculated the Law of 1892, labor continued its endeavors to secure an effective law. Bills were introduced each session, and frequent hearings were held by both Senate and House Committees on Labor, at each of which organized labor and organized employers repeated their diametrically opposed stands. Labor was helpless when these bills were killed in committee. Gompers denounced the Committee on Labor as a Committee on Indolence, and arraigned Speaker Cannon for packing the Committee with members hostile to labor.[41] With the change in the political complexion of the House in 1910, an amendatory bill was reported out of committee. It was passed after discussion, which emphasized its need because the Act of 1892 had been interpreted so differently "from that which was intended by the law-making body."[42]

The Act, passed June 19, 1912, is too long to quote in full, due to the effort made to prevent the weaknesses which the Law of 1892 had exhibited. Suffice it to say that it provided that every contract to which the United States was party must contain an eight-hour-day clause,

[40] *New York Tribune,* November 14, 1906.
[41] *American Federationist,* 1911, Vol. 18, p. 216.
[42] *Congressional Record,* Vol. 48, p. 381.

except "contracts for transportation by land or water, or for the transmission of intelligence, or for the purchase of supplies, . . . or for such materials or articles as may usually be bought in the open market, except armor and armor-plate, whether made to conform to particular specifications or not, or to the construction or repair of levees." Its final provision permitted the President to waive the Act "during time of war, or when war is imminent." The duty to report violations was placed on the government inspectors who were supervising the work performed under the contract. The penalty, provided by this Act, was cumulatively far greater than that of the Law of 1892. It fixed a fine of five dollars for each laborer for every calendar day on which more than eight hours of work was required or permitted.[43]

Despite the efforts to achieve an unassailable law, this Act, like the earlier ones, was weakened by interpretation. On October 3, 1912, the Attorney General ruled that "no penalty could be collected . . . if the laborer or mechanic were required to labor more than eight hours per day upon some other work than that contemplated by the contract."[44] This nullified the law for plants working on public and private contracts by making it a practical impossibility to obtain evidence. A second opinion, which excepted workers dredging rivers and harbors from the terms of the Act, later led to an amendment which specifically brought such laborers under its provisions.[45] On the other hand, the Attorney General's reasoning in an opinion on a reported violation in the construction of the Lincoln Memorial was such that labor held it would be "helpful

[43] 37 Stat. 137.
[44] 29 Op. A. G. 538, 1912.
[45] 37 Stat. 726.

in the future in securing the enforcement of the plain reading and intent of the Federal Eight-Hour Law."[46] However, the peaceful course of a slowly developed body of opinions as to interpretation and enforcement was disrupted by the war.

Suspension of the Act by presidential order, for which the Act itself provided, was restated in the Naval Appropriation Act of March 4, 1917, subject to the provision that in this event the wages of laborers on government contracts should provide time and one-half for all hours in excess of eight. This principle was affirmed in the Executive Orders of March 24 and April 28, 1917.[47] The substitution of the basic eight-hour day for the straight eight-hour day drew a constant fire of criticism from newspapers and employers' associations that labor wanted shorter hours not as an end, but as a means to raise wages.

In order to avoid delay in interpretations, and to secure uniform enforcement of the law, Professor Felix Frankfurter was detailed by the Secretary of War to act as an advisor on all questions that arose under the provisions of the Act of 1912, and the changes here mentioned. He issued "information and suggestions for the interpretation, administration and enforcement" of the law, and orders relative to it, "for the assistance of all officials and agencies engaged in making contracts or purchases for the War Department."[48] Despite this care, the enforcement of the law continued to be a source of discontent throughout the war. The *New Republic* of March 30, 1918, listed,

[46] *American Federationist*, 1915, Vol. 22, p. 600.
[47] National War Labor Board, *Memorandum on Eight-Hour Working Day*, Washington, 1918, p. 11.
[48] *Ibid.*, pp. 13-25.

among the causes of industrial unrest, "the misleading language of the Federal Eight-Hour Law," which had spread the belief among workers that eight hours was universal for all government jobs. A memorandum to the War Labor Policies Board of June 21, 1918, reported the same condition. It stated: "In many cases workers in the same factories engaged on different articles needed by the government were treated differently . . . rulings, which in the light of present conditions would seem arbitrary to the workers (whatever historical justification they might have) have created in the workers a sense of injustice and of unfair discrimination which has been responsible for a great many labor troubles." This memorandum stated further that manufacturers objected to granting eight hours on all government contracts, partly through fear of establishing a precedent for conditions after the war, and partly on the ground that it would so upset the organization of work on public and private contracts as to interfere " with the production of the articles needed by the government."[49]

Manufacturers saw the recognition of the basic eight-hour day only as a means to higher wages. The Metal Trades Association urged that it be abolished because it penalized firms patriotic enough to work for the government,[50] and the National Association of Manufacturers, in the same vein, said: "Never before in our history has the opportunity been presented to demonstrate to the world the real patriotism of American industry . . . neither employers nor employees should take advantage of the country's needs to change existing standards."[51] On the other

[49] *Ibid.*, pp. 27, 28.
[50] *New York Times*, April 24, 1917.
[51] *Ibid.*, May 16, 1917.

hand, labor's appreciation of the basic eight-hour day as a means of drawing some of the war profits from manufacturers, did not obscure for them the larger view that it was establishing the principle of a straight eight-hour day for the time when peace should have removed the need for excessive production. With both the immediate and the ultimate advantage of the basic eight-hour day in view, labor used its strategic position to spread its adoption. In this it was aided by the War Labor Board, which almost invariably awarded the basic eight-hour day when the question of hours was at issue. The decisions in two of the three cases, in which failure of the Board to reach an agreement led to submission to an umpire, were significant in their insistence on the need for the straight eight-hour day. In both cases, the actual eight-hour day was awarded except in an emergency, which could only be declared to exist by a majority of a joint board consisting of two representatives of the employers and two of the employees. In one of these awards, the umpire said that "very few emergencies justified the practise of exceeding eight working hours." [52]

At the close of the war, work on government contracts reverted to its former status of the straight eight-hour day. Organized labor, through the conventions of the American Federation of Labor, has continued to demand further reduction in hours for government employees. Resolutions have been passed annually since 1919, urging the passage of a law establishing the forty-four-hour week in Navy Yards, Arsenals and in the Government Printing Office. Until 1929 this was urged, as in earlier days, on the ground of "the importance of the United States Government establishing and maintaining advanced employ-

[52] U. S., *Bulletin of Bureau of Labor Statistics*, No. 287, pp. 71, 72.

ment standards."[53] Since that year, the reason for the demand has, significantly enough, been based on the fact that inasmuch as "private business has now generally adopted the Saturday half-holiday practice throughout the year," its inauguration in the "industrial establishments of the government be made an issue of primary importance."[54] Finally in 1931, statutes were enacted which established the forty-four-hour week for federal employees including those in the postal service.[54a] Thus at the end of a sixty-year period of federal legislation for government employees, the National Government was no longer a leader, a model to other employers, in the movement for reduction of hours.

REGULATION OF HOURS OF RAILROAD EMPLOYEES

The power given to the National Government by the Constitution to regulate commerce among the several States was not exerted by Congress until 1907 as a means of controlling hours of labor of employees engaged in interstate trade. The lateness of the date of federal interference in this field is not surprising when it is remembered that not until 1887 did Congress regulate railroads in any respect.

The unions and some State Legislatures, however, had attempted to regulate hours. The former, where sufficiently strong, had negotiated agreements establishing the basic ten-hour day with time and a half for over time. The agreements, which some unions had succeeded in persuading the railroads to ratify, providing that rest should be given after sixteen hours of service no matter where the

[53] American Federation of Labor, *Proceedings*, 1923, p. 346, is typical.
[54] *Ibid.*, 1929, p. 388.
[54a] 46 Stat. 1164, 1482.

trains might be, were constantly broken. Several States had passed laws which established the basic ten-hour day, and a maximum day which varied from thirteen to twenty-four hours, but the effectiveness of these laws was lessened by provision for exception in case of accident. As a result, despite agreements and State enactments, long hours were the expected order of events in the frequent emergencies "due to accidents and conditions of the weather when men were required to work continuously for thirty-six hours or more." Long hours, not in an emergency, but as a standard day, were common in those cases in which neither union agreement nor State legislation existed. For example, we read that "in the South and West rules require trackmen to work from sunrise to sunset," despite the fact that "the position of track foreman is an arduous one, and the responsibility is great." [55]

Railroad executives had no doubt, whatsoever, that this situation did not require federal regulation. Those who testified before the Industrial Commission in 1900, maintain consistent opposition, holding that it "would be very disastrous in its results," and that it was unnecesary because the tendency toward shorter hours was so marked. The attitude of organized railroad labor was not so decided. A joint reply "of the chief officers of the leading railway brotherhoods," submitted to the Industrial Commission, sometime in December, 1898, declared that: "It is impracticable to fix arbitrarily the hours of labor of train and engine-men on account of the necessity of changing crews only at established points." The contrary opinion was expressed at a meeting of the representatives of

[55] U. S. Industrial Commission, *Report on the Relations of Capital and Labor*, 1901, Vol. 17, p. 735.

five leading railroad unions, held six months later, in July, 1899, which urged Congress to pass a law restricting hours of employees in the transportation departments of interstate railroads to eight out of twenty-four, due to the increase in physical and mental strain of the job.[56] The Industrial Commission did not make any definite recommendation to Congress, but suggested that: "Probably ten hours would be a fair standard day at the present time if any general or federal legislation were contemplated." [57]

Agitation by the Railroad Brotherhoods for federal legislation continued steadily until, in 1906, President Roosevelt in his messsage to Congress advocated a law to establish shorter consecutive hours of duty for railroad men. Congress acted promptly, and the regulatory bill became law when it was signed by the President on March 4, 1907. The statute made it unlawful to require or permit any trainman engaged in interstate commerce "to be or to remain on duty for a longer period than sixteen consecutive hours," or to require or permit him "again to go on duty until he has had at least ten consecutive hours off duty." Exceptions were permitted in case of unavoidable accident or act of God. Train despatchers' hours were limited to nine in continuously operated offices, to thirteen in those operated only during the day, except in case of emergency. The law provided a penalty, not to exceed five hundred dollars, for each and every violation, and the Interstate Commerce Commission was made responsible for its enforcement.[58]

The railroads attempted to dispose of this law in two ways. The first attack, directed toward the question of its

---

[56] *Report on the Relations of Capital and Labor*, Vol. 17, p. 736.
[57] *Ibid.*, p. 737.
[58] 34 Stat. 1416.

constitutionality, was not defeated until in May, 1911, the Supreme Court handed down the decision that: "By virtue of its power to regulate interstate and foreign commerce, Congress may enact laws for the safeguarding of the persons and property that are transported in that commerce and of those who are employed in transporting them." [59] The second, which attempted to emasculate the law by interpretation, met with no greater success. When the railroads contended that the terms of the law did not include train crews gathering up loaded cars from spur lines, and placing them for movement by an interstate train, the Court ruled these crews were engaged in interstate commerce, and so came under the provisions of this Act. This decision also established a precedent for eliminating the railroads' line of defense that the sixteen-hour limit had not been exceeded when deduction was made for meals and for delays, during which the crew was idle.[60] An adverse decision of the Supreme Court prevented a further attempt to extract the teeth of the law when the railroads claimed that the over-time work of a number of employees, all due to the same delay of a train, incurred only one penalty, not a separate penalty for each employee.[61]

In the years following the passage of the Hours of Service Act of 1907, collective agreements established two systems of hours for railroad employees. One, in operation for about 15% of the roads, fixed eight hours as a standard of work and wages, with additional pay for overtime. The second, which was in operation on the remaining 85% of the roads, fixed a stated mileage task of 100 miles to be performed during ten hours, with extra

[59] Baltimore and Ohio R. R. Co. *v.* Interstate Commerce Commission, 221 U. S. 612, 1911.

[60] 197 Fed. 624, 1912.

[61] 34 S C 26.

pay for any excess.[62] This provision for over-time did not reconcile the strongly unionized railroad men to the long working hours, which were the result of the reduced speed of freight trains caused by increased tonnage per train. They blamed, in part, the Act of 1907, which had in fact ushered in a sixteen-hour day.[63] With a view to expediting the freight trains' runs, the Railroad Brotherhoods launched a movement for eight hours and double pay for over-time at their Boston session in October, 1915. Their next session submitted to a vote of the members the demand that the 100-mile task be fixed for eight hours, at the existing ten-hour wage, with time and one-half for over-time. Ninety-four per cent of the members of the four Brotherhoods voted for a general strike, if the demand were not granted.[64] When the railroads refused the demand and a strike threatened, the President of the United States called a conference of officials of the Brotherhoods and of the railroads. When the former refused to arbitrate, the President suggested that eight hours be adopted as a standard, and that the other matters be arbitrated. The Brotherhoods agreed to this, but the railroad executives refused. Thereupon, a strike order was issued to take effect September 4, 1916. To avert suffering to people and disaster to property, the President asked Congress to pass an eight-hour law, and to provide for a study of its effect on costs, with a view to giving the Interstate Commerce Commission power to increase rates, if this proved necessary.[65]

Despite widespread opposition in which even liberal

[62] Wilson v. New, 243 U. S., 340, 1917.
[63] The Academy of Political Science, *Proceedings*, 1917-1918, Carter, W. S., "Worker's View," pp. 170-184.
[64] *Public Affairs Information Service*, 1916, p. 118.
[65] *Journal of Political Economy*, 1917, Vol. 25, pp. 387-390.

papers joined, the Adamson Act, establishing the basic eight-hour day for all employees on interstate railroads, was passed. The statute made provision for the "appointment of a commission of three to observe the operation and effects of the institution of the eight-hour standard work-day . . . during a period of not less than six months, nor more than nine months . . . and within thirty days thereafter to report its findings to the President and Congress." And it fixed wages for thirty days beyond the report of this Commission at "the present standard day's wage, and for all necessary time in excess of eight hours such employees shall be paid at a rate of not less than the pro rata rate for such standard eight-hour work-day." The penalty for violating the law was fixed at from one hundred to one thousand dollars fine, or a maximum prison sentence of one year or both.[66]

The statute did not satisfy any of the parties to the dispute. In the first place, no provision was made for an increase in rates, if necessary, for which the President had asked. The Brotherhoods were dissatisfied because of the failure to pass the punitive over-time provision. Railroad officials expressed their opposition to the measure by immediately instituting suits to enjoin it. In spite of the promise to expedite a test case through the courts, it dragged on. Finally, having referred the question of a strike to the membership, the Brotherhoods announced that one would be called March 17, unless the basic eight-hour day was conceded before that time. However, at a conference of the Brotherhood and railway officials, it was agreed to postpone the strike forty-eight hours, during which time an agreement was made granting the basic eight-hour day, at the ten-hour standard rate, with over-

[66] 39 Stat. 721.

time at one-eighth of the present standard rate, no matter what the court decided. Seven hours later, the Supreme Court handed down a five to four decision sustaining the constitutionality of the law.[67] Since the Adamson Law did not restrict the number of hours railway employees should work, but through fixing a basic eight-hour day served rather as a means of fixing wages, this decision is not, in its entirety, of outstanding importance in a study of the shorter-hour movement. That part of it, however, which settled the constitutionality of this law under the terms of the commerce clause established a precedent, which should prove of great importance for future national legislation on this subject. As Professor T. R. Powell said: "The concurrence of six members of the court in the opinion that the Adamson Law is a regulation of commerce should definitely end any contention that a regulation of the relations *inter sese* of persons engaged in commerce cannot be a regulation of the commerce in which they are engaged."[68] In other words, this decision definitely broadens the scope of the commerce clause to give Congress authority to legislate on the question of hours for interstate railway employees.

Only certain parts of the Report of the Eight-Hour Commission, provided for by this Act, have any bearing on this study. Of outstanding importance was its observation that: "the eight-hour day as a basis for pay with pro rata over-time has even now caused the shortening of the time of certain trains, and these exceptions would doubtless be more numerous if there were an extra penalty for over-time." Here is evidence that the Brotherhoods were justified in their demands for punitive over-

[67] *American Federationist*, 1917, Vol. 24, pp. 282-284.
[68] *Pennsylvania Law Review*, 1917, Vol. 65, p. 613.

time rates, as a means of attaining a real shortening of hours. That these demands had the establishment of shorter hours through the elimination of over-time as their end, and were not a hold-up for higher wages as was the contention of the many opponents of the bill, was attested by another conclusion of the Report: " The immediate increase of wages . . . was not the primary motive for the movement that resulted in the law's enactment. The men want first shorter hours, and then they want all the pay they can get afterwards." [69]

Since the close of the war, the steady increase in the efficiency of the railroads has made the problem of technological unemployment of primary importance. The Report of the Committee on Recent Economic Changes states: "It is interesting to note that, although the volume of freight traffic in 1926 was nearly 8% greater than in 1923, the number of employees was 7% less, and the number of man-hours was 8% less." [70] It is of equal interest to read the laborer's way of putting the same fact: "by use of larger locomotives, longer trains, cars of greater capacity, electric car retarders and other devices, railroads have been able to decrease the number of their employees by the hundreds of thousands." [71]

Technological unemployment, intensified by cyclical unemployment, has caused the demands of the Railroad Brotherhoods for the six-hour day to become clamorous. In April, 1929, when the question of technological unemployment had not been complicated by the depression, a meeting of the Railway Labor Executives' Association was

[69] *Report of the Eight Hour Commission*, Washington, 1918, pp. 481, 419.
[70] National Bureau of Economic Research, *Recent Economic Changes*, Vol. I, p. 285.
[71] *Locomotive Engineers Journal*, 1930, p. 813.

held to plan for stabilizing employment in the railroad industry. Their program included demands for the establishment of a maximum eight-hour day, a minimum six-hour day, and a five-day week, and preventive over-time rates to discourage over-working a minimum of employees, instead of employing a maximum number at straight time rates.[72] Since that time, repeated conferences have been held to discuss this program, and the means to establish it. A joint conference of representatives of the American Railway Executives' Association and the Railway Labor Executives' Association was held on November 19, 1931, in New York City, at which proposals for stabilizing employment by shorter hours were discussed, as well as the important question of wage cuts. Nothing was accomplished because the railroad officials did not "accept the conclusion that a six-hour day is necessary, and that it must be instituted to absorb the existing number of experienced employees without reduction of compensation." As a consequence they were "unwilling to recommend the appointment of a commission to determine the ways and means of applying this principle to the different classes of employees." At later conferences, the Brotherhoods tried in vain to trade the acceptance of a cut in wages for the grant of the six-hour day.[73] Although collective bargaining has failed to press this demand for shorter hours to a successful conclusion, there is still the possibility that it may be attained by legislation. In January, 1932, the Senate and House passed resolutions ordering the Interstate Commerce Commission to make a thorough study of the practicability of the six-hour day for railroad em-

[72] *Ibid.*, 1929, p. 340.
[73] *Brotherhood of Locomotive Firemen and Enginemen's Magazine*, Dec. 1931, pp. 421-428.

ployees on the ground that unemployment had reached the point of being a grave problem. The Commission is ordered to report on or before December 1, 1932.[74]

REGULATION OF HOURS OF SEAMEN

Again in the case of seamen Congress, for many years, failed to use its constitutional power to regulate hours. The International Seamen's Union had agitated and lobbied long and unsuccessfully not merely for a measure to fix the hours of work, but for a more comprehensive bill to improve the general status of seamen on ships of American registry. The great need for legal regulation of hours was stated in a memorial to the President of the United States which was unanimously adopted at the 1914 convention of this Union. It read: " The hours of labor are discretionary with the owner and master. The seaman must work until exhausted, or go to prison for 'disobedience to lawful command.' Twelve hours' work every day, seven days a week, at sea, is the minimum often exceeded in port. Fifteen to eighteen hours a day, sometimes thirty to forty hours at a stretch, are required. Then the vessel proceeds to sea, and without intervening rest, the men begin their sea watches. Men who work thus are too much exhausted to attend to safety of ship and passengers." [75] Collective bargaining had accomplished little in regulating hours, partly because of the small percentage of seamen who were unionized, and partly because of the legal status of seamen which distinctly limited the use of the strike.

Prior to the presentation of this memorial, repeated attempts had been made to improve the status of seamen by

[74] *United States Daily,* Washington, Jan. 23, 1932.
[75] International Seamen's Union of America, *Proceedings,* 1914, p. 59, 60.

comprehensive measures, one clause of which restricted hours. In 1900 Representative Chandler, of New York, sponsored a bill including a provision for a nine-hour day, which, however, failed of passage. In 1906 the Spight Bill, a similar measure, endorsed by the International Seamen's Union, was likewise defeated. This Union's convention in 1909 again endorsed the bill, and a mass meeting was held at Cooper Union, preceded by a parade of seamen, to arouse public opinion for its support. But, although ably sponsored by LaFollette in the Senate, the bill was once more defeated. When in 1912, Congress passed it, it was pocket vetoed by President Taft.[76]

In the presidential campaign of 1912, both platforms contained planks endorsing remedial legislation for the seamen. The LaFollette Bill, which regulated hours of labor at sea by dividing the sailors into, at least, two, and the firemen into, at least, three watches, and in port by establishing a nine-hour day except on Sundays and holidays when unnecessary work was prohibited, was again introduced in 1913. The active campaign of the Seamen's Union gained great publicity for a joint letter of endorsement from the Secretary of Commerce, W. C. Redfield, and the Secretary of Labor, W. B. Wilson.[77] This letter stated that the hours, which the LaFollette Bill aimed to establish, were those that had already been established by statute in the leading European countries. The LaFollette Bill was passed, and signed by President Wilson, March 4, 1915.[78]

Mr. Andrew Furuseth, President of the International Seamen's Union, wrote in reply to questions on the ade-

[76] Albrecht, A. E., *International Seamen's Union of America*, Washington, 1923, pp. 33-36.

[77] International Seamen's Union of America, *Proceedings*, 1914, pp. 75-77.

[78] Albrecht, *op. cit.*, p. 37.

NATIONAL LEGISLATION 93

quacy of this law that it was not complied with by the owners so far as seamen were concerned, though it was for firemen. His statement, made in the latter part of the letter, that the union has been actively lobbying for an amendment which would provide an eight-hour day for seamen leads to the conclusion that legal regulation of hours in the field has had some measure of success.[79]

SUMMARY

Limitations in the Constitution of the United States have restricted very narrowly the field in which the National Government can enact hours' legislation. But even within these limits, the power has been used very sparingly. Congress has enacted only three statutes regulating hours on government work. It is noteworthy that, despite the tremendous industrial changes which have occurred from 1865 to the present, the later statutes did not decrease the length of the work-day, but merely attempted to provide more effective means of enforcing the eight-hour regulation. In the field of interstate and foreign commerce, Congress has also enacted only three statutes which regulate the hours of work. Continued pressure of labor organizations for further reduction in the two fields has, as yet, been steadily resisted. It can be concluded that Congress has made neither extensive nor daring use of its power.

[79] Letter to writer, Feb. 13, 1932.

CHAPTER IV

STATE LEGISLATION

DESPITE the fact that a modicum of State regulation of hours has come to be the generally expected condition in certain fields, this type of legislation was distinctly unusual until the close of the Civil War, and has not yet spread to every State. In only two States (Mississippi and Oregon), moreover, have statutes been enacted which include the greater part of the labor force within their provisions. The development of this State legislation on hours has tended to follow a very definite pattern. An insistent and persistent demand for general legislation to insure shorter hours for all, led to the passage of general eight-hour laws. When statutes of such unrestricted application proved unavailing, attempts at hours' regulation concentrated on specified classes of employees. Statutes regulating hours for State and city employees, and for persons employed on State and city contracts, were early examples of this type of enactment, as were also those which fixed the hours for women and for workers in hazardous trades. The third and most recent trend has witnessed a swing of the pendulum back to general legislation, defining a legal day's work for all with, however, a limited number of exceptions specifically exempted from the operation of the statute.

While the historical course of each type of hours' regulation has been much the same, the lack of uniformity in the actual laws passed in a multi-jurisdictional federation, such as the American, results in a difficult problem of presentation. It would be lengthy, confusing and tedious to follow through the course of legislation in each of the forty-eight States along each of the three lines of action mentioned above. Nor would it be of any particular value, because the history of such legislation tended to be repetitive. It seems to the writer that clarity on this phase of the subject can best be attained by presenting in detail the pioneer attempts, and those which have become significant through establishing precedent for the hours' legislation of today, in each of the three lines of action. Supplementing the presentation of the course which legislation followed in each of these fields, an attempt is made to give a comprehensive view of the situation today by references in the footnotes to the tables printed in the appendices which summarize the existing hours' legislation of the forty-eight States in the three fields of action: general laws, nullified by provisions which permit the worker to contract for longer hours, regulation of hours for special classes, that is, on government work, for women and for men in special industries, and late general laws, which omit the nullifying clause.

EARLY GENERAL LAWS

The agitation, which led to the formation of the National Labor Union to establish a legal eight-hour day by federal action,[1] had first created innumerable and widespread local organizations dedicated to similar ends within their respective States. For example, the Workmen's Eight-Hour League of Utica, New York, in 1866, presented a resolution to the Legislature of the State of New York demanding that eight hours should constitute a legal day's work in the State for all engaged in industry.[2] At

[1] *Cf. supra*, pp. 34-35.
[2] *New York Tribune*, Dec. 29, 1866.

96   SHORTER HOURS

the same time in the western section of the United States, a similar request was supplemented by a petition "which had been signed by eleven thousand of the citizens of San Francisco." [3] Attempts to pass this type of law had been made in vain in 1866, notably in California, where an eight-hour day bill passed the Senate with the proviso that it would take effect when Massachusetts and New York enacted similar laws.[4] But continued agitation bore fruit the next year in several States. Illinois and Wisconsin were the first to succeed "in having eight hours declared to be a legal day's work in the absence of any agreement."[5] New York adopted a similar measure a little later with "not as much opposition as was expected." [6]

At the convention of the National Labor Union, held in August of that year, it was reported that six States [6a] had passed eight-hour laws.[7] The same elements in all these laws, however, made them futile. In the first place, they all contained provisions permitting agreements or contracts for more than eight hours, clearly pointing the way to evasion. Secondly, they made no provision for enforcement. For example, when the New York Working Men's Assembly asked Governor Fenton, who had signed the bill, to issue a proclamation calling upon employers to observe the law, he replied: "It would be an act of unwarranted

[3] Eaves, L., *History of California Labor Legislation*, Berkeley, 1910, p. 199.

[4] *Nation* (N. Y.), Apr. 5 and 26, 1866.

[5] *Ibid.*, Apr. 25, 1867.

[6] *New York Tribune*, Mar. 29, 1867.

[6a] Although this statement is cited by Commons, he only mentions five States which enacted general hours' legislation in 1867. These are: Illinois, Wisconsin, Missouri, New York, Connecticut. Commons and Associates, *op. cit.*, Vol. II, pp. 108, 109.

[7] *Documentary History*, Vol 9, p. 184.

assumption to issue a proclamation requiring its observance."[8] He held such laws to be "obligatory by their own nature."[9] When these two fundamental weaknesses in the laws had shown themselves, labor's denunciation of them "as frauds on the laboring class" was not surprising. The feeble attempts of labor to "enforce" these laws by means of the strike is discussed below under the heading of direct action.[10]

In succeeding years, other States passed laws of this type. So long as the laws contained a provision permitting contracts for over-time, no question was raised as to their constitutionality. In 1891, however, Nebraska passed a law which not only declared eight hours a legal day's work for all classes of laborers, except those employed in farm and domestic work, but also provided that, if employees worked more than eight hours a day the employer must pay extra compensation.[11] A violation by a printing company raised the question of constitutionality. The aloofness of our judiciary from the flow of current opinion, which had stirred the Legislature to action, was well shown by the dicta of the Supreme Court of Nebraska: "For some reason, not necessary to consider, there has in modern times arisen a sentiment favorable to paternalism in matters of legislation." With an utter disregard for the possibility that the Legislature was justified in passing this law, the court held the law to be unconstitutional on two grounds, which had become and continued for some time to be the more or less standard means of attacking all hours' legislation. First, the court held that

[8] *New York Times*, Oct. 1, 1867.
[9] Commons and Associates, *op. cit.*, Vol. 2, p. 87.
[10] *Cf. infra*, pp. 140-145.
[11] Laws of 1891. Ch. 54.

the statute made an unjustifiable discrimination between different classes of labor, by exempting farm and domestic labor from its provisions; and second, that it infringed on freedom of contract.[12] There can be no doubt that the statute was discriminatory, and did limit the freedom of contract. Most statutes for this purpose could not be all inclusive, and so would have the first characteristic; all would necessarily infringe on liberty of contract.[13] Recognition of the principle of "reasonable classification" as applied to hours' regulation was a development which came later, as did justification for interference with liberty of contract on the grounds of a reasonable exercise of the police power for the public benefit.

The precedent established by this decision may be held partly responsible for the long period in which no effective general hours' law was passed. Meanwhile, additional States adopted the ineffectual type which the 1860's had produced. They have them on their statute books today. Since they are unenforceable, they may be considered, from one point of view, as a counsel of perfection, from another as an additional dead letter.

REGULATION OF HOURS FOR SPECIAL CLASSES

Government Work

Regulation of hours for State and city government employees can be divided into two categories: the first, for those directly employed by the State or local government, the second for those employed by contractors on State and city work.

[12] Low *v.* Rees Printing Co., 41 Neb. 127, 1894.
[13] See Freund, E., *The Police Power,* Chicago, 1904, for a most complete discussion of this subject. Prof. Freund gives two main attributes of the police power: "It aims directly to secure and promote the public welfare, and it does so by restraint and compulsion." p. 3.

STATE LEGISLATION

Baltimore initiated the movement for the regulation of hours of those directly employed by the government by passing, in 1866, an eight-hour ordinance for city employees.[14] This precedent has been followed steadily since that time by State and city governments, until in 1931 Boston took the lead by establishing a five-day week for all city employees as a means of popularizing this method of increasing employment.[15] The question of the constitutionality of this type of hour law has not been raised because, as has been said: "Regulation of free labor employed by the State, itself, is a proprietary power." [16] On the other hand, hour legislation for those employed on State and city contracts was for a long time hindered by court decisions which declared this type of legislation to be unconstitutional. The history of this legislation in New York is given in detail as being typical of the difficulties in establishing shorter hours on State contracts, despite the determination of the Legislature to achieve this objective.

The defects of early attempts to regulate hours of labor lay in the poor phrasing of the statutes which made evasion easy, and in the absence of adequate provision for enforcement. The resulting ineffectiveness may explain the fact that their constitutionality was not tested. At any rate, the New York Statute of 1870, which established an eight-hour day on all public contracts, was so ineffective that fourteen years after its passage the *New York Times* reported that its " existence was barely known: its value nil." [17] Somewhat later, in 1892, the New York State Bureau of Statistics of Labor repeated the same charge,

[14] *Documentary History*, Vol. 9, p. 278.
[15] *New York Times*, Sept. 8, 1931.
[16] Freund, *op. cit.*, p. 295.
[17] *New York Times*, Feb. 4, 1884.

and urged "action of a very positive character" in view of the widespread agitation for an effective eight-hour law on State contracts.[18] Opposition to an improved measure was based on estimates of the tremendous increase in costs which it would entail, and on the fact that it was a measure to get votes, not to accomplish social good. Nevertheless, in 1899, an improved bill passed the Senate by a unanimous vote, and in the Assembly there were only five opposing votes. Governor Theodore Roosevelt gave two reasons for signing it: first, the ease of evading the Law of 1870, and second, the need for the State "to set a good example to employers." [19]

This statute ruled that every contract for State and local work must contain a stipulation for an eight-hour day "except in cases of extraordinary emergency caused by fire, flood or danger to life or property." It guarded against a wage cut as the concomitant of the shorter hours by providing that wages could not "be less than the prevailing rate for a day's work in the same trade or occupation in the locality." To spur enforcement, the statute provided that violation or evasion by an official of the State or local government was malfeasance in office punishable by suspension or removal. The penalty for the contractor was that violation voided the contract, thereby depriving him of the right to payment for the job.[20]

Despite the careful wording of the law, and its very definite provisions for enforcement, questions of interpretation and enforcement immediately arose. It was reported by the Bureau of Labor Statistics that this law was the

[18] New York Bureau of Statistics of Labor, *Tenth Annual Report,* 1892, Part 1, p. 15.
[19] *New York Tribune,* Sept. 27, 1899.
[20] Laws of 1899, Ch. 385.

most prominent topic in workingmen's circles because of "The hostility or indifference of municipal officials to the law, which has thus necessitated strikes on the part of laborers employed by contractors on city work to secure its enforcement." The Bureau maintained that: "The law is clear as to the duty of the public officials to embody the eight-hour day and prevailing rate of wages' provisions of the Act in every contract for public work, as well as to refuse to make any payment on such contracts in case the law is violated."[21] The course of the law through the courts showed that the Department of Labor made every effort to carry out its duty in enforcing the law.

The first test arose when the Albany Branch of the State Federation of Labor, in May 1900, demanded that the State should not pay bills due to the Municipal Gas Company, and that its contract for providing light to the Capitol should be cancelled, because the Corporation had not obeyed the Eight-Hour Law of 1899. When the Attorney General ruled that the law applied to this contract, the bills were not paid.[22] Thereupon, the Company applied to the court for a mandamus to compel payment. As soon as it was granted, the case was appealed by the Labor Unions, and a final unanimous decision was given in favor of the Company.[23] Just as the Federal courts had narrowed the scope of the Law of 1892, the Court of Appeals limited the meaning of the term "public work" to public buildings and construction work.[24]

The Act was further weakened in the case of People

[21] N. Y., *Bulletin of the Bureau of Labor Statistics*, 1899, p. 82.
[22] *Ibid.*, 1900, p. 238.
[23] *Ibid.*, 1900, p. 240.
[24] *Cf. supra*, pp. 73-74.

ex rel. Rodgers *v.* Coler, which declared invalid the prevailing rate of wage provision. This case arose when the District Assembly of the Knights of Labor asked the Comptroller to stop payment to Rodgers, a contractor, grading a road for New York City, on the ground that he was violating the 1899 Labor Law by paying less than the prevailing rate of wages. When Comptroller Coler withheld payment, the contractor applied for a writ of mandamus to compel it, which the Supreme Court denied. It was taken to the Appellate Division, which reversed the Lower Court and granted the writ. Comptroller Coler appealed from this order to the highest court in the State. By a five to two vote, this court affirmed the order that the contractor be paid. The court held that the wage clause conflicted with the Constitution because it "invaded rights of liberty and property in denying the City and the contractor the right to agree with their employees on wages," and because "it virtually confiscated all property rights of the contractor under his contract—by providing to 'accept the fruits of his labor and at the same time refuse to pay for them.'"

Of great interest, since it was in line with a later decision of the Supreme Court, was the dissenting opinion which held that the contractors' "liberty is not . . . interfered with at all within the meaning of the Constitution, for he has solemnly covenanted in his agreement that he shall not be at liberty to do anything in the course of the contract contrary to the wishes of the proprietor as expressed in the written contract." The dissenting opinion also affirmed the right of the State, as a proprietor, to prescribe the condition of contracts into which its agents may enter.[25]

[25] 166 N. Y. 1, 1901.

The third attack on this statute was the testing of the constitutionality of the eight-hour clause. The State Department of Labor brought suit against a number of violators of this provision. In Tompkins County, the presiding judge advised the grand jury that the law was unconstitutional,[26] but in Orange County the grand jury indicted the Orange County Road Construction Company. At the trial, the judge held the law unconstitutional on the ground that the majority opinion in the case of People ex rel Rodgers v. Coler, while not considering the validity of this section of the Act, had dealt "comprehensively with the subject of labor legislation," and had been "decidedly adverse to its validity."[27] On appeal by the Commissioner of Labor, the Appellate Division of the Supreme Court reversed this decision, and held the eight-hour section of the law to be constitutional. The long drawn out career of this law in the courts was, however, not yet ended. When appealed, the final authority of the Court of Appeals in 1903 declared the statute unconstitutional on two grounds: first, it was not a proper exercise of the police power, because it had no relation to public health or morals, and was an interference with the right of municipal corporations to contract in matters concerning their own interests; second, it violated the Fourteenth Amendment by denying equal protection of the laws, since the State drew an arbitrary distinction between different classes of contractors, and between the same contractor working for the State and for a private party.[28]

Laws of this type, regulating hours of work on State and city contracts, were declared unconstitutional for

[26] N. Y. *Bulletin of Bureau of Labor Statistics*, 1901, p. 268.
[27] *Ibid.*, 1902, p. 47, quoted.
[28] 175 N. Y. 84, 1903.

much the same reasons in several other States.[28a] Since the State courts were protecting the citizens against violations of the Fourteenth Amendment, there was at that time no appeal to the Supreme Court of the United States. The opportunity to get this court's ruling on the question came when the highest Kansas tribunal declared a law of this kind constitutional.

The Kansas statute, enacted in 1891, "in order to provide employment for the greatest number of persons,"[29] stipulated that all contracts made by the State or local government "for the performance of any work or the furnishing of any material manufactured within the State of Kansas, shall be deemed and considered as made upon the basis of eight hours constituting a day's work." Extraordinary emergencies were exempted from the terms of the Act. Provision was made that laborers on State and local government contracts should receive not less than the daily wage current in the locality. Penalty for violation was a fine of from fifty to one thousand dollars or six months' imprisonment or both.[30] It can be seen that the statute did not differ fundamentally from that of New York except that the penalty was far less drastic.

From its enactment in 1891 until it was amended in 1899 to give the State Commissioner of Labor authority to enforce the law, the question of its constitutionality was not raised. Whether this was the result of lack of enforce-

---

[28a] Three noteworthy cases in which the constitutionality of such legislation was not upheld were: Cleveland *v.* Clements Bros. Construction Co., 65 N. E. 885, *ex parte* Kuback, 85 Cal. 274, Fiske *v.* People, 188 Ill. 205. Prof. Frankfurter (29 Harvard Law Review 354 n., 1916) remarks that "all recent important authorities now sustain such legislation."

[29] Kansas Bureau of Labor, *Fifteenth Annual Report,* 1899, p. 477.

[30] Laws of 1891, Chapter 114.

ment, or of inertia on the part of contractors, is impossible to determine with any degree of certainty. The Attorney General claimed that, as far as he was able to learn, it had "been generally enforced and conformed to." It is significant, however, that after its amendment "numerous complaints were made by working men and organizations of labor throughout the State." [31] A building contractor, who refused to abide by the Attorney General's opinion that the law was constitutional, took it to court on this question. The Supreme Court of Kansas ruled that there was "no infringement of constitutional rights. There can be no compulsion of a contractor to bid upon public work, nor is the laborer bound to take employment from a person having such a contract." [32]

In spite of a warning issued by the Commissioner of Labor, quoting this decision, continued violations by paving contractors resulted in a second test of the constitutionality of the statute. The Supreme Court of Kansas affirmed the constitutionality of the law, and held it applicable to the construction of public works, such as street paving under the supervision of cities. [33]

When the case was appealed to the Supreme Court of the United States, the opinion of that court, handed down in 1903, held the law to be constitutional and valid, thereby establishing a precedent of primary importance for future hour laws on State and city contracts. The court held that it was not its function to consider whether a restriction of hours "would promote morality, improve the physical and intellectual conditions of laborers and workmen, and enable them the better to discharge the duties

[31] Kansas Bureau of Labor, *op. cit.*, 1899, pp. 476, 477.
[32] 61 Kan. 275, 1899.
[33] State *v.* Atkin, 67 Kan. 174, 1902.

appertaining to citizenship," nor did the court consider it pertinent "that the work . . . is not dangerous to life, limb or health." Its decision rested "upon the broad ground that the work being of a public character, absolutely under the control of the State and its municipal agents acting by its authority, it is for the State to prescribe the conditions under which it will permit work of that kind to be done." [34]

Here was a very definite affirmation, twice by the State court, and finally by the Supreme Court of the right of a State not only to fix hours for employees on State and city contracts, but to make provision against any acccompanying wage cut. Mr. Lindley D. Clark's, specialist on labor legislation in the United States Bureau of Labor Statistics, commenting on the importance of this opinion said that "its general recognition will doubtless prevent any future adverse decision on the point of regulation of public employment." [35] Many States, however, not having absolute faith in the final authority of a Supreme Court precedent, have made constitutional provision that the Legislature has express power to fix all conditions of labor on public work, whether done directly by the State or through contractors.[35a] As a result, there has been a steady development of this type of legislation throughout the United States.

Women

Massachusetts was the pioneer State in establishing successful hours' legislation for women, and the efforts of this State have been a most valuable example of what

[34] Atkin v. Kansas, 191 U. S. 207, 1903.
[35] U. S. *Bulletin of Bureau of Labor Statistics*, No. 321, p. 55.
[35a] These States are: Arizona, California, Idaho, Montana, New Mexico, Ohio, Oklahoma, Utah, Wyoming. *Cf.* Appendix B.

features to adopt and what to discard if the law is to be effective.

The pre-Civil War agitation for a ten-hour law for all laborers was transmuted after the war into a demand for an eight-hour law. The failure of two commissions [35b] to render a favorable majority report caused this demand, in turn, to be changed to one for the ten-hour day for women in factories. Sound judgment dictated this change in demand. In the first place, the Legislature was more sure of its power to regulate the labor of women; second, their need was greater due to the weaker bargaining position of the women, who were largely unorganized; and last, the hours for factory work were longer than those which the trades had succeeded in establishing. From 1870 the annual reports of the Chief of the Bureau of Statistics of Labor urged a ten-hour law for women factory workers.

A bill providing for such a limitation of hours had passed the lower house of the Massachusetts Legislature in 1871, 1872 and 1873, only to be defeated in the Senate. In 1874 the Governor's message recommended the bill, stating: "That the strength of the operatives in many of our mills is being exhausted, that they are growing prematurely old, . . . are facts that no careful and candid observer will deny." In that year, the law was passed in the House by a vote of 111 to 19, and in the Senate by

[35b] In 1865 a house committee unanimously reported in favor of a decrease in hours. As a result, a commission of five was appointed in 1866, which stated on the hours' question that "the change desired can be better brought about by workingmen outside the state house than by legislators inside." The minority report of the commission appointed in 1867 recommended a ten-hour law for factory and farm work, and an eight-hour day for mechanical labor, in the absence of contract. *Bulletin of the Women's Bureau*, No. 66, p. 16.

one of 21 to 11, and was signed by the Governor.[36] This statute provided that no woman or minor under eighteen should be employed in a factory for more than ten hours a day, but permitted an apportionment of the time to allow one shorter day a week provided that the total weekly hours did not exceed sixty. Longer hours were permitted when time had been lost because of necessary repairs on the machinery. A maximum fine of fifty dollars was the penalty fixed for "wilfully" employing women or minors more than the hours established by the statute.[37]

The judicial history of the law was brief. The freedom of contract theory, which became the stumbling block of later hours' regulation, was not invoked. Professor Frankfurter says that the law was sustained as a matter of course.[38] The Supreme Court of Massachusetts held that the law "merely provides that in an employment which the Legislature has evidently deemed to some extent dangerous to health, no person shall be engaged in labor more than ten hours a day or sixty hours a week. There can be no doubt that such legislation may be maintained either as a health or police regulation, if it were necessary to resort to either of those sources of power." [39]

While its history in the courts was brief and eminently satisfactory, the course of the interpretation, enforcement and amendment of the Law of 1874 was long. Weaknesses, inherent in the law, had to be removed to make it an effective measure. These were: first, the necessity of proving that the violation was "wilful"; second, the permission granted to employers to extend the hours on any

[36] U. S., *Bulletin of the Women's Bureau,* No. 66, pp. 19, 20.

[37] Laws of 1874, Ch. 221.

[38] *Harvard Law Review,* Frankfurter, Felix, "Hours of Labor and Realism in Constitutional Law," 1916, p. 354.

[39] Commonwealth *v.* Hamilton, 120 Mass. 383, 1876.

one day provided another day of the week was correspondingly shortened; and third, the right to over-time when necessary to make repairs. These last two provisions made it a practical impossibility to detect violations of the law, since evidence could not be obtained unless an inspector was stationed in each factory every day in the week. Labor, the Bureau of Statistics of Labor and the Chief of Police, who was responsible for enforcing the law, agitated for legislation which would eliminate these defects.

During the succeeding years, a series of amendments were passed. In 1879, the Legislature struck out the word "wilfully," thereby immeasurably increasing the possibility of obtaining convictions. The next year, an amendment was passed requiring that printed notices be posted of the hours of labor for each day of the week, in order to prevent declarations that time in excess of ten hours was worked in order to make one shorter day. Despite this improvement, this provision continued to be a means of evasion, until 1912, when the law provided for days of equal length. To prevent illegal lengthening of the workday by claiming stoppage for repairs, the Legislature in 1877 passed a law, permitting over-time only for stoppages of thirty minutes or more, which had to be reported to the Chief of the District Police. Further abuses such as double duty, while half the workers had lunch, and early starting to get up the proper speed for production, were eliminated. The first was made impossible by the Law of 1877, which required, at least, a half hour for lunch, taken at the same time by all who began at the same time, and which prohibited the tending of additional machines. The second was prevented by an amendment requiring that the hours for beginning and stopping work be posted.[40]

[40] *Bulletin of the Women's Bureau*, No. 66, pp. 13-24.

The enforcement of the law was originally entrusted to the State Police, although this group was insufficient in size and training for the work. Proof of their inadequacy was given when the Chief of Police in 1899 told the Legislative Labor Committee that "in only one instance since 1879 had he been able to procure evidence enough to convict a corporation of any infraction of the ten-hour law." As a result of continued agitation, and of the favorable report to the Legislature of an investigation commission, a State Board of Labor and Industries was established in 1912, to whom this work was transferred.[41]

This enactment completes the significant history of the first ten-hour law for women. Its development had been a conscious evolution from a poorly worded, inadequately enforced law, to one in which most of the means of evasion had been eliminated, and for whose enforcement a group of specialists in the labor field was designated. The Massachusetts Legislature continued to decrease the weekly hours of women very slowly: it did not experiment with any radical reductions. In 1892, the weekly hours were decreased to fifty-eight; in 1908 to fifty-six, and in 1911 to fifty-four.[42] But by this time the real pioneer spirit for shorter hours for women showed itself in the West, and the next significant piece of legislation is the California Eight-Hour Law.

Before considering this law in detail, however, it is necessary to present briefly the fate of legislative regulation of hours for women at the hands of other courts. Massachusetts would not have been able to develop an enforceable policy of restricting hours of women's labor if the court had not accepted this restrictive policy of the Legislature

[41] *Ibid.,* pp. 25, 26.
[42] *Ibid.,* pp. 28-38.

"as a matter of course." Other State courts had not concurred in this decision. In 1893, Illinois had passed a law, establishing an eight-hour day and a forty-eight-hour week for women employed in factories and workshops. This statute provided that hours' schedules be posted, factory inspectors be appointed to enforce it, and established a fine of from three to one hundred dollars for each violation.[43] The question of its constitutionality was not raised until a year and a half after its passage. Then the Supreme Court of Illinois declared the law unconstitutional not only because it discriminated against factories and against women, who "have a natural equality with men and no distinction may be drawn between them with respect to power of engaging to labor"; but also because it violated the Fourteenth Amendment depriving individuals of property without due process of law. The court held that limitation of this right could be justified only by some special condition, and that there was "no reasonable ground . . . for fixing upon eight hours in one day as the limit within which woman can work without injury to her physique, and beyond which, if she work, injury will necessarily follow."[44]

In 1909, this court reversed itself, when it sustained the ten-hour law for women, which the Legislature had enacted. At this time, it held that differences of sex "often formed the basis of a classification on which to found legislation." An attempt was made to defend the court's change of position by claiming, first, that the health argument, advanced in the latter case, had not appeared in the earlier one; and second, that this statute provided for a ten and

[43] Laws of 1893, Factories and Workshops, Sec. 5.
[44] Ritchie v. People, 155 Ill. 98, 1895.

not an eight-hour day.[45] Professor Frankfurter said: "A heroic effort is made to distinguish the first Ritchie case from the second Ritchie case. It is true that one was an eight-hour law and the other a ten-hour law, but the two cases are, in fact, irreconcilable in their underlying point of view."[46]

But before this *volte face* of the Illinois Court occurred, a Nebraska Court in 1902 had upheld the constitutionality of a ten-hour statute for women on the grounds "that women and children have always, to a certain extent, been wards of the State," and since they are " unable, by reason of their physical limitations to endure the same hours of exhaustive labor as may be endured by adult males," so "the State must be accorded the right to guard and protect women as a class."[47] This reasoning was in line with that of the Supreme Court of the United States, in 1908, in the case of Muller v. Oregon, which established beyond question the constitutionality of legislation limiting the hours of women. The Oregon Supreme Court had sustained a statute which prohibited women from working "in any mechanical establishment or factory or laundry in this State more than ten hours during any one day."[48] When appealed to, the United States Supreme Court, in a noteworthy opinion of that court, held that this was justifiable class legislation because it was obvious " that woman's physical structure and the performance of maternal functions place her at a disadvantage in the struggle for subsistance." The court further said that: "The two sexes differ in structure of body, in the functions to be performed by each,

[45] Ritchie & Co. v. Wayman, 244 Ill. 509, 1910.
[46] *Harvard Law Review*, 1916, p. 356.
[47] Wenham v. State, 65 Neb. 394, 1902.
[48] Laws of 1903, p. 148.

STATE LEGISLATION 113

in the amount of physical strength, in the capacity for long continued labor, particularly when done standing, the influence of vigorous health upon the future well-being of the race, and self-reliance which enables one to assert full rights, and in the capacity to maintain the struggle for subsistence. This difference justifies a difference in legislation and upholds that which is designed to compensate for some of the burdens which rest upon her."[49]

This opinion, as was said above, established the constitutionality of hours' legislation for women, but it remained a matter of doubt whether an eight-hour law would be sustained. None had been tested since the courts had recognized that these laws were a justifiable interference with freedom of contract. This was the case which the California Eight-Hour Law presented. This State did not begin to restrict hours for women until a late date. Agitation caused the introduction of eight-hour bills in 1905 and 1906, but the Legislature failed to pass them.[50] In 1911 a bill, which had the support of organized labor, was passed by a unanimous vote of the Lower House, but by only a narrow majority in the Senate. Despite the fact that Governor Johnson was besieged by business interests to veto the law, as the leader of the Progressive Party in the State he could not afford to do so. When he signed it, he pointed out that the economic arguments advanced against the law had been used to oppose all past progressive hour legislation, and that the evils predicted had always failed to materialize.[51] This law was noteworthy not only because it was the first to establish a maximum eight-hour day and forty-eight-hour week for women, but also because of

[49] Muller *v.* Oregon, 208 U. S. 412, 1908.
[50] Eaves, *op. cit.* p. 316.
[51] *Bulletin of the Women's Bureau*, No. 66, pp. 122-124.

the unusually wide range of occupations which were included under its terms.[52]

The constitutionality of this statute was immediately questioned. A hotel proprietor claimed that the law infringed liberty of contract, and was discriminatory since it applied to hotels, but not to rooming or boarding-houses doing the same class of business. The Supreme Court of California decided that it was a justifiable interference with freedom of contract, and that it did not make an unfair discrimination as "the conditions stated appear to be a sufficient basis for the classification made."[53] The Supreme Court of the United States sustained this opinion. In view of the importance of the precedent which this decision set, it is worth quoting at some length. On the complaint that the law infringed freedom of contract, this court said: "As the liberty of contract guaranteed by the Constitution is freedom from arbitrary restraint—not immunity from reasonable regulation to safeguard the public interest—the question is whether the restrictions of this statute have reasonable relation to a proper purpose. Upon this point, the recent decisions of this court upholding other statutes limiting the hours of labor of women must be regarded as decisive." The court's pronouncement on the length of the day was: "It is manifestly impossible to say that the mere fact that the State of California provides for an eight-hour day, or a maximum of forty-eight hours a week, instead of ten hours a day or fifty-four hours a week, takes the case out of the domain of legislative discretion. This is not to imply that a limitation of the hours of labor of women might not be pushed to a wholly indefensible extreme, but there is no ground for the conclu-

---

[52] Laws of 1911, Ch. 258.
[53] *ex parte* Miller, 162 Calif. 687, 1912.

sion here that the limit of the reasonable exertion of protective authority has been overstepped." And on the complaint of discrimination, the court held: "It can not be concluded that the failure to extend the Act to other and distinct lines of business having their own circumstances and conditions or to domestic service, created an arbitrary discrimination as against the proprietors of hotels."[54]

The trade unions interpreted the hotels' complaint of discrimination to mean that the law was not sufficiently inclusive, and secured the passage of an amendment in 1913, extending its provisions to public lodging-houses, apartment houses, hospitals with the exception of graduate nurses, and places of amusement.[55] Constitutionality was again questioned on the ground that the exemption of graduate nurses from the provisions of the law was unfair discrimination. This question also reached the Supreme Court of the United States which sustained the law, concluding that " the validity of the distinction made in the case of graduate nurses is obvious."[56]

Further Amendment in 1919, extending the eight-hour provision to elevator operators in office buildings,[57] gave California, eight years after it had entered the path of legislating on hours for women, the most comprehensive and advanced law in the field, whose constitutionality had been sustained beyond the shadow of a doubt.

The Bureau of Labor Statistics was responsible for enforcing the law until 1914, when an Industrial Welfare Commission, with wide but flexible powers of enforcement, was created. This commission has developed a most

[54] Miller *v.* Wilson, 236 U. S. 373, 1915.
[55] *Bulletin of the Women's Bureau,* No. 66, pp. 124-126.
[56] Bosley *v.* McLaughlin, 236 U. S. 385, 1915.
[57] *Bulletin of the Women's Bureau,* No. 66, p. 125.

adequate and satisfactory system for administering the law, which is based on the most advanced practices of inspection and cooperation with employers.[58] California, therefore, has been a leader not only in establishing the legal eight-hour day for women, but also in serving as one of the early examples of the efficiency of administering this law by a commission with broad powers.[58a] Her example in both respects has been followed by several States.

Hazardous Work

In spite of the fact that regulation of hours to protect the public is distinctly within a State's powers,[59] it has been used but little, and with no degree of uniformity. Restrictive hour laws for drug clerks, which have been passed by California and New York, and those enacted by many States for railway and street-car employees, are the only examples of this type of legislation.

California, in 1907, as "a measure for the protection of public health," passed a law which established a ten-hour day and sixty-hour week for all "who perform the work of selling drugs or other medicine or compounding physicians' prescriptions."[60] For many years efforts to enact restrictive legislation for these workers had failed in New York. An indication of the opposition encountered may

[58] *Ibid.*

[58a] Colorado, Kansas, Oregon, Washington and Wisconsin are among the States which have created Industrial Commissions with broad powers. *Cf.* Appendix C.

[59] It has been said of this class of legislation that it "seeks to protect the safety of the public by limiting the hours of labor of those who are in control of dangerous agencies lest by excessive periods of duty they become fatigued and indifferent and cause accidents leading to injuries and destruction of life." People *v.* Erie RR. Co., 198 N. Y. 369, 1910.

[60] Act No. 2665, as amended by Ch. 224, 1907.

be gathered from a comment in the *New York Sun* in 1898, denouncing such a measure as "an extension of arbitrary authority by the government which goes logically to the extreme of State socialism, wherein the rights and interests of the individual and his whole power of initiative are surrendered to the State."[61] Strenuous agitation resulted in the enactment,[62] in 1911, of a law establishing a seventy-hour weekly maximum for drug clerks,[63] despite the obvious need for such a protective measure, and despite its unquestioned constitutionality, California and New York remain the only States which have provided such legislation.

Despite the recognized need for shorter hours for railroad employees to decrease accidents and consequent loss of life and property, but little restrictive State legislation has been enacted. Such as was passed required definite rest periods of eight or ten hours after each tour of duty, the length of which varied in different States between thirteen and twenty-four hours.[64]

It was shown in Chapter III that widespread agitation led to the passage by the Federal Government, in 1907, of the Hours of Service Act. This enactment raised the question of the constitutionality of State laws which established shorter hours than the maximum set by the federal law. A test case arose as the result of a New York statute, which limited the hours of telegraph operators and train despatchers to eight, whereas the federal law permitted a maximum of nine a day in continuously operated offices,

---

[61] *New York Sun*, May 4, 1898.

[62] For example see, *Druggists League for Shorter Hours*, Pamphlet, New York, 1897.

[63] Laws of 1911, Ch. 45, Sec. 236.

[64] *Cf. supra*, p. 83.

and thirteen in those which operated on one shift. A violation by the Erie Railroad of the New York statute finally brought the question of constitutionality to the Supreme Court of the United States. The statute was declared invalid as an attempt to regulate interstate commerce. The court ruled that Congress had completely covered this field by the Law of March 4, 1907, stating: "Where there is conflict the State legislation must give way." [65] Since this decision, such State legislation as exists only applies to hours of work on intrastate roads. These laws, like the national law, have not attempted to fix a definite length day, but merely to provide a limit beyond which a period of rest must be given.

Several States enacted legislation establishing maximum hours for employees of street railways. The constitutionality of this type of legislation was questioned in Rhode Island. That State, in 1902, had enacted a law which provided that "a day's work for all conductors, gripmen and motormen . . . shall not exceed ten hours' work to be performed within twelve consecutive hours." [66] The Supreme Court of Rhode Island declared that the law did not violate the Fourteenth Amendment. After citing Holden v. Hardy as a precedent, the court held that the constitutionality of this law was even less questionable for: "The law has more clearly such power for the triple reason that it deals with public corporations, the use of a public franchise, and the provision for public safety." [67] This decision appears to have established beyond question the constitutionality of restrictive legislation for street-car employees; several States now have a law regulating the hours of work in

[65] Erie Ry. Co. v. N. Y., 233 U. S. 671, 1914.
[66] Laws of 1902. Ch. 1004.
[67] 24 RI 603, 1902.

this field.[67a] Need for a wider application of this legislation is shown by the request of the President of the Paramount Cab Company to the New York Taxicab Commission for a law fixing fifty hours a week for taxi drivers, on the grounds that the fatigue caused by the present eleven to fifteen-hour day resulted in a heavy accident toll.[68]

Hours of work have been limited by legal enactment in some States in employments where long hours endangered the workers directly. The justification for this legislation was that certain industries involved more than the average risk to the life or health of the worker. The Legislature with the aid of a fact-finding committee might be expected to decide in what industries this condition existed, and what hours would tend to offset this disadvantage. Actually in deciding on the constitutionality of measures to protect the workers, this function was assumed by the courts without the aid of a fact-finding body.

The movement of hours' legislation for the protection of the worker did not begin until the last decade of the nineteenth century. The passage of an eight-hour law for miners and smelters in 1896 by the newly admitted State of Utah brought forth a series of court opinions which are regarded as decisive in this field. The law, for which the Constitution of the State made provision, was enacted so promptly largely through the efforts of the Utah State Federation of Labor.[69] The statute limited working hours of all employed in mines and smelters to eight a day except in case of emergency, and made its violation a misdemeanor.[70]

[67a] Among these States are: Louisiana, New Jersey, New York, Rhode Island, South Carolina, Washington. *Cf.* Appendix D

[68] *New York Times,* May 25, 1930.

[69] *American Federationist,* 1898, Vol. 5, pp. 23.

[70] Laws of 1896, Chap. 72.

When, shortly after its passage, Holden, a mine owner, made an agreement with workers to work ten hours a day, organized labor in Utah asked that he be prosecuted. The Attorney General not only refused to prosecute, but later refused to aid in preparing the brief, and is reported as saying: "There are two classes of citizens in Utah, those who pay taxes, and those who do not; and in this case those who pay taxes don't want such a law, and I don't propose to spend their money to defend it." Thereupon, the State Federation of Labor collected funds for this purpose.[70a] The Supreme Court of Utah very promptly sustained the law in two cases, covering miners and smelters respectively, holding it to be within the police power of the State as a measure to promote the health of the workers, and so not in conflict with any provision of the Constitution of the United States.[71] Labor's comment on the mine owner's argument that the statute deprived his employees of equal protection of the law and of their liberty and property without due process of law, is somewhat obvious, but is worth quoting as showing a nice appreciation of the situation: "Very few mine owners devote so much time and energy and the expenditure of money in retaining some of the ablest lawyers, as was done in this case in the protection of the employees' interest."[71a]

Some two years later the Supreme Court of the United States sustained the decision of the State court. The opinion demonstrates such clear-cut reasoning, and has had so profound an influence on further legislation in this field, that it is well worth quoting in detail. In the first place,

[70a] *American Federationist*, 1898, Vol. 5, pp. 23, 24.
[71] 14 Utah 71, 14 Utah 96, 1896
[71a] *American Federationist*, 1898, Vol. 5, p. 25.

the court greatly extended the interpretation of the police power when it said: "It is difficult to see why precautions may not . . . be adopted for the protection of their health and morals. It is as much for the interest of the State that the public health should be preserved as that life should be made secure. The whole is no greater than the sum of all its parts, and when the individual health, safety and welfare are sacrificed or neglected, the State must suffer." Second, it recognized that the exercise of the police power on grounds of health was a function of the Legislature: "The enactment does not profess to limit the hours of all workmen, but merely those who are employed in underground mines or in the smelting, reduction or refining of ores or metal. These employments, when too long pursued, the Legislature has judged to be detrimental to the health of the employees and so long as there are reasonable grounds for believing that this is so, its decision upon this subject cannot be reviewed by the federal courts." Justification on grounds other than health suggested a new line of defense for these measures when the court said: "that the proprietors of these establishments and their operatives do not stand upon an equality . . . the employers lay down the rules, and the laborers are practically constrained to obey them. In such cases, self-interest is often an unsafe guide, and the Legislature may properly interpose its authority." The court pointed out as labor had done: "his [the employer's] defense is not so much that his right to contract has been infringed upon, but that the Act works a peculiar hardship to his employees, whose right to labor as long as they please is alleged to be thereby violated. The argument would certainly come with better grace and greater cogency from the latter class." [72]

[72] Holden v. Hardy, 169 U. S. 366, 1898.

The decision was compared to that of the Dred Scott case in importance, and was hailed as a "hopeful sign that industrial freedom may be extended by legislative measures."[73] As a matter of fact, it established the precedent which is followed today, although important decisions, immediately following, swerved from the trail the Supreme Court had begun to blaze for the development of hours' legislation.

The history of the Colorado Eight-Hour Law, which was an exact copy of the Utah law, was a case in point. The State Federation of Labor, the Western Federation of Miners, the United Mine Workers, had been active supporters in its passage in June, 1899, while powerful corporations had opposed it. One of these, the American Smelting & Refining Company, arranged to have the law violated to bring a test case to court. Simultaneously, a strike, which had commenced at one of this Company's plants on the posting of a notice that the men could work more than eight hours if they chose, spread and became a gigantic struggle. In this crisis, Chief Justice Campbell of the Colorado Supreme Court, in July, 1899, announced: "After a most careful and earnest consideration of the case we have unanimously arrived at the conclusion that the so-called eight-hour law is wholly unconstitutional and void." This announcement was a strong factor in causing the Smeltermen's Union to call off the strike.[74] The opinion which was handed down in September held that the Utah decision was not relevant to this case, because the provision in the Utah Constitution, which directed the Legislature to pass laws of this type, did not exist in that

---

[73] *American Journal of Sociology,* 1898, pp. 21-34.
[74] Colorado Bureau of Labor Statistics, *Seventh Annual Report,* 1899-1900, pp. 125-161, 181.

of Colorado. After the court had thus established that the case of Holden v. Hardy was not a precedent, it nevertheless undertook to express an opinion on the interpretation of the police power which was diametrically opposed to that of the Supreme Court of the United States in the same case. Its rhetorical question on this point must be quoted in full to illustrate the difference in viewpoint: "How can an alleged law, that purports to be the result of an exercise of the police power be such in reality when it has for its only object, not the protection of others or the public health, safety, morals or general welfare, but the welfare of him whose act is prohibited, when, if committed, it will injure him who commits it, and him only?" The conclusion of the Colorado opinion indicates clearly the opposite poles to which the reasoning of the two courts brought them: "It is manifest that this extraordinary and extreme statute is not necessary and was not intended for the protection of the public. Its sole purpose was to regulate private interests and enforce private rights. . . . In this statute we have another example of class legislation where the Legislature has attempted to improperly interfere with the private rights of the citizen. This species of legislation has been so often condemned by this and other courts as to render any further discussion of its impropriety and invalidity wholly unnecessary." [75]

This decision was a complete surprise to the people of the State, and strong disapproval resulted in agitation for a constitutional amendment. In 1901 by an overwhelming vote, the people adopted an amendment directing the Legislature to provide an eight-hour law for work in mines, smelters or places dangerous to health.[76] Al-

[75] *in re* Morgan 26 Colo. 415, 1899.
[76] Article 5, Sec. 25a.

though one was passed for miners and smelters in 1905, it was not until 1913 that an enforceable law was put on the statute books. "The essential injustice and stupidity of the employers against eight-hour legislation is strikingly shown by a letter from Mr. L. M. Bowers, Chairman of the Board of Directors of the Colorado Fuel & Iron Company, to Mr. John D. Rockefeller, Jr., stating that after they saw such legislation was inevitable, they tried out the eight-hour day in their mines, and found it was profitable." [77]

Proof that the Colorado decision was out of line with the trend of judicial opinion was evidenced, when in the cases of the Missouri Eight-Hour Law for Underground Miners, and the Nevada Eight-Hour Statute for Underground Miners and Smelters, the State courts sustained their constitutionality following the precedent set by the Supreme Court in Holden v. Hardy.[78]

It is of particular interest, at this point, to quote the United States Industrial Commission on the Utah Eight-Hour Law. Summarizing the evidence, the Commission said: "There was a general agreement among the witnesses representing both employers and employees that this Act had proved beneficial. Several employers stated that the men worked harder . . . and accomplished practically as much in eight hours as they had done in ten, especially in mines." The Commission recommended: "that the provisions of the Utah Constitution and statutes be followed in all the States." [79]

In 1895, the year preceding the passage of the Utah eight-hour statute for miners and smelters, New York had

[77] U. S. Commission on Industrial Relations, 1916, Vol. 1, p. 45.
[78] 179 Mo. 245, 1904; U. S. Supreme Court affirmed this decision without writing an opinion, 199 U. S. 602; 27 Nev. 299, 1904.
[79] U. S. Industrial Commission, 1901, *op cit.*, Vol 12, p. XIV.

enacted a ten-hour law for bakers,[80] which had a far different judicial history, and as a result a hindering effect on restrictive legislation for men in unhealthy trades. The law was passed on the advice of the Commissioner of Labor after an investigation of the bake shops of the leading cities made by him, in conjunction with the Bakers' and Confectioners' International Union. He reported: " Were it not fully established by indisputable proof, credence would hardly be given to the fact that many bakers are obliged to work more than one hundred hours per week, and in some instances they labor one hundred and thirty-two hours in a week. These unnecessary hours . . . as the investigation demonstrates, have resulted, in many cases, in great physical injury to the employees." [81]

The question of the constitutionality of this law did not arise until 1901. Like the lower courts of the State, the Court of Appeals of New York affirmed its constitutionality. This court declared on two grounds that the statute was not repugnant to the Fourteenth Amendment, since it was within the police power of the State. The first ground was the nature of the work which predisposed its members to consumption: "The published medical opinions and vital statistics bearing upon that subject *standing alone* fully justify the employees in such establishments." The second was that the health of the community was dependent on the health of the bakers who produced this necessity of life.[82] This decision was entirely in line with that of the Supreme Court of the United States in Holden *v.* Hardy, which was quoted as a precedent.

[80] Laws of 1895, Ch. 518.

[81] N. Y. Bureau of Statistics of Labor, *Thirteenth Annual Report*, 1895, Part II, p. 5.

[82] People *v.* Lochner, 177 N. Y. 145, 1904.

The Supreme Court of the United States, however, by a five to four vote, held this statute unconstitutional as an unjustifiable interference with liberty of contract. Disregarding the findings of the investigation, quoted above, and also the evidence of medical authorities, the majority opinion stated: "We think that there can be no fair doubt that the trade of a baker, in and of itself, is not an unhealthy one to that degree which would authorize the Legislature to interfere with the right to labor and with the right of free contract on the part of the individual either as employer or employee." In like manner, the court decided: "Clean and wholesome bread does not depend upon whether the baker works but ten hours per day or only sixty hours a week." The court's concluding statement was in the exact vein of the Colorado court in its decision on the Eight-Hour Law for miners and smelters: "Statutes of the nature of that under review, limiting hours in which grown and intelligent men may labor to earn their living, are mere meddlesome interferences with the rights of the individual." Justice Holmes sharply dissented on the ground that the opinion was the result of the court's laissez-faire bias which beclouded its judgment on the question of the constitutionality of statutes which embodied the principle of control.[83] This opinion demonstrates that "a common understanding" of the bakers' conditions, unconsciously influenced by the social outlook of the judges, caused the court to draw a line of distinction between work in mines and smelters and in bakeshops; on one side of the line, regulation of hours was constitutional, on the other side it was not. As had been most pertinently remarked in the New York Labor Bulletin: "Since the differences that manifest themselves in

---

[83] Lochner v. New York, 198 U. S. 45, 1905.

the several opinions as to the relative healthfulness or unhealthfulness of the occupation, one realizes as never before the need of official statistics of trade diseases and occupational mortality, such as have been begun by the English Government." [84]

The decision aroused a storm of comment which continued for a long time. The *New York Sun* approved and quoted in its defense: "If this statute were held to be valid, there would seem to be no limit to which legislation of this nature might go." [85] The *Outlook*, on the other hand, quoting Judge Harlan's dissenting opinion that this will "seriously cripple the inherent powers of the States to care for the lives, health and well-being of their citizens," prophesied a resulting increase in the power of labor leaders whose distrust of the courts was now shown to be justified. [86] The law journals severely criticized the decision. Sir Frederick Pollock's pertinent comment was: "How can the Supreme Court at Washington have conclusive judicial knowledge of the conditions affecting bakeries in New York?" [87] Professor Freund asked: "Where is the dividing line that will serve to distinguish Holden v. Hardy from Lochner v. New York?" [88] Professor Pound said: " study of the facts has shown that the Legislature was right and the court was wrong." [89] The United States Industrial Commission of 1912, which listed denial of justice as one of the four causes of industrial unrest, declared that "decisions, such as the Lochner case, in which the Fourteenth Amendment has been

[84] N. Y. *Bulletin of the Dept. of Labor*, 1904, p. 39.
[85] April 18, 1905.
[86] April 29, 1905.
[87] 18 Yale Law Journal 480, quoted in footnote.
[88] 17 Green Bag 416.
[89] 18 Yale Law Journal 480.

invoked to annul statutes designed to better conditions of life and work, must constitute just ground for grave concern not only to the workers but to every citizen who values his liberty."[90] The *American Federationist*, after a bitter criticism of the reasoning of the Supreme Court, declared the "judicial victory" of the employing bakers was barren, because the organized bakers of New York had brought about an agreement limiting the hours of work to ten per day.[91]

This decision has been labelled "reactionary," and has been of importance, like the Colorado case, rather as an exception to the general trend of court decisions in regard to hours than as a direct influence. Since it was handed down, some States have passed laws fixing the hours of labor in trades which the Legislature held to involve more than average hazard or danger to health.[91a] No statement can be made as to the Supreme Court's attitude today on this point, because the question of the constitutionality of these statutes has not arisen, probably due to the acceptance of the principle laid down by the United States Supreme Court in Holden *v.* Hardy.

LATE GENERAL LAWS

The growing elasticity of the judicial interpretation of the police power of the State in relation to regulation of hours had its beginning in the case of Holden *v.* Hardy.

[90] Vol. 1, p. 49.

[91] Vol. 12, p. 363.

[91a] Examples of such regulation are: for employees in cement and plaster mills in Colorado and Nevada; for workers under compressed air in New Jersey, New York and Pennsylvania; for employees of electric light and power plants in Arizona, and of plate-glass manufacturing plants in Missouri; and for grocery clerks in New York. *Cf.* Appendix D.

This view has continued with comparatively few exceptions, and finally has been expanded on general health grounds to include the regulation of hours for all workers, including men. When this occurred, labor at last achieved that for which it had begun to agitate in 1865. The fruit, however, was not only late in developing, but took the form of a ten-hour day instead of an eight, and appeared in only a meagre number of States.[91b]

In 1912 Mississippi, however, passed a law which established a maximum ten-hour day, except in emergencies, for all employees in manufacturing or repairing establishments, and fixed a fine of from ten to fifty dollars for each day's violation.[92] Shortly after, it was attacked on the ground of contravening the Fourteenth Amendment. The Supreme Court of Mississippi by a unanimous decision upheld its constitutionality. After declaring that Lochner v. New York was not a precedent because the New York statute had made no provision for emergencies, the court stated that the Mississippi law was a reasonable act within the police power of the State, saying: "In fact, when we consider the present manner of laboring, the use of machinery, the appliances, requiring intelligence and skill, and the general present-day manner of life, which tends to nervousness, it seems to us quite reasonable, and in no way improper to pass such law so limiting a day's labor."[93] At a hearing granted on the company's complaint of error, the Mississippi court commented, as the

---

[91b] *Cf.* Appendix E. North Carolina had on its statute books until 1931 a law which established a sixty-hour week for all factory workers. In that year it was amended to apply to women only, and the maximum hours were reduced to fifty-five per week. Laws of 1931, Chap. 289.

[92] Laws of 1912, Ch. 157.

[93] 102 Miss. 802, 1912.

Supreme Court had done [94] on the source of the appeal to protect the liberty of contract: "It is rare for the seller of labor to appeal to the courts for the preservation of his inalienable rights to labor. This inestimable privilege is generally the object of the buyer's disinterested solicitude." To this was added the promising statement that: "Some day perhaps the inalienable right to rest will be the subject of litigation." [95]

This decision is an important landmark in the development of the recognition of the constitutionality of hours' regulation. For the first time in the United States, an enforceable law regulating hours for men and women alike was sustained as a health measure. No longer was legislation of this type limited to women as "the wards of the State," or to an industry admittedly hazardous, but as a general health measure, regulation for men was recognized as a power of the State Legislature. Hope for a wider use of this method of obtaining shorter hours was confirmed when that same year Ohio's Constitution was amended to give the Legislature power to regulate the hours of labor.[96]

From one point of view, the law enacted by Oregon in 1913 was not as significant as that of Mississippi in a study of a real shorter-hour tendency, because of the permission for three hours over-time daily at time and a half pay included in the former measure. From another, the law can be viewed as one distinctly in line with the tendency towards a shorter-hour standard. The best proof is the wording of the law itself, which says: "It is hereby declared that the working of any person more than ten hours in one day, in any mill, factory or manufacturing

[94] *Cf. supra*, p. 121.
[95] 103 Miss. 263, 1913.
[96] Art. II, Sec. 34.

establishment is injurious to the physical health and well-being of such person, and tends to prevent him from acquiring that degree of intelligence that is necessary to make him a useful and desirable citizen of the State." [97] The Supreme Courts of Oregon and the United States both classed the law as primarily a regulation of hours rather than wages. The brief prepared by counsel, Felix Frankfurter, assisted by Josephine Goldmark, was a monumental piece of work.[97a] It gathered into a thousand pages the facts of common knowledge on hours' limitation for men, presenting: first, complete tables of American and foreign legislation; and second, data collected from experience all over the world, illustrative of the need for shorter hours on physiological, social and economic grounds.[98] Justice McKenna delivered the opinion for the United States Supreme Court. The claim that permission for over-time at more than the market rate proved the law to be a wage regulation, not a health regulation, was denied on the ground that the State court, which had cognizance of all the facts that led to the statute's enactment, had declared that its intent was primarily to regulate hours. The court concluded that the Act "did not transcend constitutional limits," and that it was not an unreasonable or arbitrary regulation.[99] Since the Lochner case was not cited in this opinion, which arrived logically at the opposite conclusion, Chief Justice Taft in an *ex cathedra* statement, said: "I have always sup-

[97] Laws of 1913, Ch. 102.

[97a] The brief in this case, Bunting v. Oregon, has been reprinted by the National Consumers League under the title "The Case for the Shorter Work Day." New York, n. d.

[98] This type of brief had been introduced by Counsel Louis D. Brandeis in the Oregon Ten-Hour Law Case. *Cf. supra*, pp. 112, 113.

[99] Bunting v. Oregon, 243 U. S. 426, 1917.

posed that the Lochner case was thus overruled *sub silentio,*" and Justice Holmes supposed that the Lochner case "would be allowed a deserved repose." [100]

This affirmation by the country's highest tribunal of the legislative authority to limit hours of adult males was hailed by all those who were convinced of its necessity as the beginning of a new era, inasmuch as it supplemented trade union action by the more inclusive legislative method.[101] The new era has not materialized. The Territory of Alaska referred to the voters the question of a general eight-hour day for all wage-earners and salary earners. In response to their affirmative vote, this law was passed, exception being made of cases where life and property were in imminent danger. Violation was made a misdemeanor, punishable by a fine of from one hundred to five hundred dollars, or six months' imprisonment, or both.[102] In a test case, the Supreme Court of the Territory declared the law unconstitutional, holding that, since the Organic Act under which the Territory was governed made no provision for a referendum, the original Act of 1915 was unauthorized, and therefore not binding. Aside from this, the court added that the law was an unjustifiable infringement of contract, because it made no claim that "it was necessary for the peace of society or morals of the people . . ." [103]

The States of Washington and California initiated general eight-hour laws in 1914. In both States, they were rejected by a two to one vote, apparent proof that public opinion either did not approve of the eight-hour principle,

[100] Adkins *v.* Children's Hospital, 261 U. S. 525, 1923.
[101] *Survey*, 1918, p. 494.
[102] Laws of 1917, Ch. 55.
[103] U. S. *v.* Northern Commercial Co. *et al.*, 6 Alaska Reports 94, 1918.

STATE LEGISLATION

or did not approve of it by the legislative method. The same year, the Utah State Federation of Labor canvassed all candidates on a proposal for the enactment of an eight-hour law for all classes of labor,[104] but no action was taken by the Legislature. In 1920 Michigan ratified a constitutional amendment whereby the Legislature was empowered to enact laws relative to hours for men, women and children;[105] no use has been made of this permission. In 1929, New Hampshire, amending an earlier hours' statute, enacted that: "In all contracts relating to labor, ten hours' actual labor shall be taken to be a day's work unless otherwise agreed by the parties." [106] This law, made nugatory by permission to contract otherwise, was of the type labor had denounced in the 1860's as a "farce," and as an ironic though silent criticism of all their effort, it provided for a day greater in length by two hours than the eight hours labor had tried to legislate into existence in that decade.

It would appear from this history that even when the courts were prepared to give affirmative decisions on the constitutionality of hours' legislation, in the light of realistic study of industrial conditions, the Legislatures of the States did not quickly take advantage of this method of labor reform.

[104] *Public Affairs Information Service*, 1915, pp. 114, 115.
[105] Art. V, Sec. 29.
[106] Laws of 1929, Chap. 93.

PART II
REDUCTION OF HOURS BY TRADE UNIONS

CHAPTER V

DIRECT ACTION

AMERICAN labor, organized and unorganized, has had two primary objectives: higher wages and shorter hours. While to the individual laborer the order of importance is that given, the leaders of the labor movement have stressed hours.[1] The individual laborer has been influenced by a very natural but short-run point of view. The emphasis of labor leaders on hours has been the result of their ability to view the question more broadly in terms of the relation of hours to wages. Two lines of reasoning have been influential. The less important is the theory, injected into the early hours' struggle by Ira Steward,[2] that increased leisure through creating new wants necessarily results in higher wages. The more important line of reasoning is the outgrowth of labor's attitude on hours in relation to unemployment. Since labor accepts the fundamental assumption that shorter hours will decrease the number of unemployed, the logical conclusion is that, due to reduced pressure for jobs, labor will be in a strategic position to negotiate better wage agreements.[3]

[1] "The most progressive leaders, such as Mr. Gompers, of the Federation of Labor, are constantly urging their associates to put the shorter work-day in the forefront of their demands." Report of the Industrial Commission, 1901, Vol. 17, p. XLVII.

[2] *Cf. supra*, p. 16.

[3] Report of Industrial Commission, 1901, Vol. 17, p. XLVII. Dahlberg, *op. cit.*, advocates the shorter day as a means of establishing a chronic and genuine scarcity of labor, not merely for higher wages, but as a panacea for Capitalism, pp. 221-244.

The American Federation of Labor from its inception has held to the policy that direct action was the only effective means of decreasing the work-day for men. Before the formation of the Federation, however, labor made trial of legislative enactment as a means to reduce work hours.[4] Failure to pass effective statutes was followed by an effort to use direct action in two ways. The first was the use of the strike "to enforce" the hours' legislation which the Executive Departments of the State failed to do; and the second was to rely on direct action, unaided by the medium of the law, to attain the objective, shorter hours. The decades immediately following the Civil War witnessed both uses of direct action. Thereafter, labor accepted the futility of attempting to enforce laws that were "frauds on the working class," and reliance was placed on collective bargaining to establish the shorter day for men without the medium of the law.[5]

EARLY EFFORTS 1865-1886

The attempt to trace direct action for shorter hours, prior to the American Federation of Labor's concerted action in 1886, is complicated both by the inadequacy of records and by the sporadic nature of the movement. Sparsely scattered strikes, each of small significance, were not likely to be mentioned by metropolitan papers. Not only were labor papers few in number and short-lived, but they also reflected the interest of their subscribers, by being "more political than industrial, more given to argument than to fact,—to financial reforms, than to trade

[4] *Cf. supra*, pp. 31-37, 39, 40.
[5] The American Federation of Labor excepts from this policy regulation of hours on government work and in hazardous trades. *Cf. supra.* pp. 51, 55.

unionism."[6] The creation of state labor departments, whose reports would be a helpful source, was not begun until later, and did not become universal for a considerable time. Fortunately, however, the commissioners' zeal led them to search records and publish facts in regard to past efforts, as an aid to comprehending the existing situation.

Direct action to establish the eight-hour day—in reality, any shorter day—was a steadily rising wave, which reached its high point just before the panic of 1873, and practically disappeared in the long depression that followed. The demand in Massachusetts for legislative action to reduce hours, which commenced in 1865,[7] was paralleled by direct action for the same purpose by realists. The latter, through their local labor organizations, demanded immediate action, not discussion, investigation and a slow marshalling of votes; they demanded practical action, a decrease in hours from thirteen to eleven, not the highly improbable inauguration of the eight-hour day, which the theorists like Phillips and Steward sought to establish.[8] A successful two-day strike in 1865 in the textile mills in Eastern Massachusetts caused a similar attempt in Pittsfield, where the " change of hours was finally made."[9] The following year, strikes in the textile plants of Fall River resulted in the adoption of a ten-hour day. Twenty-one months later, however, because of competition with mills on longer hours, the work-day was increased to eleven

[6] Mass. Bureau of Statistics of Labor, *Fourth Annual Report*, 1873, pp. 251, 252.

[7] *Cf. supra*, pp. 33, 34.

[8] The policy on hours adopted by the National Labor Union puts this organization in the class of theorists. *Cf. supra*, pp. 35-39.

[9] Mass. Bureau of Statistics of Labor, *Eleventh Annual Report*, 1880, p. 21.

hours with the promise to labor "that we would assist them in obtaining ten hours established as a day's labor." [10] After this failure of direct action, organizations in Massachusetts concentrated on reducing hours in the textile mills by legislation.

In the spring of 1866, a strike for eight hours by the New York ship carpenters and caulkers spread to Boston, when the trades in that city refused to do work forwarded from New York. The New York strikers held torch-light processions and mass meetings, one of which was addressed by Horace Greeley who declared the eight-hour day to be a desirable, natural and proper arrangement.[11] The Boston strikers urged the New Yorkers to hold fast to their purpose, and reported the encouraging news that the Maine carpenters had promised not to work in Boston at any price.[12] The New York master shipwrights and carpenters tried to use the eight-hour strike as a means of destroying the union. When the strike ended in June, the *New York Tribune* reported that the settlement was unsatisfactory to all: "The bosses have resisted the eight-hour day, while the men retain their organization." It was estimated that the strike cost labor one and a half million dollars in lost wages, and the cost to the fourteen shipbuilding firms was placed at ten million.[13]

The passage of eight-hour laws by several States in 1867 was greeted with exuberant rejoicing by labor, followed by attempts to enforce these measures by direct action when complete administrative indifference had been

[10] *Ibid.*, 1870, Commissioner's report gives 1866 as date, p. 45; Isaac P. Chase, a mill executive gives date as 1868, but adds "I think"; p. 501.
[11] McNeill, *op. cit.*, p. 351.
[12] *New York Tribune*, May 31, 1866.
[13] *Ibid.*, June 27, 1866.

exhibited by the executive departments.[14] In Chicago, for example, the procession to celebrate the passage of the Illinois Eight-Hour Law reads like a magnificent spectacle of the mediaeval guilds: "The Stone Cutters Union had three trucks with operatives cutting ornamental masonry. The Iron Molders Union truck was drawn by eight noble horses, and contained men at work on the finer branches of iron molding. The Ship Carpenters and Caulkers Union had a full rigged ship and yawl boat with busy workmen thereon . . ." Yet the next day the city was wild with rumors of strikes and riot because no provison for enforcing the law had been made. The *Chicago Tribune* reported that the workers were peaceful, the demand for strikes was the work of a few demagogues and unprincipled newspapers.[15] The *New York Times* commented scathingly on the use of the strike in Chicago by those who had asked for legal protection. The Chicago episode caused this paper to generalize and moralize to the effect that: "There is every reason to expect that the stimulus given to strikers of every degree by the State Legislatures will cause the movement to spread until hard experience brings the deluded workmen to their senses, and to some proper understanding of economic law."[16] The result of legislative action, supplemented by direct action, was disappointing; not quite two weeks after the celebration of the passage of the Eight-Hour Law, most of the laborers were reported to be at work under the old ten-hour rule.[17]

New York laborers celebrated the passage of the Eight-

[14] *Cf. supra*, pp. 96, 97.
[15] *New York Tribune*, May 6, 1867, quotes *Chicago Tribune*.
[16] *New York Times*, May 8, 1867.
[17] *Ibid.*, May 17, 1867.

Hour Law in their State less exuberantly, but immediately devoted great attention to the question of enforcement. A meeting of labor was called at which some advocated a general strike, and other successive strikes in each industry, but the resolution, which the meeting passed, demonstrated the essentially conservative spirit of the workers. This resolution called on the employers "to have the question considered," and recommended, "local unions to move with caution and avoid premature action, but to act, agitate and work with a view to the ultimate adoption of the eight-hour rule."[18] San Francisco apparently was the one large city where the movement met with entire success. It was reported that "the eight-hour day was quietly inaugurated after one of the largest processions the City had ever witnessed."[19]

Concerted action by the New York building trade unions, in the spring of 1868, to enforce the State Eight-Hour Law for their members did not meet with entire success. "The stone cutters of New York City, depending upon themselves alone, obtained the eight-hour rule, and have since maintained it . . . with satisfaction to both employers and workmen."[20] Likewise, the plasterers and painters obtained it, and passed a resolution to support the bricklayers who were still striking for it.[21] This latter trade had made a peaceful but unsuccessful demand for the shorter day, and had agreed to accept a 10% cut in wages. The ensuing strike led the *New York Tribune* to ask the very pertinent question: "Who knows the rela-

[18] *New York Tribune*, May 20, 1867.
[19] *New York Times*, June 8, 1867.
[20] New Jersey Bureau of Statistics of Labor and Industries, *Ninth Annual Report*, 1886, p. 234.
[21] *New York Tribune*, June 26, 1868.

tive product of an eight and a ten-hour day's work? Do we not need light on this point?"[22] The *New York Times*, on the contrary, saw no need for definite information on this subject; *a priori* reasoning led this journal to declare that the "exactions were arbitrary and unreasonable, and defied all the laws of political economy." It interpreted the failure of the strike as incontrovertible proof of the futility of any attempt to regulate hours by trade-union action.[23]

In the summer of 1868, the Pennsylvania anthracite coal fields were the scene of a general strike to compel the enforcement of that State's Eight-Hour Statute. The strike commenced July 1, and shortly after included every colliery. It was reported that the mass meetings were the largest ever held in the district, attracting an attendance of from twelve to twenty thousand workers. Although the leaders made every effort to preserve peace, violence spread rapidly. The strike was at last settled in September as a result of negotiations carried on through an association which the coal operators had formed. The State Bureau of Statistics reported that the men returned to work with good spirit, but failed to mention the hours' settlement, although this question had caused the strike.[24] McNeill states that the settlement of the strike was the abandonment of the eight-hour system.[25]

Renewal of direct action to establish in fact the eight-hour day as well as on the statute books, occurred in New York the following spring, 1869. The painters, who had

[22] *Ibid.*, Aug. 25, 1868.
[23] *New York Times*, Aug. 13, 1868.
[24] Pennsylvania Bureau of Statistics of Labor and Agriculture, *First Annual Report*, 1872-1873, p. 332.
[25] McNeill, *op. cit.*, p. 138.

won the eight-hour day by direct action in the preceding year, were forced again to join other trades in striking when the employers, encouraged by the superabundance of labor, insisted on re-establishing the ten-hour day.[26] In California, too, the increased supply of labor caused the loss of the eight-hour day which "had been so easily won." When the California Lumber Mills, in August, 1869, demanded a return to the ten-hour day, the Eight-Hour League voted that no trade would handle lumber unless stamped with the eight-hour label.[27] The attempt to stem the return to longer hours was unavailing, and this first break prepared the way for the loss of all eight-hour gains.[28]

Demand for the enforcement of the Eight-Hour Law was again active in New York in the fall of 1871. The carpenters met, and decided to strike if it had not been established by the following spring.[29] The trades' unions of the city united to hold a procession and a monster mass meeting. Despite the rain, 8,000 members marched.[30] The painters' float, preceded by a cannon, and bearing the slogans, "Peaceably if we can, forcibly if we must," and "When peaceful efforts fail, then revolution," struck a warning note. However, the monster mass meeting, held that evening at Cooper Union under the Chairmanship of the President of the New York Workingmen's Union, reverted to the panacea of all American labor's ills, the

[26] *New York Times*, Apr. 17, 1869.

[27] This is reported to have been the earliest use of the union label. *Cf.* Commons and Associates, *op. cit.*, Vol. I, p. 266.

[28] Eaves, *op. cit.*, p. 209.

[29] *New York Times*, May 19, 1872.

[30] *Ibid.*, Sept. 15, 1871. Gompers placed the number at 25,000. *Cf.* Gompers, S., *Seventy Years of Life and Labor*, New York, 1925, Vol. I, p. 53.

formation of a new political party. The platform of the party included an eight-hour plank, one for equal division of the land, and many other remedies which labor had in the past looked to as final means of relief.[31]

The following spring, however, labor returned to direct action with renewed vigor. New York was the scene of a tremendous upheaval of labor which, for a time, threatened to spread throughout all industrial centers. The carpenters, who had announced their intention the preceding September, began the strike to establish the eight-hour day.[32] In a short time, they were joined by the wood carvers, upholsterers and cabinet makers.[33] For the following month, the newspapers were filled with accounts of great organizing activity among the various trades. From day to day, announcements were made of new recruits to the movement; the bricklayers, plumbers,[34] sash and blind-makers,[35] the piano-makers,[36] the patternmakers,[37] each in turn joined the movement, which finally spread from a trade movement to an industrial one, when all the workers of concerns such as the Singer Sewing Machine Company and the Brewster Carriage Company went on strike.[38] Likewise, there were daily reports of the growth of the movement outside New York. Letters were received from the Cabinet Makers Unions of Chicago and Pittsburgh which announced plans for a strike.[39] The Jersey City Building

[31] *New York Times*, Sept. 15, 1871.
[32] *Ibid.*, May 19, 1872.
[33] *Ibid.*, May 20, 1872.
[34] *Ibid.*, May 21, 1872.
[35] *Ibid.*, May 23, 1872.
[36] *Ibid.*, May 24 and 27, 1872.
[37] *Ibid.*, May 28, 1872.
[38] *Ibid.*, June 6, 1872. Also *cf. infra*, p. 230.
[39] *Ibid.*, May 23 and 26, 1872.

Trades struck on May 28.[40] The Philadelphia Labor Reform Party called for the inauguration of an eight-hour movement in that city,[41] with the result that the cabinet-makers, upholsterers, varnishers and piano-makers went on strike.[42] Workers in many trades in Buffalo and Albany called strikes,[43] while workers in St. Louis and Boston held meetings to plan to make the eight-hour demand.[44]

The rapidity of the growth of the movement, while due in part to the intensity of labor's desire for the shorter day, can be explained by its immediate successes in New York. On May 20 the Master Carpenters Association, "under its most solemn protests hereby uttered, accedes as an experiment to the demand of the journeymen employees to consider in the future eight-hour's labor as a day's work."[45] And on the very day on which they struck, the bricklayers at a meeting, which was the "scene of almost indescribable confusion and enthusiasm," announced that they had won their demands.[46] The following days brought the same success to other building trades, and to the majority of the cabinet-makers.[47] Thereafter victories were less frequent, and the strike settled down to a drawn out struggle. In addition to the trade unions which met daily to make plans, and to arrange relief for the strikers, an Eight-Hour League, which recognized the strike as a useful weapon but condemned violence, was formed. It

[40] *Ibid.*, May 28, 1872.
[41] *Ibid.*, June 6, 1872.
[42] *Ibid.*, June 11, 1872.
[43] *Ibid.*, June 10 and 16, 1872.
[44] *Ibid.*, June 11 and 17, 1872.
[45] *Ibid.*, May 21, 1872.
[46] *Ibid.*
[47] *Ibid.*, May 22-May 30, 1872.

soon had a membership of 21,000 [48] from which it collected a weekly tax of one to two dollars to pay strike benefits.[49] The strikers, 4,000 strong instead of the expected 40,000, paraded peacefully on June 10.[50] The *New York Times'* editorial on this is reminiscent of a note often struck today: "It would be a matter of interest to inquire what proportion of the thousands forming that long column of strikers . . . were thoroughly American." [51]

The widespread nature of the strike, and the earnestness of the strikers, led the employers to unite for action. At a meeting of 300 business men, the Employers Central Executive Committee was elected to resist the strikers behind whose demands the "spectre of communism" was seen.[52] The Committee met regularly to hear reports and to advise employers; it issued an "Address to the Intelligent Workers," pointing out the folly of their demands, and warning them of the sinister influences at work.[53] Attacks on the movement on the ground that it was fostered by communists were as common as they are in strikes today.

The strike had not kept its peaceful aspect. The activity of the police in arresting strikers caused the workers to appeal to the Governor for protection in their attempt "to establish peacefully the eight-hour system in our businesses in accordance with the laws of our State." [54] Vio-

[48] *New York Tribune*, June 8, 1872.
[49] *New York Times*, June 19, 1872.
[50] *Ibid.*, June 11, 1872; *Nation*, June 13, 1872.
[51] *New York Times*, June 12, 1872.
[52] *Ibid.*, June 19, 1872.
[53] Pamphlet, New York, June 17, 1872.
[54] *New York Times*, May 31, 1872.

lent demonstrations, to prevent the return of workers under the ten-hour rule, led the police to consider calling on the National Guard for aid.[55]

The abject return to work of the unsuccessful strikers made this aid unnecessary. Early in June, the *New York Tribune* estimated that one-third of the strikers had gained their objective,[56] and two weeks later the *New York Times* announced that the movement was "not a general success or failure."[57] However, the Massachusetts Commissioner of Labor stated that the New York failure discouraged the Boston building trades from striking as they had planned. Instead, they renewed their political activity through the Boston Eight-Hour League.[58] In like manner, plans for direct action of the California Eight-Hour League, which had pledged its members to work only that number of hours on and after a certain date, came to naught. Unemployment was so common that the League did not dare to set the date.[59]

Despite the widespread interest of labor in the movement, the strike did not become a matter of outstanding importance except in New York. There its prospects for success grew very slight as soon as it had spread to financially powerful concerns such as the Singer Sewing Machine Co., the Steinway Piano Company and the Brewster Carriage Company. Even the early successes of the movement were short-lived, "only the stone cutters held it [the eight-hour day] through succeeding panic and depression."[60]

[55] *Ibid.*, June 21, 1872.
[56] June 8, 1872.
[57] June 24, 1872.
[58] Mass. Bureau of Statistics of Labor, *Fourth Annual Report*, 1873, pp. 247, 248. Cf. *supra*, p. 39.
[59] Eaves, *op. cit.*, p. 213.
[60] Gompers, *op. cit.*, Vol. I, p. 60.

Although these annual spasmodic attempts of labor to establish the eight-hour day by strikes had little direct success, they nevertheless served to keep the agitation before the public, and to draw labor together by providing a common objective. Even these ineffective struggles, however, stopped during the long depression which followed the panic of 1873. Testimony taken by the Senate Committee on the Relations of Capital and Labor in 1885 gave reduction in wages as the cause of practically all strikes between 1873 and 1879.[61] The railroad strikes of 1877, which began on the Baltimore & Ohio as a result of a 10% wage cut, and spread through the country, were representative of the goal which labor was then trying to guard.[62]

All these efforts can be classed as more or less individual attempts of unions to establish shorter hours by direct action. National organizations took little part in the movement, due either to policy or weakness, or both. The Knights of Labor advocated arbitration, but the history of the Order does not offer any proof of success in reducing hours by this method. Although the Order's opposition to strikes continued on paper, in the world of reality it found them essential. The first national strike into which the Knights of Labor was drawn was that of the Brotherhood of Telegraphers for the eight-hour day, pay for Sunday work and improved conditions.[63] After an overwhelming affirmative vote, the strike was called on July 19, 1883. Although two telegraph companies granted the demands of the strikers, the Western Union fought

[61] Vol. I, p. 451.
[62] Perlman, S., *A History of Trade Unionism in the United States* New York, 1922, pp. 58, 59.
[63] Wright, C. D., *The Battles of Labor*, Philadelphia, 1906, p. 125.

them bitterly.[64] Financial weakness — the Order added only $3,600 to the $58,000 which the strikers had raised[65] —caused the union to declare the strike over on August 17. Return to work was arranged with the disastrous condition that membership in all labor organizations was prohibited. This was the sole national attempt of the Knights of Labor to establish the eight-hour day by direct action.[66]

Like the Knights, the International Molders Union had no faith in strikes as a means of reform. Under Sylvis's leadership they had adopted the policy of "agitation, education and legislation" as the means of inaugurating the eight-hour day. The failure of this policy led the Union in 1876 to adopt a rule which fixed ten hours "as a legal days' work," but left the enforcement to the local unions. What measure of success they achieved is shown by the president's statement in 1895 that ten hours was supposed to be the rule, but in many foundries little if any attention is paid even to this.[67]

The Brotherhood of Carpenters and Joiners, organized in 1881, favored strikes by locals to establish the shorter day.[68] The Bricklayers and Masons International Union showed itself in a more practical role than the locals, which had been struggling for years to establish the eight-hour day, when it voted to enforce the nine-hour system.[69] McNeill in 1885 stated that the powerful Amalgamated

[64] Ware, *op. cit.*, p. 129.

[65] Wright, *op. cit.*, p. 125, estimates total expenditures at $62,000. Figure in text is resultant of information in Wright and Ware.

[66] Ware, *op. cit.*, p. 129.

[67] Stockton, F. T., *The International Molders Union of North America*, Baltimore, 1921, pp. 161, 162.

[68] McNeill, *op. cit.*, p. 357.

[69] *Ibid.*, p. 372.

Society of Engineers had "many years ago succeeded in fixing nine hours as the standard for a day's work," but he does not give any information as to the method by which this was established.[70] The National Silk and Fur Hat Finishers Association, established in 1854, permitted locals to make their own rules, subject to the final control of the national body. The hours' question had not been a cause of agitation in this organization—the men worked by the piece, and had "no stated hours of labor."[71]

The Furniture Workers Association of North America was formed largely as a result of the shorter-hour movement. The United Cabinet Makers of New York, who had been leaders in the unsuccessful strike of 1872 in that city, were active in establishing this Union to prevent repetition of failure due to lack of organization. The constitution of this Union held "the establishment of the eight-hour normal working day to be indispensably necessary," and the Central Committee directed a steady agitation to this end,[72] with the result that the Furniture Manufacturers Association in 1876 voted to adopt the eight-hour day with no reduction in pay if two-thirds of the manufacturers would sign the agreement. They took this action because the already overstocked market was being further disrupted by the supply of goods made at home by unemployed cabinet-makers. This attempt at a national agreement failed.[73] Local collective bargaining in Chicago had a very brief success. In 1879 the Furniture Workers of that city were very active in the July

[70] *Ibid.*, p. 375.
[71] *Ibid.*, p. 388.
[72] *Ibid.*, pp. 376-379.
[73] Memorial of the Central Committee of the Furniture Workers Union of North America, *The Normal Workday of Eight Hours*, New York, 1879.

4th eight-hour day demonstration. On the fifth, nine furniture factories granted it, on the sixth the number had increased to forty, but the movement was stopped by the Brunswick & Balke lockout of their employees until they consented to work the ten-hour day. Thereupon, the owners of thirty-five concerns met, and voted that "the interests of the manufacturers as well as the workingmen's will be most secure as long as the ten-hour day remains in force." [74]

The International Typographical Union did not join as an active national organization in these attempts to establish the eight-hour day.[75] Such negotiations were left to the local unions. The New York local, for example, was "well represented in the 1871 demonstration," but in 1872 it limited its action to a vote of sympathy for the trades which were on strike. Later in that year, this local tried to negotiate the eight-hour day, but peacefully accepted the employers' refusal.[76] The International Typographical Union also remained aloof from the concerted effort of the American Federation of Labor to inaugurate the eight-hour day.

THE AMERICAN FEDERATION OF LABOR

Since the Federation has made reduction of hours for men one of its primary objectives [77] and has steadily op-

[74] *Illinois Centennial History*, Vol. 4, pp. 451, 452.

[75] *Cf. supra*, pp. 140-147.

[76] Stevens, G. A., *New York Typographical Union No. 6*, Albany, 1913, pp. 368-370.

[77] It is significant that the propaganda purposes to which the publication of the Proceedings of the Annual Conventions is put are limited to the trade union label and the hours' question. The first inside cover of this publication bears two slogans in large type: first, "Eight hours for work, eight hours for rest, eight hours for what we will"; and second, "Whether you work by the piece or work by the day, decreasing the hours increases the pay."

posed the use of the legislative method in this field, it might be expected that the officials of this organization would constantly exert great thought and care in studying the most effective use of the strike and in planning and carrying out centralized campaigns. The early history of the Federation offered some examples of such preparation, but a drifting policy characterized by alternating periods of inactivity and of unplanned efforts was soon discernible. Finally, at the turn of the century, the Federation withdrew completely, not only from all planning for a national hours' movement but also from all action, leaving the questions of strategy and tactics to the national unions. The central organization then devoted its energies to placing a firm check on all attempts to supplement direct action by legislative action in the field of men's hours, to an endless reiteration of the need for agitation and education on the hours' question and to an equally endless repetition of the past successes of the trade union method.

The Federation of Organized Trades and Labor Unions was responsible for the inauguration of the first movement, which was almost national in scope, to obtain the eight-hour day by direct action. This body, organized only in 1881, grew in its early days to a position of importance, largely as a result of the programs which it planned and carried through for this objective. The crux of its plan, a general strike as of a fixed date, was not original with this organization, having been suggested by the California Eight-Hour League in 1873,[78] and by some of the Knights of Labor.[79] Rejecting legislative action because "in the world of economic reform the working classes must depend upon themselves for the enforcement of

[78] Eaves, *op. cit.*, p. 214.
[79] *Cf. supra*, pp. 41, 42.

measures, as well as for their conceptions," the 1884 convention voted to submit to all labor organizations the question of the feasibility of a universal strike for a working day of eight (or nine) hours to take effect not later than May 1, 1886.[80] The next convention asked all unions which did not vote to strike to extend financial aid to the others, providing that these " in asking for decreased hours do not request an increase in wages." [81]

The Federation did not wait for an affirmative vote before officials set in motion machinery for peaceful negotiation. The Legislative Committee made contacts with employers by circular letters which proposed mutual agreement to adopt the eight-hour day. They urged the unions to hold mass meetings for discussion, agitation and expression of opinion, and to follow these meetings by conferences with employers. The following agreement blank was prepared for submission at these conferences:

"Entered into between.................and............Union hereby agree that on and after May 1st, 1886, his establishment shall be restricted in its working hours to eight hours per day. .... Union hereby agrees not to ask any increase on the present rate of wages until such time as the same is warranted by the conditions of the trade. Signed this ...... day of .... 1886.
.... for firm
.... for Union " [82]

In the event of failure of these peaceful attempts at collective bargaining for shorter hours, the general strike was to be used as a last resort.

This plan of action was sent to the Knights of Labor with a request for their cooperation. Since no answer was received, the Federation officials remained in doubt

[80] American Federation of Labor, *Proceedings*, 1884, pp. 10-13.
[81] *Ibid.*, 1885, p. 12.
[82] Gompers, *op. cit.*, Vol. I, p. 291.

as to the Order's position on the question until Powderly issued the so-called secret circular of March, 1886, ordering the Knights to refrain from participating in the movement.[83] Most of the local assemblies, however, were swept by the intense feeling of their members into playing an active role.

The weakness of the Federation, which was both inexperienced and poorly organized, necessarily left the burden of the work to the local unions. Gompers wrote later that, though the movement was general, it was most aggressive in New York, Chicago, Milwaukee, Cincinnati and Baltimore.[84] It is important, therefore, to review contemporary reports from each of these centers in order to estimate the worth of this first concerted direct action to shorten hours.

The New York Commissioner of Labor in his report for 1886 wrote that: "The great May movement of the past year was nominally for an eight-hours' day, really for shorter hours." He stated "meetings of various trades were held," addressed by Henry George and other popular speakers; that employers met their employees, and discussed the matter without arousing any "fire of antagonism" because the employers wisely took no concerted action. Since, however, these peaceful means accomplished little, strikes were common. He estimated that approximately 74 of the 256 strikes, which were called, were successful. The building trades, ironworkers and machinists generally succeeded in compromising on a nine-hour day " due to good management, old organizations and a well-filled treasury." He added, however, that in " the majority of cases nothing was gained." [85]

[83] Commons and Associates, *op. cit.*, Vol. 2, p. 378.
[84] Gompers, *op. cit.*, Vol. 1, p. 292.
[85] pp. 656-661.

In Chicago, where "the movement had absorbed the efforts of all classes of labor agitators to the exclusion, for the time being, of every other consideration," [86] the tension increased as May Day approached. "Squads of police guarded the larger factories, and galloped unexpectedly through quarters where laboring men assembled." [87] The Labor Department reported, however, that the day was peaceful; of approximately 110,000 workers agitating for the eight-hour day, about 47,500 (including meat packers, cigar makers, machinists and building trades) gained satisfactory concessions without striking.[88] But peace and success were disrupted when on May 3 at the McCormick Works, an attack on strike-breakers caused a counter attack by the police in which four workers were killed and many wounded. At the protest meeting in Haymarket Square, called by the leaders of the International Working People's Association—or Black International, for short—the peaceful order of denunciatory speeches was interrupted by the advance of a large squad of police. A bomb was thrown at them; they fired on the crowd.[89] In the panic which followed this catastrophe, as might be expected, sympathy for the eight-hour movement disappeared, and it collapsed.

The successive steps of the Federation program were carried out in Milwaukee by local assemblies of the Knights of Labor, assisted by the well-organized Central Labor Union, which was largely composed of foreign

[86] Illinois Bureau of Labor Statistics, *Fourth Annual Report*, 1886, p. 479.
[87] Staley, E., *History of the Illinois State Federation of Labor*, Chicago, 1930, p. 65.
[88] Illinois Bureau of Labor Statistics, *op. cit.*, 1886, pp. 479, 480.
[89] Centennial History of Illinois, Vol. 4, p. 168; Commons and Associates, *op. cit.*, Vol. 2, p. 392.

born. A mass meeting attended by 3,000 workmen roused such enthusiasm for the movement that on March 15 the Common Council passed an Eight-Hour Ordinance for all city employees. This action was followed by an announcement from all the tobacco manufacturers that they would put into operation an eight-hour day with no reduction of pay. It was a matter of surprise to the Wisconsin Labor Commissioner that after this preliminary success the demand on May 1 was not more general. He claimed that on that day the only strikers were the building trades, some unskilled laborers and socialists and anarchists, but that by May 3 the strikes had spread to other trades. Demonstrations and riots were so violent that it was necessary to call out the militia, whose presence was required until the middle of the month to maintain order. The Commissioner listed "with sorrow" the results of the movement. Although five people had been killed and two wounded, and forty-five laborers had been indicted for riot and conspiracy, "no benefits whatever have been derived from the agitation by any class of workingmen"; business was conducted on the ten-hour basis, even the Common Council repealed the Eight-Hour Ordinance.[90]

The Federation's program of preparation was not carried out in Cincinnati where, according to the Commissioner of Labor, "many of the best organized trades gave it the cold shoulder." Despite this apparent lack of interest, on May 1 some 32,000 striking workers paraded with "music and banners," while large crowds followed them. Although there was no "cause for fear of violence," the police force was doubled, and "excitement was

[90] Wisconsin Bureau of Labor and Industrial Statistics, *Second Biennial Report*, 1885-1886, pp. 314-371.

kept at fever heat" by the curious mobs that followed the shifting squads of police. When the Mayor "lost his head," and had the Governor send two brigades of infantry and two batteries of artillery, nearly every trade held meetings to denounce this act on the ground that labor was peaceably demanding that the eight-hour day, already provided for by law, be inaugurated, and that the law-breakers were "those who refused to comply with its terms." Despite the protest, the troops stayed on, and strikes continued through the early part of the month. These were, with two exceptions, unsuccessful: in one case, a nine, and in the other, an eight-hour day was established.[91]

In Baltimore, as in Milwaukee, the Federation's program was carried out to a great extent by local assemblies of the Knights, and by the German-speaking unions. Beginning January 8, meetings were held, circulars were addressed to employers (in most cases asking for the nine-hour day), and conferences were called. The bricklayers, plasters, tin and sheet-iron workers and slate roofers succeeded in establishing the nine-hour day before May 1. On that day, the carpenters and furniture workers began strikes for the eight-hour day, which dragged on to failure. The Commissioner of Labor reported that the movement had been " a success for the trades demanding nine hours, and a failure for those demanding eight hours." [92]

Considering the movement as a whole, the general consensus of opinion seemed to be that it promised more on paper than it accomplished in reality. This can be explained in part by the fact that the newspapers had ex-

[91] Ohio Bureau of Labor Statistics, *Tenth Annual Report*, 1886, pp. 27-63.

[92] Maryland, Bureau of Industrial Statistics, *Second Biennial Report*, 1886-1887, pp. 66-69.

aggerated its importance beyond all reasonable bounds, and in part by the lack of adequate machinery—not to mention the lack of strength—to carry out the daring program of the Federation. Although its success cannot be measured in numbers, because in many cases it was but short-lived, it is of interest to note that two weeks after the commencement of the strike Bradstreet estimated that 150,000 of the 325,000 workers in the movement had gained the eight-hour day without striking, and another 35,000 with the aid of the strike.[93] The real success of the movement lay not in the reduction of hours, but in the tremendous upheaval of the working class throughout the nation, and in the establishment of an objective sufficiently powerful to cause the rapid growth of trade-union organization. Gompers, writing at a considerably later date, still thought only in terms of the immediate failure of the movement, which he blamed on the Haymarket disaster.[94] The judgment of the Illinois Commissioner of Labor, based on the full facts of this catastrophe, is probably a far fairer and less biased estimate of the whole movement. He said: "On the whole, the tendency of the year's experience has been to strengthen the convictions of the original adherents, to educate a large number of others in the considerations making for shorter hours of labor—not only among working men as a class so called, but among the thoughtful of all classes."[95]

When in 1890 the American Federation of Labor[96] put in motion a modification of its earlier program of direct

[93] *Nation* (N. Y.), May 13, 1886.
[94] Gompers, *op. cit.*, Vol. I, p. 294.
[95] Illinois Bureau of Labor Statistics, *op. cit.*, 1886, p. 498.
[96] Federation of Organized Trades and Labor Unions had reorganized and adopted this title in 1886.

action to attain the eight-hour day, it was clear that a more skillful and far stronger organization was managing the campaign. Plans were adopted at the convention of 1888 and 1889, "amid tumultuous cheers and enthusiastic applause." As before, provision was made to rouse a favorable public opinion and enthusiasm among the workers during a long period, then to strike while the iron was hot.[97] In this plan, however, a strike by the carpenters, who had volunteered to take the lead, was substituted for the general strike.[98] This union, under the leadership of P. J. McGuire, was in a strong position, due to both the size of the organization, and the large fund it had accumulated in past years with the eight-hour objective in view.[100] About a thousand mass meetings were held on holidays, in 1889, throughout the country, addressed by Gompers, Foster, McNeill, Gunton and Henry George. Sixty thousand copies of pamphlets on the "Economic and Social Importance of the Eight-Hour Movement," "History and Philosophy of the Eight-Hour Movement" and an "Eight-Hour Primer," written by Gunton, Danryid and McNeill, respectively, were distributed. In addition to these steps, salaried organizers travelled throughout the United States holding meetings at all times and all places and letters were sent to public officials, economists and industrial leaders.[99] The American Federation of Labor officials again tried to enlist the cooperation of the Knights, though by this time that organization was distinctly on the wane.[101] Of greater interest, although

[97] American Federation of Labor, *Proceedings*, 1888, p. 24; 1889, pp. 14, 29.
[98] *Ibid.*, 1890, p. 13.
[99] *Ibid.*, 1889, p. 14.
[100] Commons and Associates, *op. cit.*, Vol. 2, p. 475.
[101] *Cf. supra*, p. 46.

of less importance, was the request for sympathetic action sent to the International Workmens' Congress in Paris, which caused that body to resolve that an eight-hour demonstration should be held in every country on May 1. This is the origin of the European (Labor) May Day.[102]

May 1, 1890, toward which all these plans were directed, was "a quiet day through the country" because the carpenters had succeeded in making satisfactory agreements before that day.[103] That there was comparatively little trouble is attested by Labor Department reports. For example, that of New York says that the success of the carpenters in gaining the eight-hour day was "unaccompanied by trouble of any kind," [104] and the Ohio Commission comments on the eight-hour and in some cases nine-hour contracts established by the carpenters without "long and bitter struggles with employers." [105] The *New York Times* described a monster but peaceful parade in Chicago, and lent a homely touch to the scene in New York by remarking that householders were too busy with "the annual moving" which occurred on that day to have time or interest for demonstrations.[106]

The success of this limitation of demand to one trade was shown by McGuire's report that shorter hours had been gained in 137 cities by approximately 46,000 carpenters. An indirect result of the widespread agitation was the reduction of hours in many places after local strikes which had not been included in the plan of the

[102] Gompers, *op. cit.*, Vol. 1, pp. 296-298.
[103] *New York Times*, May 2, 1890.
[104] New York Bureau of Statistics of Labor, *Eighth Annual Report*, 1890, p. 997.
[105] Ohio Bureau of Labor Statistics, *Fourteenth Annual Report*, 1890, pp. 29, 30.
[106] May 2, 1890.

American Federation of Labor.[107] The *New York World* urged the carpenters to aid the general movement by increased efficiency during work hours, and by wise use of leisure, proving that the shorter day "means progress in intelligence and good citizenship."[108]

The original plan had provided that, when the carpenters had succeeded, the coal miners were to strike for eight hours, and the other industries were to follow in quick succession. Due to "unpropitious conditions, this action was postponed until May 1, 1891."[109] But as the day approached, the United Mine Workers decided not to strike since their position was weak as a result of both a long drawnout strike in the coke fields, and the determined opposition of the United Coal Operators, who had voted almost unanimously for the nine-hour day and a cut in wages.[110]

For several years following the campaign for direct action by successive trades under the leadership of the central organization, the Federation's conventions did little more than reiterate the need for shorter hours, largely on the grounds of technological unemployment. The weakened condition of the unions, as a result of the panic of 1893, was in part responsible for this inactivity. Finally, 1896 was set as the time for a determined renewal of the 1890 program. Despite the fact that mass meetings were held, and laborers and employers circularized, the unique quality of the Federation's plan was lost because of the failure of the Executive Council to carry out the convention's orders to appoint one trade on whose demand all

[107] American Federation of Labor, *Proceedings*, 1890, p. 13.
[108] May 6, 1890.
[109] American Federation of Labor, *Proceedings*, 1890, p. 14.
[110] *New York Times*, April 28, 1891.

should concentrate. As a result, there was no concerted movement, but a number of scattered strikes, some of which were successful.[111] Uncoordinated action occurred again the following year.[112] Dissatisfaction with this scattered effort caused the Federation to attempt to repeat the more unified program. The Executive Council was active in organizing the campaign of action. It organized Labor Day demonstrations; it published an eight-hour pamphlet; and finally it selected the machinists to strike for the eight-hour day on May 1, 1898. This was an error of judgment. When the machinists declined the honor, the movement for that year came to naught.[113]

For the last time, and then only as a feeble imitation of the really spirited attempts of 1886 and 1890, the program was carried through in 1900, when the granite cutters struck for the eight-hour day.[114] The complete victory which this strike gained was more the result of the strength of this union, and of the fact that eight hours was the next step in a carefully conceived and executed program for a progressive reduction of hours, than of any decisive aid which the Federation gave.

With this strike at the turn of the century, the American Federation of Labor ended all centralized programs for advancing the universal adoption of the eight-hour day by direct action. Gompers, looking back from the vantage point of 1925, placed the close of this type of action in 1891,[115] utterly disregarding the slow petering-out of confidence in it, the rather pitiful flare-ups of

[111] American Federation of Labor, *Proceedings*, 1896, p. 23.
[112] *Ibid.*, 1897, p. 19.
[113] *Ibid.*, 1898, p. 21.
[114] *Ibid.*, 1900, p. 21.
[115] Gompers, *op. cit.*, Vol. I, p. 310.

renewed effort in 1896 and 1897, and finally the strike of the granite cutters, which, though nominally in line with the earlier program, was in reality the seed of a new Federation policy in regard to shorter hours. The new program was to leave the entire question of initiating and carrying through efforts to inaugurate them to the separate unions, with the assurance that such movements would receive encouragement from the central organization. The efficacy of this method for well-organized trades will be shown through the study of a type case in the next chapter. It is necessary here, however, to point out the significant announcements of the central body in regard to shorter hours by direct action.

At no time was the policy of uncertainty and lack of leadership on the important question of plans for direct action to reduce hours more evident than in the period 1901-1914. Although the statement made at the 1901 convention that "the eight-hour day is a perennial subject of discussion and commendation," [116] was all too true in that discussion had been substituted for action, nevertheless at five conventions in this period, the subject of a shorter-hours' program was not mentioned. Unlike the launching of the comprehensive—if somewhat ambitious— programs of 1886 and 1890, the Federation in 1902 drifted into an inactive policy, merely recommending "that at each succeeding national and international convention of trade unions, the eight-hour day and means for its achievement shall occupy a most prominent place in discussions; that local unions and central bodies give the eight-hour day special consideration at every opportunity." [117] At this convention an enduring precedent was set for such

[116] American Federation of Labor, *Proceedings*, 1901, p. 186.
[117] *Ibid.*, 1902, p. 222.

future conventions as discussed the hours' question to include a declaration in favor of this plan of "agitation and education." When the Typographical Union in 1904 was preparing to inaugurate its nation-wide movement for the eight-hour day, there was added the principle of endorsement by the central organization of any such attempt made by national unions.[118] While this policy of withdrawal from leadership and action in the struggle was being evolved, the rank and file continued to propose resolutions which demonstrated a continued faith in the earlier policy. None received favorable action.

A steadily growing dissatisfaction with the "do nothing" program of the central body probably caused the determined stand for the use of the legislative method of obtaining the eight-hour day at the conventions of 1914 and 1915. Since this struggle has been discussed in Chapter II,[119] it is sufficient to say here that, although the principle of direct action was sustained by a majority vote, yet the minority expressed a most decided dissatisfaction with the results that the Federation had obtained by this method.

The war years showed the American Federation of Labor in its most business-like and opportunistic role in regard to the attainment of shorter hours. In 1916, opposition to the legislative method changed to the extent of cooperating with the Railroad Brotherhoods to obtain the passage of the Adamson Law.[120] Then followed a period which is difficult to classify as to the method by which shorter-hour gains were made, and which, at any rate, is not of primary importance in this study, as the gain was

[118] *Cf. infra*, p. 180.
[119] *Cf. supra*, pp. 52-57.
[120] *Cf. supra*, pp. 86, 87.

the establishment of the basic eight-hour day, which is to a great extent a wage question. Insofar as the awards in the timber industry, the meat packing industry, etc., of a basic eight-hour day with time and a half for over-time were made by governmental bodies, the gain cannot be ascribed entirely to direct action. On the other hand, the unions supported by the Federation were making wise use of their strategic position to bring conditions to such a state that these decisions were necessary. That the acceptance of the basic eight-hour day illustrated the Federation's opportunism, rather than expressed any real satisfaction in it, is shown by an article in the *American Federationist,* which after citing gains and the employers' belief that labor was satisfied by them, said: "This is not the case. . . . It is the opinion of the vast body of American workers that the eight-hour day ought to be a reality." [121] A resolution to this effect was unanimously adopted at the convention of 1918.[122]

Since the close of the war, the Federation has not modified its policy of limiting its activities for shorter hours by direct action to "education and agitation." Its significant declarations have dealt with the question of the number of work hours toward which this agitation should be directed. In 1919 it adopted a forty-four-hour week resolution,[123] and in 1926 one which set the five-day week as the goal;[124] in neither case was a program of action mapped out. When the forty-four-hour week demand was announced, organized labor was still in a dominant position. The condition, however, was so changed by the de-

---

[121] Vol. 25, 1918, p. 999.
[122] American Federation of Labor, *Proceedings,* 1918, p. 220.
[123] *Ibid.,* 1919, p. 449.
[124] *Ibid.,* 1926, p. 197.

pression of 1921 that the convention of that year voted down an insistent demand to endorse still shorter hours as a means of relieving unemployment, not as the Committee said, because of a lack of belief in this measure, but because "many trade unions are now on the defensive, battling for their very existence," and in no state "to take an advanced position."[125] Faced with the growing strength of the so-called American plan of company unions,[126] and the increasing prosperity of which labor was given a share in the form of shorter hours and higher wages, the Federation's conventions did little but feebly suggest the need for a scientifically calculated work-day as a means of "balancing production and consumption," and renew the offer to assist any union in its attempt to get a shorter day. But, by the 1926 convention, although not yet moved from words to action, the declaration for the five-day week was made on the ground that changes in the method of production had resulted in an excess capacity to make goods, and in a greater strain on the physical and nervous condition of the laborer.[127] In 1927, the convention again merely reiterated the usual statement of the need for a campaign of education to bring about the universal establishment of the five-day week.[128] It must be stated here that a great deal of publicity in newspapers, magazines and pamphlets was given to the Federations declaration in favor of shorter hours, and to the movement in general. It cannot be determined, however, whether this was the result of the skill and assiduity of the Federation's press agents, or of a growing interest on the part

[125] *Ibid.*, 1921, p. 420.
[126] *Cf. infra*, pp. 241, 242.
[127] American Federation of Labor, *Proceedings*, 1926, pp. 197-207.
[128] *Ibid.*, 1927, p. 400.

of the public at large in all labor questions, including the shorter-hour movement.

The Executive Council's report to the 1928 convention, admitting what the protagonists of the legislative method had claimed, that the unorganized were not "enjoying the benefits and blessings of the eight-hour day," offered as their solution that all should organize and gain it "through collective action." [129] It is almost too obvious to point out that this statement—like the whole policy of the Federation on the hours' question— is the result of unwillingness or inability to face facts. Accepting their assumption that direct action is the only effective method of gaining shorter hours, the least that could be expected would be an admission of the difficulty of organizing the unskilled, accompanied by a vigorous program to overcome this obstacle. Again, in 1929 the Executive Council smugly pointed to "the steady progress being made toward a fuller and freer and more enjoyable life under the policy of the American Federation of Labor." At the suggestion of the Committee on Shorter Hours, the convention unanimously subscribed to this statement.[130]

At the 1930 convention, however, a resolution to name a day on which all labor would refuse to work as an expression of determination to obtain the five-day week showed that the rank and file still had faith in the efficacy of a national demonstration. It was vetoed at the Committee's suggestion as an unsatisfactory means of "agitation and education." At this convention James O'Connell, President of the Metal Trades Department, stressed the need for the five-hour day, which his Department had long advocated, to counteract the unemployment caused by

[129] *Ibid.*, 1928, p. 43.
[130] *Ibid.*, 1929, p. 388.

DIRECT ACTION 169

technological improvement. No action was taken because the Committee voted to submit his suggestion to the Executive Council.[131]

Again in 1931, desire for a nation-wide expression of labor's will on hours led to the introduction of a resolution to set aside a Proclamation Day on which not only the five-day week but also the six-hour day would be inaugurated. The Committee vetoed this both because it was an unsatisfactory method, and because the Federation had taken no official stand for the six-hour day. Instead of action, the Committee on Shorter Hours called on the convention "to give renewed devotion" to the efforts of the Executive Council to obtain universal observance of the five-day week.[132] These efforts had centered in the construction of a program for remedying unemployment in which the immediate inauguration of the five-day week and the shorter work-day in all public and private industry had been suggested.[133] The Federation has since been represented at all conferences on unemployment, the plan has been presented and has received great publicity,—beyond that nothing has been accomplished by the central body of organized labor in America.

[131] *Ibid.*, 1930, pp. 261-265.
[132] *Ibid.*, 1931, pp. 278-281.
[133] *Ibid.*, p. 163.

CHAPTER VI

DIRECT ACTION: TYPE CASES

SINCE the American Federation of Labor, the mouthpiece of organized labor in this country, has continued to insist through depression and prosperity that direct action is the only effective means of decreasing hours for men, and that the strategy and tactics can be most effectively planned and carried out by the national unions, it is essential to survey the work of these organizations. The hours of organized labor and those of labor in general, given in Appendix H are convincing proof of the marked success of this method for the organized. The figures, which are available only from 1914, show that the average weekly hours of tradeunion members have tended to be from four to six less than those of labor in general. Nor can the numerical figure be taken as the full measure of the success of this method. In the first place, the figure representing the hours of all workers is influenced by the inclusion of trade unionists in the data used to obtain this average. And second, there is the indirect and non-measurable influence of the standard, established by trade unions, on legislative bodies in the enactment of hours' statutes and on liberal employers in making voluntary reductions.

Although the Federation can be considered the mouthpiece of organized labor in America, important union developments [1] outside it must be included in a survey of direct action to reduce hours. This is necessary to determine,

---

[1] The action of the Railroad Brotherhoods has already been discussed. *Cf. supra,* pp. 82-91.

DIRECT ACTION: TYPE CASES 171

first, if there is any essential difference in collective bargaining on hours as carried on by industrial unions, unaffected by the Federation's philosophy; and second, if the Federation's support is of any real importance in the hours struggle.

To survey direct action to reduce hours by all unions would be impossible, tedious and unprofitable, because it is so repetitive. It has been decided, therefore, to use the case method to present the history of direct action for the shorter day in a typical Federation craft union, in a non-Federation industrial union, and in an unorganized industry. For the first, the International Typographical Union has been chosen for two reasons: its age—it is the oldest union in the United States—which made possible a study of the successive steps taken by this Union toward shortening hours since the Civil War; and the fact that it presents collective bargaining on the subject under what has been held to be the most desirable condition, namely, a strong, intelligently led union, negotiating agreements with an association of employers.[1a]

The Amalgamated Clothing Workers seemed to be the logical choice for a non-Federation union, placed as it is in the forefront of the new unionism. The hours' question has been one of tremendous importance in the clothing manufacturing field. Furthermore, the failure of the craft-conscious United Garment Workers to reduce hours in the industry is in sharp contrast to the new organization which has obtained results for skilled and unskilled, and so points to a badly needed reform in the Federation's policy of craft unionism.

Choice of a typical unorganized industry is complicated by the fact that non-union labor is, for the most part, neces-

[1a] U. S. Commissioner of Labor, *First Annual Report*, 1886, p. 287.

sarily inarticulate on the question of excessive hours. If this situation is brought to light, it holds attention only for a short time unless public opinion develops to force reforms. Inasmuch as such a condition arose in the steel industry, the struggle for shorter hours in this field offers an unusual amount of valuable material for detailed study. For that reason, it has been selected here. Yet it must be remembered that in our economic and social system such powerful forces could not often be expected to aid the unorganized in the struggle for shorter hours.

A TRADE UNION : INTERNATIONAL TYPOGRAPHICAL UNION

Certain facts in regard to the organization and composition of this Union must be given in order to understand its policy in regard to attaining shorter hours. Control is divided between the International officials and the local unions. The power of the officials to direct trade union opinion, their ability to meet and negotiate with employers, their responsibility for supporting strikes, give them a major role. On the other hand, the local unions, of which there is only one in each city, do not play an insignificant part. In the first place, the question of establishing a new standard of hours must be referred to them, as must the levying of a strike assessment, without which a united demand for shorter hours would be feeble. In the second place, the local unions negotiate and sign agreements with the employers' association of their jurisdiction, subject only to the limitation that these must embody the maximum hours or less, which have been established for the entire jurisdiction by the officials of the International Typographical Union. Reference must be made also to the fact that these local unions include all workers connected with printing—the machine compositors, proof-readers, mailers, machinists—in newspaper offices, commercial offices, and combination offices in small towns carrying on both newspaper and book and job work.² Separate agreements are negotiated for members in newspaper offices, and for those in book and job offices; combination offices are ordinarily included with these. The former have usually been able to negotiate shorter-hour agreements in advance of the book and job workers largely because of the comparatively few hours in which the greatest amount of work in a newspaper composing-room must be accomplished.

Printers had established ten hours as a standard day's work fairly generally before the Civil War. At its close they, like the rest of the working population, began to agitate for the eight-hour day. Between 1865 and 1886, however, this remained a matter of discussion which, as might be expected, was no more effective than the action of the other organizations in this period. In 1865 the convention of the Typographical Union voted to have local unions consider the negotiation of agreements to establish an eight-hour day as of May 1, 1866.³ The convention of 1866 sent a resolution to Congress, urging the passage of a national eight-hour law,⁴ and the meetings of 1869 and 1872 again urged that locals consider the adoption of an eight-hour day.⁵ In the long depression which followed the panic of 1873, reduction of hours was not considered by this Union, but with the revival of business and the general interest in this question subsequent to 1881, the Typographical Union renewed its discussion on the ground that shortening hours would increase wages through decreasing the available supply of labor. Although it accepted this doctrine,

[2] Barnett, G. E., "The Printers," *American Economic Association Quarterly*, Oct., 1909. For details of organization, pp. 29-69.
[3] Tracy, G. A., *History of the Typrographical Union*, Indianapolis, 1913, p. 213.
[4] *Ibid.*, p. 231.
[5] Barnett, *op. cit.*, pp. 145, 146.

the Typographical Union did not recommend that local unions join the concerted action for the eight-hour day planned by the American Federation of Labor for May 1, 1886.[6]

The Typographical Union, however, at its 1886 convention embarked on a hastily conceived, inadequately planned variation of the Federation's program, which was doomed to failure. The local unions were urged to discuss the feasibility of the inauguration of a nine-hour day by the printers, alone. The next convention, in 1887, passed a law [6a] that locals with a minimum membership of sixty arrange to establish the nine-hour day as of November 1, 1887, on all book and job work.[7] Certainly this scheme showed that the Typographical Union had no comprehension of the need for strength and for unity of action to enforce such a change. This demand caused the local Typothetae, the name taken by employers' associations, to call a meeting in Chicago, October, 1887, to establish a national organization.[8] This call, combined with unfavorable reports from locals, led to a special gathering of Union representatives in Cincinnati, who ordered the Executive Council to release the unions from enforcing the law, and arranged to meet the employing printers. At the meeting, the newly organized United Typothetae of America refused the compromise of a nine-hour day with a proportionate decrease of wages, and voted to aid all local Typothetae that withstood the Union's demands. Despite release from the nine-hour order, some of the larger locals determined to strike. These were unsuccessful although the Typographical Union tried desperately to raise sufficient funds to aid them.[9] In Chicago the employers

[6] *Ibid.*, p. 146.
[6a] The term "law" is used by this union instead of "rule."
[7] Tracy, *op. cit.*, pp. 409, 410.
[8] Brown, E. C., *Book and Job Printing in Chicago*, Chicago, 1931, p. 41.
[9] Tracy, *op. cit.*, pp. 413-416.

DIRECT ACTION: TYPE CASES 175

turned the strike into a determined and fairly successful effort to establish the open shop, which left the Union in a weakened condition.[10] The address of the President of the Union to the convention of 1888, in which he stated that this effort had "awakened us to the important fact . . . that our actions should be controlled by a careful consideration in commencing hostilities; that we should study the situation as to the probabilities of success," [11] indicated the path of the future policy of this Union.

Just as the 1887 episode demonstrates the weakness of a hasty, ill-considered attempt, so agitation and negotiation for the nine-hour day, which commenced in 1890 and terminated successfully in 1898, point to the value of long considered, slowly moving plans of action. At the direction of the 1890 convention, the Typographical Union officials tried unsuccessfully to gain the financial support of the American Federation of Labor for a nine-hour strike in 1891.[12] A referendum in that year on the nine-hour day lacked only 332 votes of the three-fourths' majority required on any strike measure. Continued agitation led to unsuccessful attempts in 1893 and 1894 to vote assessments to raise a large strike fund, which the officials held essential for success.[13]

The need for shorter hours appeared to the union to be emphasized by cyclical unemployment caused by the depression of 1893, and by the technological unemployment caused by the wider adoption of the linotype machine. This machine, which had been invented in 1884 but did not become an important factor until the nineties, might have led to the substitution of unskilled labor and the eventual over-

[10] Brown, *op. cit.*, pp. 45, 47.
[11] Tracy, *op. cit.*, p. 417.
[12] *Ibid.*, pp. 446, 447.
[13] *Ibid.*, pp. 466, 501.

throw of the Union, had it not been for the Typographical Union's acceptance of the innovation subject to the proviso that it be worked by a union man, and be regarded as a means to "secure decreased hours of labor at a fair rate of wages."[14] Due to these conditions, the local unions became very active in their efforts to negotiate agreements providing for shorter hours. They were most successful in the case of newspaper offices since the real work of the composing-room had always been done in the few hours before the paper went to press, while the linotype machine saved the time which had formerly been needed to distribute type. Further encouragement was given to the movement by successful negotiations for shorter hours in the book and job trade, particularly in New York, where a nine-and-a-half-hour day was instituted with the promise of the nine-hour day whenever the Typographical Union was able to enforce it generally.[15]

With this proof of a growing nine-hour sentiment, the Shorter Hours' Committee of the Union issued monthly circulars urging local unions to negotiate and to raise defense funds, despite the failure of the 1897 referendum to sustain a national assessment. When in August, 1898, this Committee announced that it had set a date for the inauguration of the movement, the United Typothetae of America arranged a conference at which it agreed to establish the nine-and-a-half-hour day as of November 1, 1898, and the nine-hour day as of November 1, 1899, except in cases where agreements had already established shorter hours. Circulars to this effect were sent to local unions advising them to call meetings to make arrangements for wage adjustments,

[14] *Typographical Journal,* Sept., 1931, Dumas, C. J., "When the Linotype Came." This resolution was introduced by New York Typographical Union No. 6.

[15] Barnett, *op. cit.,* pp. 149-153.

DIRECT ACTION: TYPE CASES 177

which were left to the local jurisdictions.[16] Compared with the long period of agitation and negotiation, the length of time required for enforcement was short. Despite the fact that the Typothetate offices in Pittsburgh and San Francisco repudiated the agreement, the nine-hour day was generally established in the book and job offices of the United States within the year of the date set.[17] This peaceful climax stands as a monument to mutually helpful collective bargaining. As the President of the Typographical Union said: "Formerly, employer and employee got together with a club; now they meet in a friendly and business-like way." [18]

As if to prevent an enduring confidence in the possibility of continued peaceful adjustment of hours by fairly equally matched employer and employees' associations, the eight-hour struggle was an expensive, long drawn-out fight, typifying the use of war-like methods of collective bargaining. Since the nine-hour day had been sought only because it was more easily obtainable, it was natural that agitation for the eight-hour day, the goal this Union had set in 1865, should immediately begin. Although an eight-hour resolution, introduced at the 1901 convention, failed to pass, decisive action was taken at the next convention. The Executive Council was directed to make plans for establishing the eight-hour day, and to discuss it with the United Typothetae to the end that it be inaugurated without friction. The local unions were advised to make contracts that provided a fifteen-minute decrease in the length of the day for each of the succeeding four years. They were ordered under no other circumstances to make a contract for more than an

---

[16] Tracy, *op. cit.*, pp. 563, 564.
[17] U. S. Industrial Commission, 1901, *op. cit.*, Vol. 17, pp. 94-96.
[18] Tracy, *op. cit.*, p. 565.

eight-hour day beyond October 1, 1905.[19] The Typographical Union took this definite stand because the eight-hour day had been successfully negotiated by most of the newspaper offices, and even by some of the book and job offices.[20] Besides, increased membership gave it added strength, which was in turn increased by new members attracted by the eight-hour demand.

The United Typothetae, however, were also growing in membership, and felt that they were prepared for a test of strength. So much so that when the Union asked for a conference, the employers' association refused to grant one. Thereupon the 1903 convention fixed January 1, 1905, as the date for the inauguration of the eight-hour day. The Typothetate answered by a "Declaration of Policy," which besides restating the right of its membership to conduct "an open" office, said that the organization was "opposed to any further reduction of the working time to less than fifty-four hours per week for day work."[21] This open-shop declaration, in conjunction with membership of several local Typothetae in manufacturers' associations openly hostile to the closed shop, and with the breaking off of union relations by the Chicago Typothetae as contracts expired,[22] injected the fear of organized effort at union dissolution into the struggle.

After repeated unsuccessful conferences, the 1904 convention of the United Typothetae voted that it would " resist any attempt on the part of the Typographical Union to reduce the present hours of labor."[23] The convention of

[19] Powell, L. M., *The History of the United Typothetae of America,* Chicago, 1926, pp. 50, 51.
[20] Barnett, *op. cit.,* p. 156.
[21] Powell, *op. cit.,* pp. 53-56.
[22] Brown, *op. cit.,* p. 117.
[23] Tracy, *op. cit.,* p. 778.

the Typographical Union, held later in the same year, girded itself for action "since overtures for peace . . . were refused and declined, and replied to with a threat." To gain time to prepare for an open struggle, the date for inaugurating the eight-hour schedule was postponed to January 1, 1906, and to build up an adequate defense fund a referendum on a ½% assessment on earnings was submitted to the membership.[24] When it is recalled that a measure providing a smaller assessment had been defeated three times in the nine-hour struggle, and that a large proportion of the members, having already negotiated eight-hour contracts—those in newspaper offices and a few book and job offices—would gain little direct advantage from the struggle, the majority vote given to this assessment shows the strong feeling which the movement had engendered. While making careful provision for action, the Union officials did not fail to make every effort for peaceful negotiation. Conferences held through the summer of 1905 failed to provide a basis for conciliation.[25]

Hostile action commenced in August in Chicago; a strike was called when non-union workers were employed. Similar action in Detroit and San Antonio led the Typographical Union officials to instruct all locals, not bound by contract, to demand the eight-hour day immediately, for fear that the effectiveness of concentrated action would be lost. As the inevitability of a widespread strike became more evident, the Union by the tremendous majority of 25,046 to 6,945 voted a 10% assessment on earnings. By January 2 strikes were fairly general throughout the United States. Thousands of copies of strike bulletins were distributed to keep the union members united by a common fund of knowledge. Single men on the strike roll

[24] *Ibid.*, pp. 782, 783.
[25] Powell, *op. cit.*, pp. 65, 66.

were paid $7.00 a week, married men $10.00, making a staggering total expenditure of $1,500,000 by June 1, 1906. Despite the heavy burden of assessment success in many jurisdictions led the 1906 convention to vote unanimously for a continuation of the struggle.[26] At the convention of 1907 it was announced that the eight-hour day had been established in all but two large centres, Nashville and Kansas City. The assessments, which had been gradually reduced beginning in November, 1906, were finally ended in March, 1908.[27]

The victory had been gained at a heavy indirect and direct cost to the Union. The average paying membership decreased from 46,734 in the fiscal year 1904-1905 to 42,357 in the year 1906-1907.[28] Many of the larger shops became non-union. In addition, many locals had to compromise on the question of pay for over-time, that is, they permitted it at the ordinary rate instead of one and a half times, thereby interfering with an important policy of this Union to minimize over-time by punitive rates as a means of spreading work.[29] It is impossible to estimate the direct cost of the strike to the workers, much less to the employers, but the fact that the special assessments alone exceeded $3,500,000 gives some concept of the tremendous monetary burden of the establishment of the eight-hour day in the printing trade.[30]

The American Federation of Labor did not take an active part in this struggle. At Gompers' suggestion, the 1904 convention endorsed the strike, agreed to give financial aid,

[26] Tracy, *op. cit.*, pp. 872-879.
[27] *Ibid.*, pp. 895, 897, 914.
[28] Barnett, *op. cit.*, p. 157.
[29] *Ibid.*, pp. 158, 221-227.
[30] *Ibid.*, p. 81n. Gompers placed the cost at $4,000,000. American Federation of Labor, *Proceedings*, 1907, p. 66.

DIRECT ACTION: TYPE CASES

and appointed a committee to cooperate with the Typographical officials.[31] The Executive Council carried out the convention's order by placing an assessment on each member of one cent a week for four weeks, which netted a total contribution to the strike fund of $52,619.[32] Beyond this admittedly small financial aid, the Federation limited its activities to the moral support of commendatory resolutions. Fortunately the Typographical Union was in a financially strong position, since the Federation's assistance amounted to practically nothing in the establishment of the eight-hour day.

The eight-hour day, won with such difficulty, did not prove to be entirely satisfactory due to the question of the Saturday half-holiday. To keep this shorter work-day, which had long been established in the book and job trade, it was necessary to work eight and three-quarter hours each day. Many members of the Union opposed this compromise on the eight-hour day.[32a] Discontent, almost from the date of the inauguration of the eight-hour day, led to ever-increasing friction in making new contracts, which finally culminated in the initiation of negotiations for the forty-four-hour week in 1919 by the International Joint Conference Council.[33] The purpose of this organization was to provide a permanent means of settling labor difficulties in the entire printing industry. It had been formed, only in February of that year, by employers' associations, including the Closed Shop Branch of the United Typothetae and the Printers' League, and by the Allied Printing Trades' Council of which the International Typographical Union was a mem-

[31] *Ibid.*, 1904, pp. 22, 118, 180.
[32] *Ibid.*, 1905, p. 77.
[32a] Brown, *op. cit.*, p. 137.
[33] *Typographical Journal*, Jan., 1921, p. 1.

ber.[34] The preliminary steps gave every promise that a peaceful and satisfactory conclusion would be reached. In April, 1919, the Joint Conference voted to submit a referendum on the adoption of the forty-four-hour week as of May 1, 1921.[35] This proposition was strongly opposed by large locals, particularly in New York and Chicago, which advocated the inauguration at an earlier date. The officials of the Typographical Union, however, won a vote of 24,389 to 11,919 by stressing both the fact that the forty-eight-hour week had been gained "only after a struggle that will live forever in the history of the Union," and the fact that the forty-four-hour week was being gained "without the necessity of assessing our members."[36] When the Printers' League and the Closed Shop Branch of the Typothetae Association had also ratified the referendum, negotiations were practically complete.[37] The Joint Conference left the question of wages to the local unions as always merely recommending that no reduction be made because of the change in hours.[38]

Employers outside the Joint Conference opposed the change. The Open Shop Branch of the Typothetae Association passed a resolution disapproving "any action which would even imply that the United Typothetae Association as a body endorses such a policy."[39] Hostility grew, fostered by the activities of various manufacturers' associations, advocates of the American (Open Shop) Plan, who threatened to boycott any printer who conceded the forty-

[34] Powell, *op. cit.*, p. 146.
[35] *Typographical Journal*, Jan., 1921, p. 1.
[36] *Ibid.*, Supplement, Aug., 1919, p. 52.
[37] *Typographical Journal*, Oct., 1919, p. 372.
[38] *Ibid.*, May, 1920, p. 575.
[39] Powell, *op. cit.*, p. 150.

four-hour week, and by the business depression of 1920-21.[40] This latter was without doubt the final reason why the negotiations did not bear fruit in peaceful enforcement.

By September, 1920, the International Typographical convention recognized the possible need for more than peaceful means of collective bargaining by providing that, in the event of failure to inaugurate the new schedule on the date fixed, local unions were to notify the Executive Council, which was given "full power to carry out the forty-four-hour program according to agreement."[41] Hope for a peaceful outcome was lessened when the United Typothetae convention of October, 1920, recommended resistance on the ground that the Union was misrepresenting the situation by stating that the whole association was bound by the action of the Closed Shop Branch.[42]

The Joint Conference continued in vain to make every effort for a peaceful outcome. It voted that the "members were morally bound" to adopt the forty-four-hour schedule,[43] and at its last meeting, held in April 1921, it passed a resolution which reaffirmed the fact that wages were to be decided locally "notwithstanding the fact that the Joint Conference recommended that there should be no reduction in wages because of the installation of the forty-four-hour week." A final unavailing attempt at conciliation was made at a meeting held in the office of Secretary of Labor J. J. Davis.[44]

When the strike commenced on May 1, the Typographical Union had arranged for a strong defense fund by placing

[40] *Typographical Journal*, Apr., 1921, pp. 381-400.
[41] *Ibid.*, Supplement, Sept., 1920, pp. 281, 282.
[42] Powell, *op. cit.*, p. 153.
[43] *Typographical Journal*, Jan., 1921, p. 2.
[44] Powell, *op. cit.*, pp. 155, 156.

a 10% assessment on earnings by a vote of 40,703 to 11,-499,[45] an amazing exhibition of solidarity in view of the fact that the strike would benefit directly only the book and job workers who numbered approximately one-half of the Union. The Executive Council arranged for the immediate admission to the Union of all strike-breakers who thereupon were entitled to the strike benefit,[46] which was set at $12.00 a week for single and $17.00 a week for married men.[47] It was reported that there were 9,000 on the strike roll in May, 1921,[48] between 8,000 and 9,000 in August, 1921,[49] and 6,000 in August, 1922.[50] After that date the Union did not publish strike roll figures. Significant, however, were the resolutions passed at the convention of August, 1923, to continue the struggle until it was entirely successful,[51] and the strong opposition which tried in vain to prevent the arrangement to suspend benefit payments in August, 1924.[52]

In this strike, as in that for the eight-hour day, it is impossible to measure either the indirect or direct costs even to the Union. In the first year of the strike, the Union was faced with a decrease in membership of 6,000, which it did not regain until 1927.[53] An even greater penalty was the widespread growth of open-shop sentiment which the rather weak Printers' League, composed of employers who advocate the closed shop and collective bargaining through peace-

[45] *Typographical Journal*, June, 1921, p. 671.
[46] *Ibid.*, May, 1921, p. 538.
[47] *Ibid.*, June, 1921, pp. 671, 672.
[48] *Ibid.*, p. 671.
[49] *Ibid.*, Supplement, Aug., 1921, p. 9.
[50] *Ibid.*, Supplement, Aug., 1922, p. 5.
[51] *Ibid.*, Supplement, Sept., 1923, pp. 58, 59.
[52] *Ibid.*, Supplement, Sept., 1924, pp. 74-78.
[53] *Ibid.*, Supplement, Aug., 1929, p. 101.

fully negotiated agreements, has tried to combat.[54] When the President of the Typographical Union reported an expenditure of $8,863,578 at the close of the first year of the strike, he said that the "cost makes it almost prohibitive."[55] The estimated total expenditure of the Union has been placed at $17,000,000,[56] a figure which proves beyond a doubt the futility of this method for any but a strongly organized, rich trade.

The role played by the American Federation of Labor in the establishment of the forty-four-hour week was not of any apparent significance. It "unequivocally" endorsed the campaign.[57] It also passed a resolution which called on all its members and their friends to boycott non-union printed matter. The Executive Council was directed to aid in every practicable manner when called on to do so.[58] The Typographical Union, however, was sufficiently strong to force the adoption of the shorter-hour schedule without demanding other than moral support from the central organization.

Despite the selection of the International Typographical Union largely because of its long history, time has not yet sufficed to encompass the attainment of the five-day week nationally. The desire for it has been keen, and has strained against the check which the controlling group has placed due to caution, learned from carrying on a strike for shorter hours in a previous depression, and to the fear of costs, monetary and otherwise, left by the still recent forty-four-

[54] Powell, *op. cit.*, pp. 159, 160.
[55] *Typographical Journal*, Supplement, Aug., 1922, p. 7.
[56] *New York Herald-Tribune,* Nov. 1, 1931. This statement was made by Harvey Kelly, an official of the American Newspaper Publishers' Association.
[57] American Federation of Labor, *Proceedings*, 1921, pp. 421-426.
[58] *Ibid.,* 1922, p. 319.

hour struggle. Although at the close of the strike the Executive Council devoted its entire energy to an active reconstruction campaign to rebuild membership, to organize new locals, and to establish friendly contacts with employers,[59] yet the Typographical Journal showed the continued interest in further reduction by giving complete reports on the adoption of the five-day week in various industries throughout the United States. Not until 1928, however, did the question attain a position of prominence in this Union. When five-day week resolutions were offered at the convention of that year, the difference of opinion was not on the need but on the method. One group favored that of earlier struggles, that is, the passage of a five-day law which would necessitate active participation by the central organization in negotiations and in enforcement; the other, which included the officials, advocated that each local union negotiate the question in its own jurisdiction. The latter won the approval of the convention.[60]

Contrary to all earlier hour movements in this Union, members from newspaper offices were most active in the shorter hours' discussions at the convention of 1929. As a result, resolutions were sent to the American Newspaper Publishers Association, expressing the hope that this organization would abandon its hostile attitude toward the five-day week in view of the cooperative spirit which past relations had developed, and that it would either reduce hours voluntarily, or cooperate with the Union to "make the readjustments that are necessary owing to the changing methods of production."[61] The Association replied then[62]—and it

[59] *Typographical Journal*, April, 1926, p. 518.
[60] *Ibid.*, Supplement, Sept., 1928, pp. 74, 75.
[61] *Ibid.*, Supplement, Sept., 1929, pp. 55, 56.
[62] *Ibid.*, Supplement, Aug., 1930, p. 5.

DIRECT ACTION: TYPE CASES 187

still maintains this position [63]—that without its cooperation the union can inaugurate the five-day week since union law allows members in newspaper offices to engage a substitute at will.

When the five-day week was discussed at the 1930 convention, the Shorter Week Committee urged the rejection of a referendum on its mandatory adoption on the ground that "adoption without due preparation is unwise and unsound." In its place, the Committee secured the passage of a resolution by which the Executive Council was "requested to assist and encourage all local unions to gain the five-day week."[64] The parallel with the American Federation of Labor is obvious. Both organizations after a period of vigorous, active campaigns for shorter hours reached a stage of cautious passivity—later in the case of the Typographical Union, to be sure, and after a far rougher course and a greater achievement—and assumed the role of an encouraging onlooker. At the convention of 1931 the official group was again supported in what the minority called a "vacillating," "platitudinous" plan which "passed the buck to the local union."[65]

In this period in which the attempt to force a national mandate was defeated, a few strong locals negotiated the five-day week. It is interesting to note that these successes were in the book and job trade, which had a record of successful hours' strikes, and not in the newspaper offices where adjustments of hours had been made by peaceful collective bargaining. After the Chicago book and job trade

[63] *New York Herald-Tribune*, Nov. 1, 1931. This attitude has compelled Typographical Union No. 6, New York City, to pass a referendum which restricts "the situation holder to five days' work, the sixth to be given out by him." Vote taken Feb. 25, 1932.
[64] *Typographical Journal*, Supplement, Sept., 1930, pp. 68-71.
[65] *Ibid.*, Supplement, Sept., 1931, pp. 88-94.

had established a forty-hour week for night workers, it successfully negotiated in January, 1930, an agreement which provided the five-day week for the three summer months of 1931 and 1932, and its permanent establishment on April 1, 1933.[66] Two months later, the book and job workers in San Francisco signed an agreement for the inauguration of the forty-hour week for night workers on November 1, 1930, and for day workers on November 1, 1933, at the wage prevailing at that time.[67] The following month the adjacent City of Oakland adopted a contract with the same provisions.[68] These three cases, however, are distinct exceptions. Local negotiations have in general not succeeded in establishing the shorter-hour week.

For the time being, the original problem of collective bargaining for shorter hours to relieve technological unemployment has been obscured by the unemployment which is the result of the depression. This has led most locals to adopt the rule that a substitute must be employed one or even more days a week; that is the general case in newspaper offices. Since the rule cannot be so easily applied in book and job offices, on account of the nature of the work, the situation has been met not by decreasing the days worked, but by an unemployment assessment. Both acts are admittedly makeshifts to relieve the burden of cyclical unemployment. As previously stated, the earlier issue of shorter hours as a means of decreasing technological unemployment, which has receded temporarily, has yet to be faced by this Union.

[66] *Ibid.*, Feb., 1930, p. 130; *ibid.*, July, 1931, p. 5 reports the plan went into effect.
[67] *Ibid.*, Apr., 1930, p. 361.
[68] *Ibid.*, May, 1930, p. 628.

AN INDUSTRIAL UNION: AMALGAMATED CLOTHING WORKERS

The organization of the Amalgamated Clothing Workers, in 1914, was the outcome of long smoldering dissatisfaction with the United Garment Workers. While the root of this was the fundamental question of inclusiveness of organization, yet among contributing surface causes discontent with its failure to accomplish a reduction of hours was by no means unimportant. The record of the United Garment Workers had been distinctly poor. To be sure, in New York alone, four successful strikes won reductions of hours, but they proved to be only paper victories, not enforceable "because there existed no adequate organization of employers and employees."[69]

The action of the United Garment Workers in the Chicago strike of 1910, and in that of New York in 1913, is illustrative both of the general conditions which led to the break, and of the hours' situation. In both cities the percentage of organized clothing workers was small due to the failure of the Union to attempt to bring in the unskilled workers. The Chicago strike was a spontaneous movement of the unskilled that began in the Hart, Schaffner & Marx shops, and spread rapidly through the entire trade, organized and unorganized. Because of the spontaneous nature of the strike and the lack of an effective organization as a mouthpiece, its causes were not formulated until the strike was in progress. Then a committee of the strikers listed as the first cause—long hours.[70] The struggle was intense and protracted. The strikers were greatly aided both by the Chicago Federation of Labor, of which the United Garment Workers was a member, and by the Women's Trade Union League. The latter organized a Citizens' Committee which obtained wide-

---

[69] U. S. Bureau of Labor Statistics, *Bulletin* 198, p. 99.
[70] *Ibid.*, p. 17.

spread publicity for the shocking working conditions, collected funds, picketed, and supplied speakers for the daily mass meetings that were held to keep the strikers both informed and united. Public opinion, stirred by the facts broadcasted by the Women's Trade Union League, was further roused by the conditions that were disclosed in the report of the investigation of the trade by the Illinois Senate.[71] Yet when this interest gave promise that the employers would be forced to improve conditions, the United Garment Workers suddenly called off the strike with no explanation, and with nothing gained for the trade as a whole.[72] Hart, Schaffner & Marx, however, inaugurated an arbitration agreement with its employees which, among other conditions, established a fifty-four-hour week.[73]

Unlike the Chicago strike, the great New York strike of 1913 was called by the Union. But as the membership of the United Garment Workers numbered 5,000, and the strikers in the first week totalled 50,000, a number which had grown by the fourth week to 110,000, it can be seen that in this case, too, the strike was an upheaval of the unorganized.[74] As in Chicago, the first demand of the strikers was for shorter hours, specifically, the forty-eight-hour week.[75] One of the frequent attempts at mediation showed the importance that strikers placed on hours when they refused even to vote on a compromise which provided a fifty-two-hour week with the promise of forty-eight hours as soon as competitive conditions justified it.[76] Very unex-

[71] Wolman, Leo, *The Clothing Workers of Chicago*, Chicago, 1922, pp. 28-42.
[72] *Ibid.*, p. 46.
[73] Bureau of Labor Statistics, *Bulletin No. 198*, p. 25.
[74] *Ibid.*, pp. 99, 100.
[75] *Ibid.*, p. 101.
[76] *Ibid.*, pp. 108, 109.

pectedly, and with no expression of opinion from the strikers, the United Garment Workers called off the strike, accepting Marcus M. Mark's offer to mediate. With his assistance a settlement was made with the three largest manufacturers' associations by which, among other conditions, a work week of fifty-three hours was established until January 1, 1914, when it was to be decreased to fifty-two.[77] Agreements with smaller organizations fixed the hours at fifty and fifty-one per week.[78]

The resentment of the great mass of clothing workers at the action of the United Garment Workers in these two strikes was fuel added to an accumulating mistrust of this organization, due not only to its failure to organize the tailors, but also to its autocratic administration of union business, and its misuse of the union label. An open break resulted in 1914 when a convention city, financially inaccessible to the unskilled, was chosen, and when many were refused admission on the ground that their locals were in arrears, and so not entitled to representation. The excluded and others long dissatisfied organized their own convention.[79] In the group were men who had profited greatly from experience in successful negotiations with Hart, Schaffner & Marx, since 1911. Although the first conventions were necessarily devoted to the work of regularizing their position and to organization, the hours' question, which had been a sore spot in the trade for years, rapidly came to the front. The second resolution adopted at the New York convention of the Amalgamated Clothing Workers, held in the fall of 1914, advocated the establishment of the eight-hour day as a means of relieving the unemployment which was steadily

[77] *Ibid.*, pp. 110, 111.
[78] *Ibid.*, pp. 116, 119, 121.
[79] Wolman, *op. cit.*, p. 74-91.

increasing because modern machinery was "displacing our members."[80] Here was no attempt to base the demand in part at least on higher grounds, as older and more sophisticated organizations are prone to,[80a] but a statement of a condition for which the obvious remedy—to labor, at least—was suggested.

Tremendous organizing activity occurred in 1915.[81] Its fruit was a reduction in hours though the Union was still too young to enforce a national standard. Its method was to organize, present demands, fight as a last resort only, then opportunistically make the best bargain possible. New York was the scene of a series of strikes and lock-outs in the spring and summer of 1915, which led to agreements with the American Clothing Manufacturers Association, and with the Associated Boys Clothing Manufacturers, on wages, employment of union men, and on the establishment of machinery for the adjustment of disputes. A one-week strike in November in the boys' clothing trade, caused by the failure of this Association to set up machinery to adjust disputes, not only satisfactorily settled the point at once, but also resulted in the adoption of the forty-nine-hour week in this branch.[82] In Chicago the manufacturers did not reply to the Amalgamated's request for cooperation in establishing peaceful collective bargaining. A strike, therefore, was called in September, 1915. Like that of 1910, it was greatly aided by the Women's Trade Union League. It was unlike the earlier strike, however, in that the United Garment Workers were actively hostile to the extent even of

[80] *Documentary History of the Amalgamated Clothing Workers*, 1914-1916, p. 92.

[80a] The Amalgamated, itself, by 1918 had reached this stage of rationalizing on the need for the shorter day. Cf. *infra*, p. 196.

[81] *Documentary History*, 1914-1916, pp. 111, 113.

[82] *Ibid.*, pp. 134-137, 159.

DIRECT ACTION: TYPE CASES 193

acting as scabs, and in the successful settlement which established the fifty-hour week.[83]

Almost equally successful strikes took place in other cities. When the largest clothing manufacturer led the way, the other Baltimore firms signed agreements which established the fifty-hour week in place of the former one of fifty-four hours.[84] A strike in Philadelphia, early in 1916, resulted in the adoption of a fifty-one-hour week by some, but not all, of the firms.[85] In Rochester, the Clothiers Exchange granted the forty-eight-hour week a concession which, according to the union officials, aimed at "counteracting the effects of our organization propaganda."[86] With this record of activity and success, the President at the 1916 convention very simply said: "Hours were shortened throughout the country."[87]

The convention, which listened to this unboastful announcement, clamored for more reductions. Many resolutions calling for the establishment of the forty-eight-hour week were introduced, one of which even fixed the date of its inauguration as not later than January, 1917. The resolution that was adopted in no way bound the Executive Board to action, simply stating that the convention went on record as favoring the establishment of the forty-eight-hour week throughout the industry, and that efforts be made in that direction at every opportunity.[88]

For the next two years the Executive Board worked incessantly to establish this standard nationally. Its plan of campaign was simple; negotiations between the Executive

[83] *Ibid.*, pp. 141-157.
[84] *Ibid.*, pp. 161, 162.
[85] *Ibid.*, p. 173.
[86] *Ibid.*, p. 188.
[87] *Ibid.*, p. 114.
[88] *Ibid.*, p. 195.

Board, in cooperation with the local union, and the employers' associations at well-organized centers, were carried on in as rapid succession as was possible. Those in New York were successful. Conferences with the Associated Boys Clothing Manufacturers led to an agreement to inaugurate the forty-eight-hour schedule December 25, 1916 —a charming, sentimental touch. The employers in the men's trade, however, remained "inflexible in their opposition," and a strike was called for December 13, 1916. Very shortly the employers accepted offers of mediation which resulted in an agreement to establish the new standard as of January 22, 1917.[89] This auspicious beginning was followed by a victorious forty-eight-hour movement throughout the clothing centers. The leadership of Hart, Schaffner & Marx and other union factories in adopting it in Chicago was followed by the non-union houses of that city.[90] In January 1917, a three-week strike in Philadelphia resulted in its establishment by one manufacturers' association and by several individual firms.[91] Almost simultaneously, but "without the necessity of resorting to strikes," it was inaugurated in Baltimore.[92] Not until September, 1917, did peaceful negotiations with the Boston Clothing Manufacturers Association conclude an agreement which made "the forty-eight-hour week definite and general." [93] Three firms in Cleveland, which had been organized considerably later than the other centers, agreed to adopt this standard in March, 1918.[94] In the smaller centers there was less success. Some plants in Louisville established it,

[89] *Documentary History*, 1916-1918, pp. 71-77.
[90] *Ibid.*, p. 119.
[91] *Ibid.*, p. 109.
[92] *Ibid.*, p. 87.
[93] *Ibid.*, pp. 115, 116.
[94] *Ibid.*, p. 128.

while others reduced hours to fifty-one per week.[95] Negotiations followed by strikes failed in Cincinnati and Milwaukee.[96] Rochester, which had the forty-eight-hour week through the voluntary act of the Employers Association, continued to prove difficult to organize.[97]

This amazing record of the establishment of the forty-eight-hour standard by comparatively peaceful collective bargaining was supplemented by successful negotiations between the Executive Board, aided by the National Consumers League and the government on the question of conditions of work on contracts for uniforms. It was arranged that contracts be limited to all firms that established and enforced sound industrial conditions under the supervision of a Board of Control. As a result, union firms and those with union standards of hours and wages could bid successfully whereas up to this time contracts had been bid in by manufacturers with the lowest labor standards. As Secretary of War Baker said: "The privates' uniforms of the Army of the United States are not being made in sweat shops; ... under arrangements which have been made for the manufacture of the clothing of the Army, it is now substantially all being made under sanitary conditions ... under suitable restrictions as to hours of labor and under proper wage scales, so that for once at least the Government of the United States assumes the character of a model employer in a vital industry."[98] With every recognition of the unusually strong position of labor at the time, this was a remarkable achievement viewed in the light of previous protracted struggles for the eight-hour day on government

[95] *Ibid.*, pp. 125-127.
[96] *Ibid.*, p. 128.
[97] *Ibid.*, p. 129.
[98] *Ibid.*, pp. 132-141, 13.

contracts which had resulted in provisions, emasculated by exceptions.

The report of this successful work in hours' reduction to the 1918 convention was not as modest as that to the previous convention. Looking back over the events, the officials interpreted the forty-eight-hour resolution of the 1916 convention as a "mandate," and announced that "it has been carried out faithfully and successfully."[99] In addition, time to rationalize causes that made shorter hours a "compelling necessity," resulted in the presentation of a fuller justification of the movement. While this statement stressed increased production, the gain to employer and consumer, it emphasized to a far greater extent the workers' need for relief from fatigue, caused by the intense, exacting, uninteresting work—the result of division of labor; his right to a happier, fuller life; and last, the higher wages that shorter hours would bring.[100]

The men's clothing industry, on account of the late date at which successful organization was accomplished, was so far behind well-organized trades in attaining shorter hours that each convention showed them turning from jubilation over the decreases of the past to immediate plans for further reduction. So after the report of the inauguration of the forty-eight-hour week to the 1918 convention, six forty-four-hour week resolutions were introduced. Four of these urged it on the grounds that introduction of machinery and speeding-up methods of production were increasing unemployment and were shortening the season, one on the ground that the increased pace of production was undermining health, and the last evidently considering the need its own justification, on no grounds at all. After a lengthy discus-

[99] *Ibid.*, p. 61.
[100] *Ibid.*, pp. 68, 69.

DIRECT ACTION: TYPE CASES

sion, it was unanimously voted that "this convention goes on record for establishing the forty-four-hour week and that the General Executive Board start an agitation throughout the country."[101]

The General Executive Board, in cooperation with the local boards of the various clothing manufacturing centers, immediately initiated negotiations to establish the forty-four hour week. Shortly after the inception of the movement, the end of the war gave a further and immediate justification to the demand. Just as the close of the Civil War had caused a revival of the shorter-hour movement, so the need for providing work for the returned soldiers was used by the Amalgamated as a "compelling force behind our demand for the forty-four-hour week."[102]

This, however, was reasoning developed after the event as the first demand for the forty-four hour week was made in August, 1918, by the New York Joint Board of the Children's Clothing Trade. The American Men's and Boys' Clothing Manufacturers based their refusal on the ground that the movement aimed eventually to include the manufacture of men's clothing, in which branch they held it to be impossible due to the need for large war production.[102a] This answer was accompanied by a refusal to confer with the Union, but the employers offered to submit the question to the War Labor Board. The Union rejected this offer, allegedly because of the hostility of one member, but more probably because of the Board's well-known policy of establishing the forty-eight-hour week. The outcome was that the children's clothing workers struck on October 28, and

[101] *Ibid.*, pp. 178-181.
[102] *Documentary History*, 1918-1920, pp. 5, 6.
[102a] This reason, given in a letter of Oct. 18, 1918, was hardly convincing in view of the fact that conditions pointed to a speedy conclusion of the war in the near future.

on November 9 the Employers' Association locked out the workers on men's clothing. So well organized was the industry that the use of strike-breakers was at a minimum, and the newspapers reported it as a quiet, orderly strike. As the soldiers returned from draft camps, they joined the ranks of the strikers, thus giving proof of the timeliness of the demand. Repeated attempts at mediation resulted in the appointment of a commission acceptable to both parties. This commission unanimously recommended the adoption of the forty-four-hour week, and expressed the hope that it would be established throughout the industry "in view of the desirability of bringing about its proper standardization." With the acceptance of the ruling by both parties, the shorter week was inaugurated on January 23, 1919.[103]

During this course of events in New York, the General Executive Board was taking action to achieve the same objective in other clothing centers. Negotiations with Hart, Schaffner & Marx resulted on January 7, 1919, not only in a forty-four-hour week agreement, but also in a wage increase that was made retroactive to December 1, 1918. The solidarity, which is an outstanding characteristic of the Amalgamated, was demonstrated by the gift of this back pay, totalling $60,000, to the New York strikers. The agreement was of immeasurable importance because the growth of Hart, Schaffner & Marx, which had paralleled the development of its very liberal labor policy, had made that firm a leader in trade-union dealings in the clothing trade throughout the country. Hence "the victory in Chicago hastened the day of triumph in New York." In like manner, it led the other manufacturers through the Wholesale Clothiers' Association to announce the inauguration of a forty-four-hour week as of April 28. Whether to show

[103] *Documentary History*, 1918-1920, pp. 6-23, 25, 26.

the strength of the Union, and so to prevent any undermining of its power by these apparently voluntary grants, or because of insistence by the members on a more speedy adoption, the Union in this case and in other well-organized centers demanded and won the immediate adoption of a new schedule.[104] In Rochester, where organizing work had been vigorously carried on, the Clothiers Exchange granted the forty-four-hour week the day after it was obtained in New York. By peaceful collective bargaining the Joint Board persuaded the employers to advance the date of its establishment from May 1 to April 1, 1919.[105] On the 12th of February the Joint Board and the Manufacturers' Association of Boston agreed that the forty-four-hour week should go into effect March 1.[106] The Clothing Manufacturers' Association of Philadelphia, on February 25, announced the inauguration of a shorter week of May 1. When negotiations for advancing the date failed, the Joint Board by a one-day strike arranged its inauguration for March 31.[107]

The Central Executive Board followed up this success in the leading clothing centers by a campaign to increase membership in the smaller districts, and gave them every aid in establishing the forty-four-hour week, with the object of making it a national standard. This campaign was distinctly successful. In Indianapolis, a strike in a plant employing 1,000 workers resulted in the establishment of the forty-eight-hour week, followed in quick succession by the forty-four-hour week.[108] The Cincinnati employers voluntarily granted the forty-six-hour week, which was almost

[104] *Ibid.*, pp. 23, 24, 34, 119, 120.
[105] *Ibid.*, pp. 34, 44, 45.
[106] *Ibid.*, p. 110.
[107] *Ibid.*, p. 101.
[108] *Ibid.*, pp. 144, 145.

immediately reduced to the forty-four. The attempts of the Amalgamated, however, to unionize the plants brought about a lock-out which soon developed into a general strike that was financed by the general organization. The outcome was the establishment of collective bargaining agreements with ten firms.[109] When the request for a forty-four-hour agreement in Cleveland elicited no reply from the manufacturers, a strike was called on March 13, which shortly brought about the desired reduction in hours.[110] A four-day strike in Buffalo in May brought the same result from the union firms.[111] In St. Paul and Minneapolis, newly organized districts, comparatively short strikes led a number of firms to enter collective agreements which provided the forty-four-hour week in June.[112] The Milwaukee Joint Board and manufacturers peacefully inaugurated the new standard week in July,[113] while in August the same success followed renewed efforts at organization in St. Louis.[114]

The following table sums up more effectively than words the remarkable success of this forty-four-hour-week movement:

PERCENTAGE OF WAGE-EARNERS IN THE CLOTHING INDUSTRY WHOSE FULL-TIME HOURS PER WEEK WERE:[115]

	44 and less	Over 44, including 48	Over 48, under 54	54 and over
1914	...	8.7	74	17.3
1919	7.4	85.1	7.5	...
1922	96.1	3.9	...	...
1924	92.5	5.5	1.6	.3

[109] *Ibid.*, pp. 75-84.
[110] *Ibid.*, pp. 84-86.
[111] *Ibid.*, pp. 67-69.
[112] *Ibid.*, pp. 145-150.
[113] *Ibid.*, pp. 139, 140.
[114] *Ibid.*, p. 142.
[115] *American Federationist*, 1927, Vol. 34, p. 1246.

These figures demonstrate the inclusiveness of the victory of the Amalgamated Clothing Workers, hailed as the first union to secure the forty-four-hour week for an entire industry. Many members of the 1920 convention, to which was reported the phenomenal success of the forty-four-hour week movement, introduced resolutions advocating still further reductions. Ten resolutions urging a forty-hour stand failed to pass due to the efforts of the Committee on Resolutions, which advocated a wiser and more restrained policy, and carried a resolution that referred the question to the General Executive Board, and gave it full power to act in accordance with general conditions of the market.[116]

Conditions were such for the next few years that the Amalgamated had to concentrate all its energies on maintenance of the *status quo*. The combined force of the depression and the general open-shop movement, which was sweeping the country, led the New York Employers' Association in August, 1920, to present a series of demands to the New York Joint Board, which not only provided for a reduction in wages, but presaged a return to individual bargaining. In only one case was the return to the forty-eight-hour week mentioned, but any weakening of the principle of collective bargaining foreshadowed a general increase in hours. The failure of conferences to produce satisfactory terms resulted in a lock-out in New York on December 8, which soon spread to Boston and to the smaller manufacturing firms in Baltimore. The lock-out was long and severe. The whole industry helped to bear its cost, paying $2,000,000 to the General Executive Board for the purpose. At the end of six months' bitter struggle, the Union began to enter into agreements with individual manufacturers. By June 1 the

---

[116] *Documentary History*, 1918-1920, p. 339.

Joint Board, acting in accordance with a referendum vote of the membership and the Manufacturers' Association signed a one-year agreement which continued the forty-four-hour week, subscribed to the principle of the union shop, and provided for a cut in wages.[117]

While the New York Manufacturers' Association had precipitated an open break based on the need for changed conditions due to the times, the change was brought about by peaceful negotiations in Chicago. On February 14, 1922, the Employers' Association submitted twelve demands, one of which provided "the hours of work must be extended to the former basis of forty-eight per week." Conferences held during the next two months resulted in a three-year agreement in which there was no compromise on hours. The importance attached to this question was shown by the position of the forty-four-hour-week provision as the first item.[118] At the same time, the Clothiers Exchange of Rochester presented to the Union the need for a new basis of negotiation which should include a forty-eight-hour week. The negotiations resulted in a peaceful settlement which provided for the forty-four-hour week.[119] In other centers in which forty-four-hour agreements had been signed, this length week continued to prevail.[120]

Realization of the amazing feat of the Union, in keeping its hour position intact, had not sunk through to all the rank and file by the convention of 1922. Resolutions were introduced, therefore, which continued to urge a stand to establish the forty-hour week. The convention, however, accepted the strong, adverse recommendation of the Committee on

[117] *Ibid.*, 1920-1922, pp. 7-83.
[118] *Ibid.*, pp. 136-143.
[119] *Ibid.*, pp. 161-165.
[120] *Cf.* Table *supra*, p. 200.

Resolutions, and did not concur.[121] By the 1924 convention the impossibility of a further decrease of working hours was accepted by all, and no resolutions on the subject were introduced. In fact, as the above table shows, the forty-four-hour week had lost some ground, probably due to the movement of industry to non-union centers.[122]

The 1926 convention, however, was the scene of a vigorous demand for an active campaign to establish the forty-hour week. Eighteen resolutions were introduced on this subject. The Committee on Resolutions recommended the adoption of one which stated that, since technological unemployment could be remedied to a certain extent by shorter hours, the organization should "bend every effort" to establish the forty-hour week. After a discussion, which showed the members' insistence on action, the resolution was unanimously carried.[123]

The General Executive Board decided to attempt to carry out this "mandate" in January 1928. They concentrated their initial efforts on Chicago and Rochester. This choice was made, it was claimed, because these centers were the recognized leaders of the industry's labor policy. The fact that union conditions in these two cities were highly favorable may have influenced their selection. Conferences developed the fact that the manufacturers, on the one hand, unalterably opposed any increase in costs due to highly competitive conditions both with union and non-union firms, and that the Union representatives, both the national officials and those from the local organizations, on the other hand, considered that a reduction in hours without a corresponding increase in wages would be a loss rather than a gain to

[121] *Documentary History*, 1920-1922, p. 397.
[122] *Cf. supra*, p. 200.
[123] *Documentary History*, 1924-1926, p. 273.

the workers. The outcome in both cities was a surrender by the Union of its demand for the immediate inauguration of the forty-hour week for an agreement to refer "to the representatives of the parties to this agreement with instructions to consider the feasibility of instituting the forty-hour week in the industry." When these negotiations were being concluded, two non-union firms in Rochester established the forty-hour week for their workers.[124]

The record of these unsuccessful negotiations was reported to the 1928 convention. Nevertheless the convention affirmed the earlier insistence on action for this objective by introducing many resolutions. A substitute resolution was introduced by the Committee on Resolutions, which recommended that the officers take action to establish the forty-hour week " as soon as practicable "—one which was susceptible either of active or passive interpretation—on the ground that the increasing unemployment in the industry made the shorter week necessary. This resolution was unanimously passed.[125]

The history of the Union activities from 1928 to 1930 evidence a gain in strength through growth in numbers, and in territory in which collective agreements were in existence.[126] Despite this, and despite the expressed will of the membership, practically nothing was accomplished in the forty-hour-week movement. The only gain was that the New York Clothing Manufacturers' Association had joined the ranks of those agreeing to consider its feasibility.[127] Lack of success in this case, as in the Typographical Union, may be attributed to many causes. That the officials felt the demand too radical to warrant an open struggle seems

[124] *Ibid.*, 1926-1928, pp. 16-20.
[125] *Ibid.*, p. 215.
[126] *Ibid.*, 1928-1930, pp. 9, 12, 13.
[127] *Ibid.*, p. 61.

improbable in view of the wide spread of the five-day week in other industries [127a] during this period. Moreover, the fact that the Amalgamated Clothing Workers had not hesitated to make the far more radical forty-four-hour demand in 1918 makes it seem that the more likely cause was a growth of caution, which age and experience had produced. A supplementary cause may be that the spread in the activities of the Union—a growing emphasis on the need for unemployment insurance, development of banks and cooperative housing schemes—had weakened, if not the bargaining strength, at least its concentration on the question of hours. Another possibility may be that factionalism, which had been reported as less harassing in 1928,[128] has actually continued to weaken the Union.

Whatever the causes of this failure to take action, the membership has continued to insist on the need for further attempts. At the 1930 convention twenty-five resolutions on the forty-hour week were introduced. Again, the Committee's substitute resolution, which pointed to the inevitability of the forty-hour week due to "persistent unemployment and the introduction of machinery," but left the choice of the time to the General Executive Board, was unanimously passed. President Hillman's promise to make every effort to establish it "at the earliest possible moment" was greeted by prolonged applause. The moment, however, no longer seemed to be an immediate one when he added that the forty-four-hour week, which was not being strictly observed in some markets, must be made effective before "we can ask honestly and conscientiously for the forty-hour week."[129]

[127a] The American Federation of Labor reported that in Oct., 1928, 514 locals, with a membership of 165,029, had five-day week agreements. *Proceedings*, 1928, p. 44.

[128] *Documentary History*, 1926-1928, p. 7.

[129] *Ibid.*, 1928-1930, pp. 276, 277.

Except for the honesty of this admission, it appears that the Amalgamated Clothing Workers has joined the ranks of those who give lip service to the need for shorter hours, but not action.

AN UNORGANIZED INDUSTRY: STEEL

Regulation of hours by the Amalgamated Association of Iron, Steel and Tin Workers, a consolidation in 1881 of three unions in these fields,[130] was not uniform for the three trades. The puddlers' work was fixed by established custom at five heats a day which took approximately ten hours to complete. These workers resented suggestions for an eight-hour day, which would decrease wages since they were paid by the heat. Employers who introduced it in the depression of 1893, as a means of dividing work on the furnaces left in operation, were aided by the Union officials, but the men continued to be hostile to the shorter day as a permanent measure.[131] Work in the sheet mills was put on an eight-hour schedule in 1885, despite the opposition of the workers, when technical changes in production had made the three-shift system an economic necessity.[132] Although workers in plants that had experimented with the eight-hour day advocated it, not until the convention of 1890 was a resolution passed that the steel workers should establish it wherever practicable.[133]

During this period the employers' policy on hours was in a state of flux. Conditions at the Edgar Thompson Mill, a union plant, though not a strongly organized one, from

---

[130] Robinson, J. S., *The Amalgamated Association of Iron, Steel and Tin Workers*, Baltimore, 1920, pp. 9, 10.
[131] Fitch, J. A., *The Steel Workers*, New York, 1910, pp. 91, 96.
[132] *Ibid.*, pp. 93, 94.
[133] *Ibid.*, pp. 95, 96.

1882 to 1888,[134] illustrate the vacillating policy. By 1879 the eight-hour day had been inaugurated in this mill because "it was out of the question to expect human flesh and blood to labor incessantly for twelve hours."[135] Although it was reported by the Superintendent to have "proved to be of immense advantage to both the Company and the workmen,"[136] after a shut-down the men were forced in 1885 to accept the twelve-hour day and a "heavy reduction in wages," because of the competition of longer hours and lower wages in other steel mills. A strike of the entire plant in the following spring resulted in the reestablishment of the eight-hour day in April, 1886. But at the end of 1887 the men were again offered a cut in wages and the twelve-hour day. They held out until May, when they were forced not only to accept the 50% increase in hours at lower pay, but also to sign an agreement not to join the Union, which ended collective bargaining at this mill,[137] just as the defeat of the Homestead Strike in 1892 [138] struck "the death knell of unionism . . . . . for the steel mills of the United States."[139]

From this time until 1919, there was no real effort to organize the steel workers. To be sure, the Amalgamated Association of Iron, Steel and Tin Workers still functioned, but the membership figures are witness to its failure: its maximum membership, 24,068 in 1891, from an eligible group of approximately 100,000 workers, had fallen to 4,355

[134] *Ibid.*, p. 111.

[135] *Ibid.*, p. 112n. Quotation from a letter written by the Superintendent of the mill.

[136] Bridge, J. H., *The Inside History of the Carnegie Steel Company*, New York, 1903, p. 188.

[137] Fitch, *op. cit.*, pp. 112-115.

[138] The issue in this case was wages, not hours.

[139] Fitch, *op. cit.*, p. 132.

in 1911.[140] During this period the average sized plant was growing steadily larger, the percentage of unskilled labor was increasing, and technological improvements in the steel industry had confirmed the tendency to continuity of process which made a compromise on hours impossible. In those operations where the work never ceased, choice had to be made between an eight-hour day with three shifts and a twelve-hour day with two shifts. Almost without exception, in the absence of collective bargaining or of a restraining law, the employer's choice was the longer day, to which was added a twenty-four-hour turn every second Sunday at the change of shifts.[141]

The results of excessive hours, as well as other evils in the steel industry, were brought to public attention in the startling revelations of the Pittsburgh Survey, which was made under the direction of the Russell Sage Foundation, and to which John A. Fitch contributed his masterly and understanding study, "The Steel Workers." The Bethlehem Strike in 1910, caused by the excessive amount of compulsory over-time, led to a government investigation whose report also stirred public opinion. The United States Bureau of Labor, which made this investigation, reported that 51% of the employees had a twelve-hour day, and that the remainder had a standard day of from ten and five-twelfths to eleven hours. Over-time was quite usual.[142] Shocked attention had not had time to subside when the four-volume report on "Conditions of Employment in the Iron and Steel Industry in the United States" was published. This comprehensive investigation was made under the direction of

[140] Robinson, *op. cit.*, p. 21.
[141] Fitch, *op. cit.*, pp. 168-176.
[142] U. S. Senate, *Report on Strike at Bethlehem Steel Works*, 1910, p. 9-14.

the Labor Department at the order of the Senate. Summarizing the hours' situation, this report stated that it was "in striking contrast to this general tendency [decreasing hours] in other industries to find in a great basic industry . . . . . that approximately only 14% of the 173,000 employees worked less than sixty hours per week, and almost 43% worked seventy-two hours or over per week."[143]

These reports roused a group of stockholders of the U. S. Steel Corporation to insist on the appointment of a Stockholders' Investigating Committee. The report of this Committee first discussed the need for shorter hours on physical, moral and social grounds, and then respectfully recommended "a reasonable and just arrangement . . . . . of reducing the hours of labor . . . . . to the intelligent and thoughtful consideration of the proper officers." As a result, the Finance Committee of the Steel Corporation appointed two of its members as a committee, to "consider what, if any, arrangement with a view to reducing the twelve-hour day insofar as it now exists among the employees of the subsidiary companies is reasonable, just and practicable." The indefinite recommendations of these last two reports were in striking contrast to that of the Special Commission on Hours of Labor in Continuous Industries—composed of representatives of Great Britain, Germany, France, the United States, and nine other countries—which in this same year strongly recommended "the eight-hour shift in continuous industries as the best system" from both the worker's and society's point of view.[144]

Private investigation, government investigation, stockholders' investigation and their respective recommendations,

[143] U. S. Senate, *Report on Conditions of Employment in the Iron and Steel Industry*, 1911, Vol. I, p. xvi.

[144] *Ibid.*, Vol. 3, pp. 161-163.

supplemented by the force of public opinion that they had roused, had small success in obtaining a reduction of hours. It is true efforts were made to eliminate the seven-day week, which was done at a cost to the employees of 14% of their wages, and at no cost to the steel companies. But the eight-hour day, the companies claimed, could not be adopted on account of increased costs, the impossibility of obtaining sufficient workers for three shifts, and the opposition of the laborers who resented the deprivation of the right to earn more wages. One company only was reported as experimenting with the eight-hour shift in the blast furnaces, and this concern had established the eight-hour day in other continuous departments prior to this time.[145] The Finance Committee of the Steel Corporation in 1913 asserted the impossibility of the eight-hour day when it reported that the Corporation could not eliminate the twelve-hour day until its competitors did likewise, and yet tabled a resolution which proposed cooperation to this end by the entire industry.[146] It was later said that the Steel Corporation, despite this unfavorable action, made continued efforts to eliminate the two-shift system, which resulted in a 3% decrease in 1914 in the number of employees on the twelve-hour schedule.[147] Since the U. S. Steel Corporation was the leader in establishing the labor policies for the greater part of the steel industry, this figure is fairly representative of the extent to which agitation, investigation and public opinion succeeded in reducing hours.

During the war, with increased pressure for production, increased pay, and decreased supply of labor, the question of shortening hours receded into the background. When it

[145] *Ibid.*, pp. 170-175.
[146] *Christian Science Monitor*, June 18, 1923.
[147] Tarbell, Ida, *The Life of Elbert H. Gary*, New York, 1925, p. 291.

came to the front again in the 1919 strike, the average weekly hours for the industry were 68.7 as compared with 67.6 in 1910, an increase in a period when the normal tendency was downward, and in an industry where the average weekly hours at the earlier period had been far above those prevailing throughout industry in general. There were no official figures of the number of employees on the twelve-hour shift, but the Inter-Church World Movement Report, made after a careful survey, estimated that 52.4%[148] of the Steel Corporation's employees were on this schedule.

The strike of 1919 was the direct result of the attempt of the American Federation of Labor to organize the steel industry,[149] but it was the indirect result of a number of contributing causes among which that of excessive hours was of primary importance.[150] The Committee, entrusted with the work of organization, made every effort to use peaceful methods of collective bargaining. This was rendered difficult by the discharge of union workers,[151] which roused the men to demand immediate action, and by the failure of the Steel Corporation even to answer the Committee's request for a conference. As a result, a strike vote set September 22 for the commencement of the strike. Thereupon the Committee again asked for a conference, which was refused by Elbert H. Gary on the ground that the Committee was not authorized to represent the sentiment of a majority of the employees of the U. S. Steel Corporation. When presentation of proof of the percentage organized failed to convince Gary of its representative authority, the

---

[148] Commission of Inquiry, Inter-Church World Movement, *Report on the Steel Strike of 1919*, New York, 1920, p. 71, 49.
[149] Resolution to this effect was passed at the 1918 convention. *Proceedings*, 1918, p. 207.
[150] Inter-Church World Movement, *Report*, p. 4.
[151] *Ibid.*, p. 171.

Committee asked President Wilson to arrange a meeting. His efforts, too, were in vain.[152]

On September 22, 300,000 [153] steel workers went on strike for the right to collective bargaining to fix reasonable hours and wages in the face of a united and powerful attack against them as radicals, communists and revolutionists. During the strike further efforts at negotiations failed: first, when the proposal for a tri-partite strike commission, made at the October Industrial Conference, was defeated: second, when Gary declined the offer of a committee from the Inter-Church World Movement as mediators or arbitrators; and third, when the suggestion of the Senate Investigation Committee that a board of conciliation be appointed came to naught.[154]

The strike ended January 8, 1920. Its failure can be blamed on both capital and labor. From the beginning, the strike had small chance of success because the power and wealth of the Steel Corporation, supported by the "independent companies," made it possible to control the newspapers, and so sidetrack public opinion by the "red herring" Bolshevism, and to continue uninterrupted production in some plants with the aid of strike-breakers. Chance for success was minimized also by the American Federation of Labor's failure to organize the industry as a comprehensive industrial union. In accordance with their philosophy they preferred to follow craft lines, relying on a central committee to unify the work of the twenty-four trades.[155] At

[152] U. S. Senate, *Report on Investigation of Strike in Steel Industries*, submitted Nov. 6, 1919, pp. 2-5.

[153] Inter-Church World Movement, *Report*, p. 176; American Federation of Labor estimated 365,000 on strike shortly after it commenced. *Proceedings*, 1920, p. 195.

[154] American Federation of Labor, *Proceedings*, 1920, p. 195.

[155] Inter-Church World Movement, *Report*, pp. 20-43, 176-188.

the 1919 convention they voted to continue the plan even though glaring defects had become apparent.[156]

The failure of the strike was followed by several investigations which finally led to action to eliminate the twelve-hour day. Judge Gary appointed a committee to investigate the feasibility of the eight-hour day. The fact that its findings were not published, then or later,[157] is negative evidence of the improbability of the change if left to the efforts of the employers. The report of a group of experts, on the basis of an investigation made at the request of the impartial Inter-Church World Movement, recommended that the Federal Government set up a commission representing employers, employees and the public, "to inaugurate immediate conferences between the Steel Corporation and its employees for the elimination of the twelve-hour day and the seven-day week, and for the readjustment of wages."[158] The report was given widespread publicity in newspapers, churches and colleges.

The findings and recommendations of the Inter-Church Movement Report in regard to hours were confirmed by an investigation made by Horace Drury for the Engineering Societies. This report, made by an expert in scientific management, aided by expert engineers, on the basis of an investigation of the operation of the eight-hour day in twenty steel plants, and of the twelve-hour day in other plants, found "no outstanding obstacle to putting the steel industry" on an eight-hour day. Drury estimated that the change would entail only a 3% increase in costs. He pointed out that the large amount of unemployment offered a par-

[156] American Federation of Labor, *Proceedings*, 1919, p. 301.
[157] *Christian Science Monitor*, June 18, 1923.
[158] Inter Church World Movement, *Report*, p. 17.

ticularly favorable opportunity for making the transition.[159] It is of interest to note that the money for the investigation was provided by the Cabot Foundation, established by Charles Cabot, one of the United States Steel stockholders who had instigated the unfruitful stockholders' investigation of 1912.[160]

In 1922, two publications focused attention on hours in the steel industry. C. R. Walker's "Steel: The Diary of a Furnace Worker," through vivid personal narrative, proved the shorter day to be a human necessity; while the investigation of the twelve-hour shift in all continuous industries, made by the Federated American Engineering Societies with the aid of a grant from the Cabot Fund, established the practical feasibility of the eight-hour day. This publication was prefaced by President Harding with the statement that "the old order of the twelve-hour day must give way to a better and wiser form of organization of the productive forces of the nation, so that proper family life and citizenship may be enjoyed suitably by all of our people." [161]

To promote action, President Harding invited the executives of the steel industry to a dinner at the White House at which he urged the abolition of the twelve-hour day. In doing this, he made articulate the will of the public whose conscience had been roused by the bombardment of facts which the failure of the steel strike had produced. Complying with his request, the American Iron and Steel Institute appointed a committee on May 22, 1922, to consider the possibility of changing hours. On May 23, 1923, the

[159] Taylor Society, *Bulletin*, Feb., 1921. The Colorado Fuel and Iron Co., was one of these plants; for its adoption of the eight-hour day, *cf. infra*, pp. 244-247.
[160] *Cf. supra*, p. 209.
[161] *The Twelve Hour Shift in Industry*, New York, 1922.

Institute unanimously adopted this Committee's adverse report. The Committee declared that the elimination of the twelve-hour day was not feasible, first, because it would require 60,000 additional workers who were not available due to the restrictive immigration policy; second, because it would increase the cost of production 15%, which would be an unfair burden to the consumer; and last, because it was opposed by the workers who objected to a decrease in wages. Furthermore, the Committee expressed the conviction that the twelve-hour day "was not of itself an injury to the employees, physically, mentally or morally." The report, however, admitted the possibility of the eight-hour day at a future date when all conditions were favorable.

The publication by the Iron and Steel Institute of this report, which not only flouted the expressed social will, but also continued the Steel Corporation's policy of making the unsupported statement that the twelve-hour day was not harmful, was followed by a bitter attack from the Church —Catholic, Protestant and Jewish united to form a commission which denounced it. The President of the United States again intervened—though this time less decisively— and suggested "that the hours of work be shortened before any labor is discharged." Ten weeks later, the Iron and Steel Institute reversed its decision. The statement read: "that the manufacturers of iron and steel, representing substantially the entire industry of this country, will now begin the total elimination of the twelve-hour shift . . . wages will be so adjusted as to afford earnings equivalent to a 25% increase in hourly and base rates." [162]

The results of the adoption of the shorter day were admitted by the leaders of the industry to be satisfactory. The increase in costs, so convincingly put at 15% before

[162] *American Labor Legislation Review*, 1923, pp. 179-186.

the change, proved within six months of the adoption of the new schedule to vary between 3½ and 5½%.[163] That the change did not mean a general eight-hour day is shown by a survey made under the auspices of the Cabot Fund eight months later, which stated that 75% of the blast furnace laborers, and 55% of the open-hearth laborers, worked more than sixty hours. The survey reported that even these conditions were held by the men to be a tremendous change for the better.[164]

The following table serves to illustrate both the decided change that followed the full blast of public opinion in 1923, and the present hours' standard in the still unorganized steel industry.

AVERAGE HOURS FOR EACH SPECIFIED YEAR FOR ALL EMPLOYEES IN NINE OPERATIONS [165]

	Blast Furnaces	Bessemer Converters	Open-Hearth Furnaces	Puddling Mills	Blooming Mills	Plate Mills	Bar Mills	Standard Rail Mills	Sheet Mills
1914	74.8	68.4	74.5	53.2	70.5	69.	61.7	70.1	52.3
1920	72.1	70.3	68.7	53.9	67.5	68.8	61.8	61.2	50.3
1924	59.7	52.3	58.	55.7	54.6	57.2	55.6	57.4	50.2
1931	57.2	53.3	53.8	53.	52.6	56.7	55.	54.9	47.8

SUMMARY

The history of hours' reduction in the two unions presented as cases, supported by the figures in Appendix H, shows the effectiveness of the method of direct action in

[163] *New Republic,* March 26, 1924.
[164] *Ibid.,* Sept. 10, 1924.
[165] *Monthly Labor Review,* Nov., Dec., 1931; Jan., 1932. The *New Republic* (Feb. 19, 1930), published the results of a survey of the hours' situation in the Steel Industry made by two theological students. They reported that the eight-hour day is still a myth; more than 50% of the 300,000 workers included in the survey worked ten hours or more a day.

achieving results. The insignificance of the aid rendered by the American Federation of Labor to the Typographical Union, and the entire success of the Amalgamated without this support, suggests the unimportance of the Federation's present role in the use of direct action for reduction of hours. The history gives no evidence of any essential difference in the tactics of collective bargaining for shorter hours as between an old line Federation union and a representative of the new unionism. Both adopt national standards of hours, both use every possible effort to introduce the change peacefully, both support local strikes by a national assessment, and both even before the depression appeared to have reached a stage characterized by a temporizing attitude on the hours' question which was in sharp contrast to their early vigor. This attitude is easily explainable as a growth of caution forced by the staggering financial burden of strikes for shorter hours. Since, however, the two cases point repeatedly to the need for the strike, a long continuation of unwillingness to bear its cost will nullify the efficiency of direct action even for the organized.

The struggle for shorter hours in the steel industry, chosen as a type case in the unorganized field, shows the utter impossibility of placing any reliance on direct action alone to reduce the work-day of the unorganized. The failure of the American Federation of Labor to organize this and other predominantly unskilled fields emphasizes the inadequacy of its craft-dominated philosophy today, and points to a vitally needed reform if the Federation is to be justified in continued insistance on direct action and opposition to legislative action to reduce hours.

PART III
REDUCTION OF HOURS BY EMPLOYERS

CHAPTER VII

Voluntary Action of Employers

EMPLOYERS and employers' associations, when opposing the enactment of hours' legislation or negotiations of trade unions for a shorter work-day, commonly refer to a "natural evolution" of shorter hours as the only desirable means of achieving this objective. The difficulty is that "natural evolution" used in this sense has never been defined. It seems obvious, however, that reference is made to voluntary reduction of hours by employers, but here again no definition is available. In the purest sense, it should mean a lessening of hours brought about by the employer's own will, not subjected to outside forces seeking this end. Actually, this "voluntary" concession of hours may be the resultant of direct pressure, not in itself strong enough to produce the change, or of indirect pressure, or of both. The former comprises requests of employees, either entirely unorganized, or united in some form of company union. The latter includes public opinion, the tendency to shorter hours in the same or allied trades in the district, or the threat of unionization against which shorter hours are granted as a more or less prophylactic measure. Since it is obviously impossible to separate and measure the influence of any one of these interacting forces, voluntary shortening of hours must necessarily be interpreted to include all reductions which are not the immediate and obvious result of trade union effort or of legislative action.

The purpose of this chapter is to present the evidence of how widespread the practice of voluntary reduction of hours has been. That it must cover a broad field is clear in view of the practically universal reduction in hours in the period under survey despite the fact that legislative and trade-union action necessarily affected but a part of the laborers. Trade-unions, even in 1920, the year of maximum membership, only included approximately 20% of the wage earners of the country.[1] That is, only one fifth of the working population at the most could have obtained shorter hours directly by trade-union bargaining. As may be concluded from the chapters on hours' legislation, it is not so easy to arrive at an estimate of the per cent whose hours have been decreased by law. Certainly the number so affected is greater today than at any other time, and this mainly for two reasons. In the first place, the hours' legislation of today is an accumulation of all the laws of the past. And secondly there has been a steady increase in the number of government employees and women in gainful occupations, the two classes for which the enactment of hour laws has been most common. Although no very satisfactory data are available, it might be estimated that about three-tenths of the wage earners are affected directly by hours' legislation.[2] Approximately one-half of the wage earners, then is the greatest proportion whose hours could have been reduced directly by trade-union action and legislation.

The nature of the material makes it necessary to subdivide voluntary action into two parts. In the first part must be included all unreported decreases in hours for which consequently there is no specific evidence. Such changes were voluntary as the term is defined in this study. They were,

[1] Wolman, Leo, *Growth of American Trade Unions, 1880-1923*, New York, 1924, p. 85. Dr. Wolman uses an estimate of the total wage-earners excluding agriculture to obtain the above-mentioned figure. It is in this sense that the term total wage-earners is used in this study.

[2] *Cf.* Appendix I.

however, the result of general conditions rather than of any pioneer action of the employers. General conditions which played an important part in the spread of reduction of hours are almost too interrelated to separate them and to estimate their importance. That business prosperity combined with scarcity of labor has been the outstanding influence is shown by the fact that the biggest decrease in hours for any five-year period, for which figures are available occurred in 1914-1919.[3] In addition, improved machinery, more efficient management, the new attitude toward leisure, and the force of example and competition of the better hours standards established by legislation, trade-unions and pioneer employers have been factors contributing to the spread of shorter hours. In the second part must be placed all cases in which pioneer employers adopted shorter hours as a matter of conscious policy, and all statements of American entrepreneurs on imitating changes in hours. While the voluntary reduction of hours brought about by general conditions is of great significance in the long run, the more direct means are legislation, trade-union bargaining and that type of voluntary action in which pioneering employers take the initiative. This chapter will be confined to a presentation of the evidence of this latter type.

It would seem that the question of voluntary reduction of hours as above delimited, is an unworked field; no material has been found which deals with it directly. This lack may be due either to the burial of such records in the minds of countless small-scale intrepreneurs, or in the files of large-scale enterprises or again to the comparative rarity of such action. There is, however, a vast amount of material indirectly bearing on the subject, a search of which should present a fair picture. Since higher wages and shorter hours have alternately been given first and second place as the causes of industrial unrest, all adequate mediums for

[3] *Cf.* Appendix H.

reporting and interpreting the labor situation should have included accounts of voluntary reduction of hours. Inasmuch as these records touch on this question from time to time, the paucity of the references is strong negative evidence that voluntary reduction of hours—except as a temporary measure to spread work during a period of unemployment—was and is an unusual act for the American entrepreneur.

Division into periods is hardly warranted by any significant difference in the tempo of reduction or attitude of employers. For purposes of clarity of presentation, however, a division has been made. The first period covers from the Civil War to the turn of the century, which offers a somewhat logical and convenient transition; the second continues from the opening of the twentieth century to the World War period, when, as might be expected, an increase in the tempo of voluntary reduction occurred; and the last period brings the evidence down to the present.

1865-1900

The comparatively small size of the average business enterprise in the decades immediately following the Civil War might have proved an insurmountable obstacle to obtaining reliable evidence of voluntary reduction of hours in this period had it not been for the indefatigable zeal of the newly-appointed Massachusetts Bureau of Statistics of Labor. This Department's annual reports of investigations of the hours' situation, when allowance is made for lack of training in statistical methods, paralleled in thoroughness the enthusiasm of the laborers and intellectuals of this State for the establishment of shorter hours. The value of the 1870 to 1873 reports, which dealt exclusively with the situation in Massachusetts, is immeasurably increased by that for 1881, which reported a thorough sur-

VOLUNTARY ACTION OF EMPLOYERS 225

vey of the situation in New York and the New England States other than Massachusetts. Since this area represents one of the largest and most industrialized parts of the country, voluntary action to reduce hours in this district can be taken as a fair sample of the situation throughout the country.

The Bureau's report for 1870 included an account of the hearing held on the hours' question. To the great disappointment of the Bureau's officials, no executives were present, "yet we have been assured that there are treasurers, agents and superintendents of mills, as well as clergymen and physicians, who favor reduction to ten hours of daily work."[4] The report also presented the replies of seventy-four manufacturers to the question: "What, in your opinion, would be the effect of a limitation of the hours of labor?" Although the value of the inquiry was lessened by the indefiniteness of the question, which left unknown the number of hours which the correspondent had in view, the results are important in showing the employer's attitude at a time when a ten-hour day in factories was a rare and highly-prized schedule, and when agitation by labor for the eight-hour day was active. Sixty-two employers were definitely opposed; eleven, while not favorable, yet showed a doubt which gave some hope of conversion; and one had " no objection to ten hours' work if all the United States adopt the same hours." The Bureau remarked that "those employers who required the greatest number of hours are the most opposed to any reduction whatever." A fairly typical explanation of this opposition was that given by the owner of a bleachery who had "invariably noticed that when men are kept at work until

[4] Massachusetts Bureau of Statistics of Labor, *First Annual Report*, 1870, p. 111.

10 P. M. they live in better health, as they keep indoors instead of sitting round doors smoking."[5] None of these replies had reported any voluntary reduction of hours, but in answer to the Bureau's question on strikes, a paper manufacturer reported one which had resulted from his reduction of the day's work to eight hours. This case with no explanation of causes leading to the change, or of the wage situation which may have forced the strike against the reduced hours, is of little significance compared with the overwhelming expression of hostile opinion.[6]

Unlike the 1870 report, that for 1871 presented little information on the hours' situation. Oral testimony on work and home-life of factory operatives of three mill executives was reported in detail. Mr. Perry, of the Everett Mills of Lawrence, employing 900 workers, was the only one to mention reduction of hours. He said: "Of spinners as a class, I believe them to be a rowdy, drinking, unprincipled set, and that any concession of time to them would only be wasted and rioted away. If they were kept at work fourteen hours a day, it would be better for them." The only other reference to the subject was that the Lowell Bleacheries had inaugurated a sixty-three-hour week in place of the sixty-six-hour week, and that the change had not caused any decrease of production.[7]

The second inquiry of the Bureau in regard to results of decreases in hours on wages, on production, on profit, etc., received only one complete and nine partial answers. The complete answer was made by a rubber thread company, employing approximately 100 workers. A reduction in hours from sixty-six per week to sixty had increased costs

[5] *Ibid.*, pp. 223-234.
[6] *Ibid.*, p. 208.
[7] *Ibid.*, 1871, pp. 467-473.

in this mill about 2%, but had improved the quality of the goods. Of the incomplete answers, six favored a reduction to ten hours a day, two gave no opinion, and one opposed it. Only one of these companies explained the voluntary reduction of hours. A chair manufacturer reported that his employees, not imperatively, but in a "friendly" manner, requested that the customary eleven-hour day of the summer season be reduced to ten. The firm consented, and after four years' experience stated that production had been maintained. None of these concerns had reduced the hours to less than ten per day.[8] Another questionnaire—not summarized here because it included answers of workmen as well as of employers—was answered by a manufacturer of nitro-glycerine, employing only ten workers, that he had established the eight-hour day, apparently because of the "special difficulties" and danger of the work;[9] and by a leather manufacturing concern that they had changed "voluntarily several years ago to ten hours," but were opposed to further reduction.[10]

The 1873 report yields comparatively little information on employers' action or attitude on this question, because it is devoted in large part to an exposition of the economists' viewpoint on hours, wages and poverty, and to a resumé of the hours' situation in England. It does, however, report the successful—and apparently voluntary—inauguration of the ten-hour day in the Atlantic Mills at Lawrence, which with the renovation of the plant, and the introduction of new machinery, had resulted in an increase of 6.13% in the number of operators, and of 50 to 60% in the product. Mr. Gray, who testified, pointed out

[8] Ibid., 1872, pp. 218-225.
[9] Ibid., p. 139.
[10] Ibid., p. 231.

the need for shorter hours because "to run these machines required more activity, more skill, and a greater tax upon the strength." Despite an occasional example of this type, the report stated that "even manufacturers who are said to be efficient in their efforts to improve the condition of their people," continue to oppose a reduction of hours.[11]

From the passage of the Ten-Hour Law for women in 1874 [12] until the Legislature ordered an investigation of the hours' situation in the other New England States and in New York in 1880, the Bureau's reports do not yield further information on this subject. The survey, which the Legislature ordered, was carefully planned and carried out. Data for it was gathered by agents, supplied with two schedules of inquiries, from 246 textile manufacturing establishments, and 545 employees. The summary stated that "some mills have voluntarily adopted ten hours . . . , by far the greater portion of the manufacturers, however, consider that a reduction of hours to ten would result in a diminution of product." Only six mills were specifically mentioned as having voluntarily adopted the ten-hour day, and one the eleven-hour day. In the first group, one successful carpet manufacturer, employing 1700, had reduced his hours from twelve to ten a day in 1855; a woolen mill had done the same in 1870, and continued to compete successfully with mills on an eleven-and-a-half-hour schedule; a linen mill had made the change with success in 1878; and the three other mills reported no date for the change, but did testify to satisfaction with the result. The cotton mill, which had reduced hours from thirteen to eleven, had made the change under a new manager in 1865, and "with the same machinery" had increased out-

[11] *Ibid.*, 1873, pp. 495-500.
[12] *Cf. supra*, pp. 107, 108.

put 33 1/3%. The testimony of the employers who had experimented with shorter hours is convincing, but there are amazingly few examples, considering the length of time during which agitation had had an opportunity to exert indirect pressure.[13]

In the same year as this report was issued, the Continental Iron Company of Greenpoint, Long Island, the builder of the "Monitor," reduced hours from sixty to fifty-six per week as a summer experiment. The results were so satisfactory that the shorter week was continued, and five years later its owner reported that "it makes no real difference in the cost of the work done."[14] At this time, too, the steel mills were experimenting with the shorter day.[15] Carnegie stated later that he had spent $50,000 in an effort to introduce the eight-hour day, but had been compelled by his competitors to revert to the twelve-hour day.[16]

The United States Senate in 1882 ordered an investigation of the relations between capital and labor for which four volumes of testimony were taken from manufacturers, workers, clergymen, journalists and doctors in New England, the Middle States and the South. This work was completed and published in 1885. If any material should yield examples of voluntary reduction of hours, this survey which, by order of the Senate, dealt with "the wages and hours of labor" should do so. It must be remembered that in this period the agitation for the eight-hour day was mounting each year toward the attempt at forcing its acceptance by means of a general strike in 1886. Under

[13] *Ibid.*, 1881, pp. 323-327, 459-462.
[14] Ohio Bureau of Labor Statistics, *Tenth Annual Report*, 1886, pp. 48, 49.
[15] *Cf. supra*, pp. 206, 207.
[16] *American Federationist*, 1904, Vol. 11, p. 591.

these circumstances, the three examples of voluntary reduction mentioned in the testimony bear witness to the inefficacy—and even more to the uniqueness—of voluntary action as a means of attaining shorter hours: a fact which was further emphasized by the niggardliness of the reduction in each case. The first example was that of Brewster & Company, the New York carriage-makers, whose President stated that they had a ten-hour day, and testified: "We have made some voluntary concessions: for instance, on Saturday night we let the men off a little earlier, and in the extreme hot weather we give them a little longer time than usual at noons. That is done voluntarily."[17] The insistence on the voluntary nature of this reduction is explained by earlier testimony on the eight-hour strike of their employees in 1872. At that time, the workers had valued the really shorter day so highly that, though warned by the management of what the strike would cost them, they sacrificed the accumulated profits due them from the Brewster Industrial Association, a company union, which the firm had established in 1869.[18] The second case was that of a jute bagging manufacturer of Columbus, Georgia, whose employees worked a ten-hour average day through the year, because the hours in winter were shorter as the result of a policy of not lighting up morning or evening. The testimony did not indicate whether the factory possessed lighting equipment which would have permitted the longer day, but this manufacturer appeared sincere in his statement that hours in the South were "excessive," causing applicants for jobs to "appear to be

[17] United States Senate Committee, *Report upon the Relations between Labor and Capital and Testimony taken by the Committee*, 1885, Vol. 2, p. 1120.

[18] *Ibid.*, pp. 1104-1109.

VOLUNTARY ACTION OF EMPLOYERS 231

worked out, as mules sometimes are."[19] The last case of voluntary change, which the testimony produced, was a reduction from a twelve to an eleven-hour day made in 1865 in the Enterprise Mills in Augusta, Georgia. The decrease, which was made conditional on maintenance of former output, was caused by "public sentiment and increasing development of machinery." It was followed by an immediate increase in production with the same machinery. No further reductions had been made, although the Superintendent of this mill was convinced that the ten-hour day would be more productive.[20]

While it is possible that the paucity of examples resulted from the employers' failure to call attention to their voluntary reduction of hours, their general testimony would not lead to this conclusion. Only one firm reported a workweek of less than sixty hours. This, the Manchester Print Works, had established a fifty-eight-hour week.[21] In fact, the sixty-hour week was comparatively rare: Pierre Lorillard & Company testified that it treated its employees "with kindness and forbearance," and cited the sixty-hour week as proof.[22] A sub-committee, visiting four mills in New England, reported a ten-hour day at the Cheney Silk Mills,[23] a ten-and-a-half-hour day at another plant which was interested in welfare work, eleven hours at the third, and eleven and a half at the fourth.[24] A paper manufacturer, who subscribed to the need of taking "the best care of the help," said that "of course, each set of hands works

[19] *Ibid.*, Vol. 4, pp. 532-533.
[20] *Ibid.*, Vol. 4, pp. 748-752.
[21] *Ibid.*, Vol. 3, p. 230.
[22] *Ibid.*, Vol. 2, p. 1152.
[23] This mill was cited in the survey made by Massachusetts in 1881. *Cf. supra*, p. 228.
[24] U. S. Senate Committee, *op. cit.*, Vol. 3, pp. 671-675.

twelve hours."[25] The eleven-hour day was most commonly reported, and the possibility of decreasing it by voluntary action seemed slight when many employers testified that "as far as they knew" labor did not want any reduction.

1900-1915

In 1901 the report of the Industrial Commission was published. This body had been appointed by Congress to investigate many subjects, among which the question of the relations between labor and capital was important. The tendency of employers to reduce hours voluntarily had not increased in the fifteen years that had elapsed between this investigation and that referred to in the previous section: this survey brought to light one more example. William C. Redfield, Treasurer of the J. H. Williams Company, manufacturers of steel products, reported that on March 1, 1901, this firm "voluntarily and unasked," changed the hours from ten to nine per day, with no reduction of pay.[26] Perhaps the announced intention of the International Machinists' Union on May 20, 1900, to establish the nine-hour day as of May 1, 1901, and its continued negotiations to this end, exerted an indirect pressure on the policy of the Williams Company.[27] Mr. Redfield, however, denied any outside influence, stating that the firm employed relatively few machinists. Moreover, his exposition of the labor policy of the firm was convincing proof of a continuous endeavor to establish good conditions "not as charity, but as matters of justice, as privileges, and as sources of profit." He reported that the reduction of hours had been accompanied not only by

[25] *Ibid.*, Vol. 3, p. 380.
[26] U. S. Industrial Commission, 1901, *op. cit.*, Vol. 14, p. 659.
[27] *American Federationist*, 1901, Vol. 8, p. 200.

an increased rate of hourly output, but also by a slightly larger average daily output "though in every respect the work was done under similar conditions." He attributed the increased daily output to the pride and interest of the workers, who were anxious to prove the nine-hour day an economic success.

Quite the contrary to Mr. Redfield's testimony of the actual effect of decreased hours was the conclusion, based not on actual experience but on theory, of Mr. Frank Cheney, of the progressive Cheney Silk Mills. He held that in any industry where "machinery comes in as a heavy element," any reduction in hours would necessarily decrease output. It is surprising considering the liberal labor policy of this firm that the theory was accepted without further test, and lends color to the probability that the lack of examples of voluntary reduction of hours is the result not of a failure to give testimony, but of the rarity of such action.[28]

Benevolent employers have always existed. With the growth of unions and larger-scale strikes in the closing decades of the nineteenth century, their number and efforts increased. While witnesses testifying before the Industrial Commission had referred to this tendency, a monograph "Industrial Betterment," prepared for the Paris Exposition in 1900, presented details of this movement in more concise form. The work was explained as "a study of what employers are doing to improve the conditions of their operatives," [29] and the author's thesis was that capital

[28] U. S. Industrial Commission, 1901, *op. cit.*, Vol. 14, p. 733. This firm, which had been a pioneer in hours' reduction, from this time remained outside the movement, not adopting the forty-eight hour week until "about August, 1927." *Industrial Activities at Cheney Bros.*, prepared by the National Industrial Conference Board.

[29] Tolman, W. H., *Industrial Betterment*, New York, 1900, p. 4.

had recognized its responsibility to improve labor's working conditions. Not one example of a reduction in hours to attain this end is cited. This omission by an author, chosen to present to the world an exposition of industrial relations of liberal companies in the United States, showed either that he was unfitted for the work, or that the earnestness of labor's long continued demands for the shorter day had not impressed him or employers as a feasible demand of any real importance.

"Betterment of Industrial Conditions," published in the Bulletin of the United States Department of Labor in 1900 yields so little evidence of voluntary reduction of hours that it, too, helps prove that employers did not seriously consider this a means of improving industrial relations. The author stated that the purpose of the pamphlet was to study plans looking "to industrial improvement and the elevation of working men," and summarized these various measures for improvements under fifteen heads.[30] It is significant that reduction of hours was not one of these, despite the fact that it was one of the two major demands of labor. His report of individual companies' policies, however, gave information on reduction of hours by the National Cash Register Company of Dayton, Ohio, and by Fels & Company, the soap manufacturers of Philadelphia. The former had in force an eight-hour day for women, and a nine-and-a-half-hour day for men.[31] This inauguration of the eight-hour day for women is a noteworthy example of voluntary action long in advance of its establishment by law even in the most liberal States. On the other hand, it was proven that the nine-and-a-half-hour day for men was an unsatisfactory concession when the

[30] U. S. *Bulletin of the Dept. of Labor*, Nov. 1900, pp. 1117, 1118.
[31] *Ibid.*, p. 1132.

VOLUNTARY ACTION OF EMPLOYERS

machinists of the concern struck in the general nine-hour demand of this trade in 1901.[32] Fels & Company, according to the author, aimed to keep working hours in their plant less than those prevailing in other industries.[33] His only additional reference to hours throws a most interesting sidelight on the attitude of employers. The Kennard Manufacturing Company, of Dayton, Ohio, reported that " during the summer of 1898 considerable trouble was encountered on account of sudden illness and fainting spells among the women, as many as seven or eight a day being frequently compelled to quit work." When physicians investigated the cause, they suggested rest periods. The firm " promptly " gave the female employees a fifteen minutes' morning and afternoon recess to be devoted to a calisthenics club, for which they generously supplied " a competent instructor." [34] Failure to mention the hours in this plant is indirect evidence that they were the accepted schedule for women of ten or eleven a day. The remedy—a calisthenics club—can be added to the mounting proof that voluntary reduction of hours was a unique action.

Interest in the question of the relations of the employer and employee led to a symposium on this subject in the Hearst papers, which was initiated and directed by the Episcopal Church of New York in the fall of 1901. The results were later published in book form. Such evidence on hours as this produced was meagre and negative. Aside from the example of Nelson & Company of St. Louis, which reported: "Our different trades are all unionized, union wages prevail, and we have a nine-hour

[32] U. S. Industrial Commission, 1901, *op. cit.*, Vol. 14, p. 729.
[33] U. S. *Bulletin of the Dept. of Labor*, Nov., 1900, p. 1154.
[34] *Ibid.*, p. 1133.

day in ten-hour trades," [35] — the only contribution of this publication to the question was the statement of a settlement worker that only well-organized trades had succeeded in establishing shorter hours.[36]

Tolman's "Social Engineering," published in 1909—the title showed the trend which later developed a new profession—was written after fifteen years' study of the numerous and varied efforts to promote better relations between capital and labor. Again it must be pointed out, as evidence of lack of voluntary reduction, that this work reported only one such incident: a pen manufacturer, employing 175 laborers, had reduced his hours from ten to eight a day.[37] Yet this book devoted a lengthy chapter to detailing the efforts of employers to improve the health of their workers.

An examination of "Human Engineering," the short-lived monthly which was described as "a magazine for Employers and Employees, published to provide a means of exchanging experiences on the human side of industry, and a forum for the discussion of the conservation of human energy," confirms the evidence so far adduced, that not only did employers fail voluntarily to reduce hours, but that they did not give the matter serious consideration. In its four issues in 1911, this magazine gave only one instance of the establishment, voluntarily or otherwise, of a shorter day. In the January number, an executive of the Carhartt Clothing Company, of Detroit, which had 700 women employees, recounted the successful experience of his firm in reducing hours from ten to eight. He stated: "The output of the eight-hour day not only equaled but exceeded

[35] Symposium: *Labor and Capital*, New York, 1902, p. 351.
supra, p. ——.
[36] *Ibid.*, p. 55.
[37] Tolman, W. H., *Social Engineering*, New York, 1909, p. 8.

that of the former ten-hour day," and "our working force is more efficient, loyal and stable than before." [38]

The two further references in the same magazine to shorter hours were made not by employers but by economists. Miss Josephine Goldmark, who had a well-established reputation as an expert on fatigue and the length of the workday, put the seal of authoritative approval on labor's demand by saying: "In the lives of working people no single factor counts so much for good or ill as the length and regularity of their working hours." [39] Professor Irving Fisher's article on "Industrial Hygiene as a Factor in Human Efficiency," stressed the need for shorter hours of labor to conserve our vital resources.[40] That his examples of the value and success of such reduction are all drawn from Europe may be taken as further proof that the movement for voluntarily establishing a shorter day was non-existent in the United States on any scale worthy of mention. The three cases which he cited, the gradual reduction from eleven to seven and a half hours a day at the Engis Chemical Works, of Liege, Belgium, the introduction of the eight-hour day in 1893 at the Salford Iron Works, of Manchester, England, and in 1899 at the Zeiss Plant, of Jena, Germany, might well be called the classic examples used by all the intellectual exponents of the movement in the United States: none fails to mention them.

Besides the examples yielded by publications dealing directly with the relations of labor and capital, other material used in this study brought to light a few additional

[38] *Human Engineering*, Cleveland, 1911, Vol. 1, No. 1, p. 21.
[39] *Ibid*, Vol. 1, No. 3, p. 150.
[40] *Ibid.*, Vol. 1, No. 4, p. 254.

instances.[41] These seem, to the writer, to be of sufficient importance to be given in detail for two reasons. First, because they show what employers had done, and insofar as possible what had led to the change, and what were the results. This is most important when it is borne in mind that to every trade union demand, and at every legislative hearing on hours, employers attested faith in reduction of hours, provided only it came by "natural evolution." And second, because the cases listed may suggest a basis for further research in this field.

In the first place, there were some outstanding examples in continuous industries which are of especial interest because of the long drawn-out struggle to change from the two-shift system in steel manufacturing. In 1892 the Solvay Process Company, of Syracuse, New York, decided that the two-shift system with eleven hours of day, and thirteen hours of night work, was uneconomical to the corporation and to the men. They changed to three shifts of eight hours each. Within two years the firm reported that the cost of production "was less than it was before the eight-hour change was made."[42] The leading Minneapolis flour mills made the same change in 1902 and 1903. Although they reported the success of the three-shift system, it was not until 1918 that the smaller mills adopted the shorter hours.[43] One of the leading cereal manufacturers

[41] See bibliography.

[42] Frankfurter, Felix, *The Case for the Shorter Working Day*, New York, Vol. 2, pp. 701-703.

[43] Committee on Work Periods in Continuous Industry of the Federated American Engineering Societies, *The Twelve-Hour Shift in Industry*, New York, 1922, p. 152. This conflicts with Mr. S. Thurston Ballard's statement in the *American Labor Legislation Review*, June, 1914, that he thought his mill, which had adopted the three-shift schedule in 1907, was still the only one on this schedule in the flour business in 1914.

of Battle Creek, Michigan, changed in 1910 to three shifts on the understanding that the cost of production was not to be increased. This condition was fulfilled.[44] The Purington Paving Brick Company, at Galesburg, Illinois, one of the largest industries of this kind in the world, changed from a ten to an eight-hour day for all workers, except the burners, in 1913. The following year, due to discontent among the workers, the company "decided to make the change ourselves before it was forced on us by our burners," and found it most successful.[45] These examples, however, were the exceptions. On the whole, it was not until the war that most continuous industries in non-unionized fields [46] or outside of the West, where several States had passed laws for smelters, changed from the two-shift system to the shorter working-day.

Besides these additional examples in continuous industries, the available material yielded a few more cases of voluntary reduction in non-continuous industries. None of them were sufficiently noteworthy to have been substituted for the classic European examples. The Armour Fertilizer Works on the Pacific Coast adopted between 1901 and 1905 first a nine and then an eight-hour schedule, and found that it did not increase costs.[47] The New Jersey Bureau of Statistics of Labor adduced as proof of the increased efficiency of shorter hours the case of a Boston shoe factory with 3,000 employees, which had successfully

[44] *Ibid.*, p. 160.

[45] *Ibid.*, pp. 109, 110.

[46] It must be pointed out that not all unions insisted on the eight-hour day in continuous trades. It was stated in 1922 that despite thorough unionization of the pottery industry, "according to the employers no complaints are made by the men or the unions regarding the twelve-hour work." *Ibid.*, p. 112.

[47] *American Federationist*, 1916, Vol. 23, p. 959.

reduced hours in 1898, reasoning that "an active nine-hour day would be superior to a more or less inactive ten-hour day."[48] The *Philadelphia Post* in an editorial commented on the "cultivation of the spirit of amity" when it reported in 1901 the voluntary reduction to eight hours inaugurated by a shoe manufacturing concern which employed 2,000 workers.[49] In 1903 the announcement was made of the adoption of the nine-hour day by the International Time Recording Company.[50] In 1910 the National Association of Lithographers, which had a few years earlier defeated the unions, by a small majority, voted to establish the eight-hour day. To get this favorable vote, the Association had carried on for two years an active educational campaign among the employers. The Association stated that they accepted the shorter-hour schedule not through fear but to make conditions so satisfactory that the men would not turn to the unions.[51] Wm. J. Crawford & Company, of Buffalo, experimented with reducing hours from ten to nine and finally to eight in 1912,[52] and reported that the individual laborer in their granite works produced more in the eight than in the ten-hour day. The same year the Commonwealth Steel Company changed from the twelve to the eight-hour day, increasing wages to compensate in part for

[48] New Jersey Bureau of Statistics of Labor and Industries, *Twenty-eighth Annual Report,* 1905, pp. 226, 227.

[49] *Philadelphia Post,* Oct. 11, 1901.

[50] *New York Times,* Sept. 30, 1903.

[51] *New York Times,* May 5, 1910. This appears to be a fairly clear case of voluntary action forced by indirect pressure, as the closely allied International Typographical Union had established an eight-hour day in 1907. Cf. *supra,* p. 180.

[52] The Granite Workers' Union had established nationally the eight-hour day in 1900. *American Federationist,* 1900, Vol. 7, p. 272.

VOLUNTARY ACTION OF EMPLOYERS 241

the change. Despite this added expense, the shorter shift proved more economical because of the increased efficiency of the workers.[53] And in January, 1914, as "an entirely voluntary act" and one "of social justice," Henry Ford reduced the hours in his plant from nine to eight a day.[54] The satisfactory results to which each of these firms testified failed to cause any sweeping movement among employers for the voluntary reduction of hours, despite their expressed faith in "natural evolution" toward this end.

THE WAR PERIOD TO THE PRESENT

It was to be expected that employers would decrease hours during the war and immediately following it. For example, when the Victor Talking Machine Company, of Camden, New Jersey, reported the voluntary inauguration of the eight-hour day in September, 1915,[55] it failed to mention the sweeping success of the eight-hour campaign of the International Machinists' Union throughout the country in that year. In this period in which the trade unions were making tremendous gains in obtaining shorter hours, action of this kind had to take place if only as a preventive measure. The field is too comprehensive to attempt an unchartered survey, but since at this time, most of the liberal-minded firms—and some not so liberal—organized works' councils, attention may be concentrated on them in order to compare the result of voluntary reduction with that obtained through trade-union action.

"Works' council" is used as an inclusive term for all forms of employee representation, such as company unions,

[53] Lauck, W. S., and Watts, C. S., *The Industrial Code*, New York, 1922, p. 154.
[54] Ford, Henry, in collaboration with Samuel Crowther, *My Life and Work*, Garden City, 1923, p. 126.
[55] *Survey*, April 1, 1916.

shop committees, industrial democracies, etc., by means of which the management and the employees of any organization discussed, and in some cases settled, the conditions of employment. Prior to 1917, there were only twelve of these organizations. But when war conditions, which strengthened organized labor's bargaining power, forced some concession to the unorganized, the growth of works' councils was widespread and rapid, so that by 1919 it was estimated that there were 225 covering 391,490 employees, and by 1922 the number was placed at 725 covering 690,-000 employees.[56] While a few might question the voluntary nature of reduction of hours by this means, the fact that employees so organized have not ordinarily sufficient strength to enforce their demands, supplemented by the fact that these councils are set in operation on the employer's initiative, and continue to exist through his will, would seem to make them a valid source of material for voluntary action in the sense in which the term is here used.

Presentation of three plans will indicate how this method worked, and what standard of hours was adopted. The Packard Piano Company, of Fort Wayne, Indiana, almost rivals the Zeiss Optical Works as a classic example of the successful results of voluntary reduction of hours, although the schedule adopted was no shorter than that which the German plant had successfully inaugurated two decades earlier. Prior to the establishment of a works' council by the President of this concern, production had been unsatisfactory both in quality and quantity. Soon after its inauguration, the council after some discussion voted to decrease hours from ten to nine a day. After a temporary drop,

[56] National Industrial Conference Board, *The Growth of Works' Councils in the United States,* New York, 1925, p. 12.

production and earnings increased, with the result that several months later a resolution was passed establishing the eight-hour day and a half-day Saturday as a two-month experiment. It proved eminently satisfactory, the resulting increase of production leading to a 16% decline in the cost of production.[57]

The works' council of the American Multigraph Company, of Cleveland, Ohio, succeeded in making remarkable adjustments of hours in the war and post-war period. This plant's council was organized on the model of the United States Government with cabinet and two houses of congress, which did much of their work through committees. The cabinet was composed of senior executives, appointed by the President. The senate—which was later dropped—was made up of supervisors and minor executives, and the lower house of employees elected at large. The initiation of hours' reduction can best be told by a quotation from a Company publication: "When the Special Eight-Hour Committee undertook to reduce the working hours of this plant (we were then a ten-hour shop), it was confronted with the biggest problem of the day—reduction in hours with increase in production was the undertaking. A detailed analysis was made of the situation, the committee investigated production methods from all angles. This included sources of supply, production control, machine production, assembling and distribution. After the management had accepted suggestions from this Committee as to production improvement—production quotas were set for a monthly output in the belief that as much work could be performed in nine hours as was being done in ten, and at less expense—the employees produced the required quotas. As soon as quotas were made, the Senate voted that

[57] Leitch, J., *Man to Man*, New York, 1919, pp. 45-48.

the plant accept the congress's recommendation that a nine-hour working-day be initiated as a basis of determining the possibilities of a future eight-hour day. This was done, with the same daily wage applying as was received for the ten-hour working-day. With this change in hours came increased production at less expense." [58]

Later, the hours were reduced to forty-four and a half by the same method. As the executives of the plant pointed out, the real test of this cooperative machinery for adjusting hours came in the depression of 1921, when the question of hours was no longer one of establishing a shorter standard day, but of spreading work with necessarily decreased earnings per worker. The congress first reduced working time to a five-day week of forty hours, and later, after a conference with the cabinet, and an investigation of the state of the business, put into effect a three-day week with no change in hourly rates. At the cabinet's recommendation, the congress later re-established the forty-four-and-a-half-hour week with a 20% cut in wages, because the three-day week was economically wasteful to the Company and to the employees.[59] From the available material it is difficult to determine whether the employees were jockeyed into the position of peacefully accepting a 20% wage cut for the same number of hours by the device of first establishing a three-day week: certainly, this is a possible interpretation of the facts.

In spite of the fact that the adoption of shorter hours by the Minnequa Steel Works of the Colorado Fuel & Iron Company was not brought about with the absolute peace

[58] Miller, E. J., *Workmen's Representation in Industrial Government*, Urbana, 1924, quoted p. 119; American Management Association, *Production Executives' Series No. 5*, 1925, pp. 42-53.
[59] Miller, *op. cit.*, pp. 124, 125.

VOLUNTARY ACTION OF EMPLOYERS 245

that prevailed in the American Multigraph Company's negotiations, yet—in the light of the history of hours' reduction in the steel industry [60] — the inauguration of the eight-hour day in the Colorado plant was indeed peaceful. The works' council, established in 1916, provided for joint conferences at which employers and employees were equally represented, held at stated periods, to "discuss freely such matters of mutual interest as the promotion of increased efficiency and production, improvement of working and living conditions, etc." Between conferences it was provided that four joint committees should function: one of these, the Joint Committee on Industrial Cooperation and Conciliation had the power to take up and report to the President " any matter pertaining to the prevention and settlement of industrial disputes, terms and conditions of employment, etc." [61] Although this machinery was provided, when the eight-hour question became a major problem, it was not used.

Simultaneously with the adoption of the plan, employer and employee signed a memorandum of agreement which established certain conditions of work. The clause dealing with hours, which were then twelve a day, provided: "The present hours of labor of employees of the several sub-divisions shall not be increased, and shall not at any time be less favorable to the employees than the hours of labor in similar operations conducted by the Company's competitors." [62] The workers were reported as keenly desiring the eight-hour day. At the joint conference held in January, 1917, a workers' representative delivered an earnest address, setting forth the arguments in favor of its

[60] *Cf. supra*, pp. 206-216.
[61] Selekman, B. M., *Employees' Representation in Steel Works*, New York, 1924, pp. 57, 58.
[62] *Ibid.*, quoted, p. 64.

inauguration. His courage was great; not very surprisingly none of the other representatives supported his request, despite their own feelings and those of their constituents. The management replied that no action could be taken until the United States Steel Corporation had introduced the shorter day. When in 1918, the latter Corporation established the basic eight-hour day with time and a half for overtime, the same terms were offered by the Minnequa Steel Works to the employees' representatives.

Dissatisfaction with this offer was brought to a head immediately when the mechanics succeeded in negotiating a straight eight-hour day with a 10% increase in wages. The rest of the plant voted for the establishment of the straight eight-hour day. The officials were opposed, and attempted to swing the workers' opinion by posting wage schedules illustrating the higher earnings which the basic eight-hour day would yield. Thereupon some employees struck, and others quit work at the end of eight hours. After the President had conferred with the various representatives, and found them unanimous in their opinion, he announced that the straight eight-hour day with a 10% increase in hourly rates would be inaugurated as of November 3, 1918. Although the change brought a considerable decrease in weekly earnings to the workers, they were enthusiastic in its support, voting each year to continue this schedule, and they praised the management for taking the initiative in reducing the hours in the steel industry, and the machinery of representation which had made it possible. The management, for its part, found the shorter hours eminently satisfactory. Five years after the change to the eight-hour shift, the President wrote: "The trend of production per man-hour, with unimportant exceptions, has been upward since the adoption of the eight-hour day, . . . almost without exception our labor cost per

VOLUNTARY ACTION OF EMPLOYERS   247

ton is lower than in the earlier periods." [63] This successful experience with the three-shift system was used in the long fight against the Steel Corporation's twelve-hour stand to cast effective doubt on their exaggerated estimates of increased costs. For this reason, if for no other, this is a noteworthy example of voluntary reduction of hours.

Mr. E. J. Miller, in his investigation of one hundred works' council plans, concluded that seventy-five of them made provision for conference on hours.[64] This provision showed an awareness of the importance of the question, but neither this compilation, nor many others of like nature, yield any outstanding examples of reduction of hours by this method.[65] It can only be said that the best of the works' councils established the standard which the most successful unions were inaugurating at the time: whether this standard would have been inaugurated, if the unions had not led the way, is a question on which differences of opinion will continue to exist.

While these three cases show the operation of this machinery in the reduction of the standard day in isolated plants, material covering a broader field is needed to establish the employers' attitude on hours at this time. From this attitude the possibility of the existence of a general movement for voluntary reduction of hours can be de-

---

[63] *Ibid.*, pp. 77-89.

[64] Miller, *op. cit.*, p. 110.

[65] Examples of hours' situation in plants with works' councils: Dennison and Co.—48 per week. *Rule Book*, dated 1921; Leeds and Northrup —basic 44-hour week. *Rule Book*, dated Jan., 1921; National Cash Register Co.—Men, 54 per week, time and a half in excess of 48 hours; Women, 43 per week. *Rule Book*, dated May 15, 1920; Fayette R. Plumb, Men, 51 per week, Women, 49½ per week. *Rule Book*, dated May 15, 1920; Westinghouse Elec. and Mfg. Co.—52 per week, night turn, 55 per week, time and a half pay in excess of 52 hours. *Rule Book*, dated 1919.

duced. That so staunch an individualist as Henry Ford advocated a federal law to make eight hours the national work-day, offers evidence that he saw small chance of any widespread establishment if left to individual employers.[66] If further proof of this were needed, it was offered by the statement of the President of the National Founders Association at their 1917 convention, and again at that of 1918, denouncing the eight-hour day, and insisting that it would have to be abolished.[67]

Still more evidence is found in the publications of the National Industrial Conference Board, which is supported by its members, who are, for the most part, manufacturers and manufacturers' associations. These publications serve two functions: first, they express the consensus of opinion of the membership; and second, they help to mold the opinion of manufacturers in general, by establishing a basis on which to form judgments. Their research into the subject of hours produced conclusions distinctly unfavorable to reduction to even that basis which labor had been demanding since the Civil War. An investigation of the shoe industry concluded that, under the given operating conditions, maximum efficiency was impossible under less than a fifty-two-hour week.[68] Reports on the wool and silk industries fixed the point of maximum output for silk factories between fifty and fifty-four hours a week;[69] for wool plants, while admitting that reduction in hours with increase in output might be expected in large plants, it was stated that reduction to a fifty-four-hour schedule

[66] *New York Times*, Oct. 7, 1916.
[67] *Ibid.*, Nov. 25, 1917, Nov. 17, 1918.
[68] National Industrial Conference Board, *Research Report Number 7*, Boston, 1918, pp. 50-52.
[69] *Research Report Number 16*, Boston, 1919, pp. 37, 38.

VOLUNTARY ACTION OF EMPLOYERS 249

involved a loss of output in the majority of cases.[70] Investigation of cotton manufacturing industries led to the same unfavorable conclusion that reduction from fifty-eight or fifty-six to fifty-five or fifty-four hours a week had, in the great majority of cases, been followed by a decreased output.[71] Conclusions on an investigation of the metal manufacturing industry, were neither so definite nor so unfavorable. It was admitted that the forty-eight-hour week had proved to be practicable in a considerable number of plants, but that there was no clear-cut line below which reduction in hours led to a uniform change in efficiency.[72]

The next year, in 1920, the Board undertook an investigation of plants which had established a forty-eight-hour week. The survey covered 436 plants, employing 373,536 workers; its findings were that, in 87.2% of the establishments, reduction to a forty-eight-hour schedule was followed by a decrease in weekly output, in 8.7% the output was maintained, in 4.1% it was increased. While admitting that it had been impossible to secure information warranting valid conclusions regarding the effect of shorter hours upon the workers' health, the Board ventured the negative statement that "in most cases no change in the health of the workers was reported." [73]

The attitude of the National Association of Manufacturers confirmed the unpromising view of the National Industrial Conference Board on the hours' question, making the possibility of any voluntary reduction by employers

[70] *Research Report Number 12*, Boston, 1918, pp. 44-46.
[71] *Research Report Number 4*, Boston, 1918, pp. 43, 44.
[72] *Research Report Number 18*, Boston, 1919, pp. 25-29.
[73] *Research Report Number 32*, New York, 1920, pp. 7, 8. Otto Lippman, in an article, "Hours of Work and Output," in the *International Labor Review*, says that existing data on this question in Europe as well as the United States is scientifically unsatisfactory. 1924, p. 481.

seem most unlikely. Many statements at their 1920 conference indicated a thinly veiled hostility to decreased hours. For example: "There is such a thing as an economic day, the hours of which you cannot reduce, . . . We seem to be moving in an endless cycle, increasing the wage and shortening hours, which necessarily increases the cost of commodities which labor, as well as the general public, must meet. . . . Labor and capitalists both realize that there is danger in its continuance, that all should unite in creating a restraining influence." [74]

Final proof that American employers opposed any reduction of hours is afforded by the vote on the referendum which the United States Chamber of Commerce sent to its members in June, 1920. The Committee on Industrial Relations prepared a statement of general labor policy, including a section on hours, on which a separate vote was taken. This recommended a careful study of the number of hours which would yield maximum output, but warned that any reduction below this point would involve loss on earnings, shortage of output and increase in cost, which would harm the "interests of the community and the nation." [75] The Committee also presented the opposite view of the case. This was the Steward-Ford philosophy [76] that society would suffer if workers were not given sufficient leisure to function as consumers. The vote left not the faintest shadow of a doubt that American employers in 1921 rejected this philosophy. It stood 1,676 votes

[74] National Association of Manufacturers of the United States of America, *Proceedings of the Twenty-fifth Annual Convention,* 1920, p. 261.

[75] *Cf. supra,* pp. 16, 17.

[76] U. S. Chamber of Commerce, *Referendum Number 31.*

for the Committee's recommendations, 3 for the negative view.[77]

Symposiums on business management, written by and with the advice of some of the recognized liberals among employers, presented the same unfavorable attitude. Take, for instance, two quotations from "Working Conditions, Wages and Profits." Sharp divergence on the question of what constituted desirable hours was shown by the complacent citation of the wool industry in which "90% of the concerns investigated work on a weekly schedule of from fifty-four to fifty-six hours," in proof of the contention that long hours were becoming rare. It must be remembered that the statement was made at a time when the war had supposedly established beyond all question the eight-hour day as the standard, and when organized labor was successfully negotiating the forty-four-hour week. Difference in viewpoint as to what labor really wanted was shown by the following interpretation of industrial unrest: "If the whole truth were known, it is probable that the basis of a good deal of the agitation for shorter hours is merely a symptom of lack of interest in the work on the part of the employees. . . . The agitation for shorter hours would seem to be a severe indictment of management, on the grounds of not making work interesting."[78] If this analysis sincerely represented the employers' understanding of the situation, voluntary reduction of hours was not to be expected.

That the employers had not changed their fundamental

[77] U. S. Chamber of Commerce, *Ninth Annual Report*, 1921, p. 53. N. B. Since voting membership is limited to local chambers of commerce and associations, this vote was far more representative of general opinion than the numbers show.

[78] Price, C. W., and others, *Working Conditions, Wages and Profits*, Chicago, 1920, pp. 14, 13.

position of prejudice and fear of any reduction of hours, despite the tremendous gain in productive capacity per worker,[79] was clearly evidenced by the outburst of criticism which greeted Henry Ford's announcement in 1926 of the voluntary adoption of the five-day week. Ford claimed he was taking the initiative in a movement which had to become widespread if mass production was to continue to find a market. He pointed out that high wages had to be accompanied by increased leisure in order to make of the workers the mass consumers that our methods of production required. Employers in denouncing this change ran through the whole gamut of arguments, that the first suggestion to reduce hours had provoked. Any hope that the competitive economic system would produce employers capable of approaching the subject, free from unreasoning prejudice and fear, immediately collapsed. In the first place every effort was made to belittle Ford's change, by insisting that it was caused by insufficient work to keep the plant running six days a week. The National Founders Association denounced the shorter week as uneconomic for employer, employee and consumer, because it would decrease production, and increase the cost of living.[80] Mr. Emery, President of the National Industrial Council, representing about 75,000 employers, criticized Ford's change on identical grounds. Yet, in the same interview, he held the five-day-week platform, which the American Federation had just adopted, most unwise because, if the change were made,

---

[79] " The volume of output for each worker engaged directly in production has, during the same period (1879-1925) increased by 76%. The increase was not an even one over the whole of the period, since output per worker increased 18% in both the first and second decades, and 27% in the six years from 1919 to 1925." *Recent Economic Changes*, Vol. 2, p. 451.

[80] *New York Times*, Oct. 12, 1926.

it should be done voluntarily.[81] The National Association of Manufacturers opposed the five-day week for the very reason that Ford had advanced, stating "it would create a craving for additional luxuries to occupy the additional time."[82] The conference of the National Association of Building Trades' Employers based their opposition on a prediction not only of increased costs of production, but also of an artificial labor shortage.[83] To put the final veto on this new standard of hours Gary quoted the commandment: "Six days shalt thou labor, and do all thy work," and added "The reason it didn't say seven days is that the seventh is a day of rest."[84] Unfortunately for the steel workers this biblical exhortation had escaped his memory when he declared it impossible to eliminate the seven-day week in that industry.

Religion has been one of the forces at work in the establishment of the five-day week. The first voluntary establishment that research has revealed was in a textile mill, with a majority of Jewish employees, owned by an orthodox Jew.[85] One of the first firms to adopt Ford's plan was a manufacturer of matzoths in New York. When this occurred, the President of the Jewish Sabbath Alliance said that he expected a large number of other Jewish business houses to do likewise in the near future.[86] Leaders of Jewish thought have combined to give publicity to the movement, and to cooperate in every way to aid in its establishment.[87]

[81] *Ibid.*, Oct. 16, 1926.
[82] *Ibid.*, Oct. 21, 1926.
[83] *Ibid.*, Dec. 28, 1926.
[84] *Ibid.*, Oct. 17, 1926.
[85] National Industrial Conference Board, *The Five Day Week in Manufacturing Industries,* New York, 1929, p. 17.
[86] *New York Times,* Oct. 28, 1926.
[87] The five-day week was urged at the United Synagogue convention. *New York Times,* Feb. 3, 1920.

It is doubtful if Ford's voluntary introduction of the five-day week led any considerable number of employers to follow suit prior to the depression of 1929. From time to time, the newspapers reported employers who had introduced the change, but a survey by the United States Bureau of Labor Statistics in 1929 showed that its greatest growth had occurred in certain highly-organized trades, with the exception of the automobile industry, which was accounted for, of course, by the change at the Ford plant.[88] Likewise, an investigation of 270 five-day-week plants by the National Industrial Conference Board brought out the fact that 57.3% of these were closed union shops, suggesting that organized labor had played an important part in bringing about its adoption. The same survey, however, pointed out that on the basis of relative size, as measured by the number of workers affected, voluntary action of employers was the more important factor in introducing the new schedule. The final conclusion of this investigation, which said that the evidence removed the five-day week "from the status of a radical and administrative experiment,"[89] was far more likely to influence employers to make the change voluntarily than the unfounded statement of the President of the National Association of Manufacturers, made in the same year, that increased leisure bred radicalism, adding the indictment: "It cannot be a mere coincidence that America is at the same time the most leisure possessed and the most crime infested nation on earth." Despite his fear of the evil social effects of more leisure, he illogically conceded the five-day week as a future possibility, provided it was the result of a "natural evolutionary process."[90] Since this organization

[88] U. S. Dept. of Labor, *Monthly Labor Review*, June, 1929, pp. 1181-1190.

[89] *Five Day Week in Manufacturing Industries*, pp. 22-24, 66.

[90] National Association of Manufacturers, *Proceedings of the Thirty-fourth Annual Convention*, 1929, p. 23, 24.

had denounced Ford for introducing the shorter week, was a consistent opponent of trade unions, and maintained lobbyists to prevent shorter-hour legislation, it is pertinent to wonder what was this natural evolutionary process to which employers constantly referred, but never defined.

From the beginning of the depression in the fall of 1929, the question of hours' reduction has been prominent. In the early stages, the five-day-week movement gained momentum: additional firms adopted it, putting in practice at a late date the American philosophy of prosperity, high wages and short hours. But when changes such as this did not restore prosperity, this philosophy was discarded, and with the introduction of wage cuts the work-week was successively shortened, not to establish a new standard of hours, but as a device to spread work. Such reduction by employers had occurred in earlier depressions, and had left no mark on the real movement toward the establishment of a shorter work-week.

Voluntary adoption by some employers of the six-hour day, which is also a product of the depression, offers greater promise of exerting a real influence on the shorter-hour movement. Its most enthusiastic exponent is Mr. Lewis J. Brown, President of the Kellogg Company, of Battle Creek, Michigan, who introduced it on December 1, 1930, to relieve unemployment, but after six months' experience he reported such success that he intended to make it a permanent policy. The plan was inaugurated after a series of meetings with the various managers and employees of the plant, at which it was discussed in detail: later meetings were held, at which all the groups agreed that it was feasible. When the four-shift six-hour schedule was inaugurated, the minimum wage of $4.00 a day was kept. Those who had been earning more received an increase of $12\frac{1}{2}\%$, the object being to establish the same purchasing power as the eight-hour day had yielded in 1928. As specific advantages to the Company, Mr. Brown reported an increase in daily output, a decrease in overhead due to the increase in packages of cereal per dollar of overhead, and a further saving through the elimination of meal periods, which had necessitated the maintenance of the cafeteria. The advantages that he had observed for the employees were a gain in health and ambition due to less fatigue, the cultivation of gardens and in some cases of farms, and a decrease in the cost of living due to the fact that they could take all of their meals at home. Mr. Brown urged the spread of the six-hour day for the same reason that Ford had advocated the five-day week, that is, as a means of increasing the consumption of goods, adding that the shorter day through making jobs more secure would encourage labor to spend instead of saving for the future.[91]

In the fall of 1931, the Manufacturing Chemists Association sponsored a six-hour-day movement in that field, with the result that many big companies introduced it. The Association stated that, though it was adopted at the time as a means of spreading work among the greatest possible number of wage earners, it might become a permanent policy.[92] The Hearst newspapers thereupon began a very active campaign of propaganda for the six-hour day, predicating its need, first, as a remedy for unemployment, and second, as the only means of sustaining an adequate home market. They emphasized the need for business leaders not limited by routine minds, and urged public utilities and manufacturers of foodstuffs, industries in which operation had remained relatively stable, to assume this role.[93] The explanation of the failure of the movement to gain disciples may be

[91] Brown, L. J., *What of the Six Hour Day*, Pamphlet, 1931.
[92] *Journal of Commerce*, New York, Oct. 2, 1931.
[93] *New York Evening Journal* and other Hearst papers, Oct., 1931.

that the Hearst circulation was predominantly among that part of the population which could support the movement by its wishes, not by action. On the other hand, as the history of the hours' movement would suggest, it may be that leaders of the employing class were not yet ready for so radical a step, so long as some of their members continued to think the ten or eleven-hour day an economic necessity. The year 1932, however, has produced a convert to the six-hour day as a means of reducing unemployment. The Goodyear Tire & Rubber Company, after testing many plans, adopted it because it provided work for 3,000 additional employees, and urged its general adoption as a means of putting millions of men to work.[94] If this leadership were followed, a good opportunity might be offered for testing out the diametrically opposed arguments of labor, on the one hand, that shorter hours would be a means to decrease unemployment, and of employers, supported by the deductive logic of economists, on the other, that unless accompanied by lower weekly wages reducing the hours of labor could have no effect on this condition, thereby removing the question from the plane of *a priori* reasoning to that of actual conditions.

The elastic work-day is another device to which the depression has brought an amount of attention which may cause it to become a permanent development, and so influence the hours' movement. The Delaware & Hudson Railroad Company, in 1922, inaugurated an understanding with their workers that no discharges would occur until hours had decreased to forty-eight per week, and that no additional men would be employed until hours had exceeded sixty per week.[95] The purpose of this elastic work-day

---

[94] *American Labor World*, March, 1932.
[95] *New York Evening World*, Sept. 2, 1925.

is to eliminate unemployment by considering this problem from the point of view of the individual plant, not from that of the economic system as a whole. The procedure is typical of the individualist approach of the American entrepreneur. The New York Commission on Unemployment Problems reported a number of firms which had adopted this elastic work-day.[96] The use of this device might tend, in the short run, to militate against a reduction of hours as an attempt to spread work: in the long run, it would apparently leave the forces fixing the limits to the work-day the same as they have always been.

While these experiments are of interest and importance as methods of meeting the problem of cyclical unemployment which the depression has created, their significance in the long run course of the hours' movement cannot, as yet, be estimated. The review of pioneer action of employers in this chapter shows that this voluntary means of reduction of hours has covered a smaller proportion of the wage earners than either trade-union or legislative action. That this situation is not likely to change in the near future is shown in the report of the United States Chamber of Commerce in 1931 on the possible means of establishing future business and employment obligation. The report, presenting an apparently well considered, dispassionate view of the question, does not preach the gospel of any immediate reduction of hours, while it does recognize the ultimate need. The statement is quoted in full as evidence that at the end of a period in which *purely* voluntary reduction of hours could not be pointed to as an outstanding characteristic of the economic system, and at a time when public attention is focused on the hours' question, there is little promise of the inauguration of a widespread program of voluntary reduc-

[96] New York, *Report of Governor's Committee on Unemployment*, Nov. 1930, pp. 65-72.

tion of hours. It reads: "It is the belief of your committee that this trend for shorter hours for workers will continue in the future and properly so. Our economic and agricultural organism, if properly coordinated, can undoubtedly provide the basis for a permanently high standard of living for our entire population, and at the same time permit a reasonable curtailment of working hours. But while we point out that such curtailment in general must come gradually, we recognize that it must come more rapidly at some period and in some lines of industry than in others. We would sound a warning, however, that any extremely radical or abrupt change in the hours of labor may bring great economic harm." [97]

[97] United States, *Hearings before Senate Committee on a Bill to Establish a National Economic Council*, p. 188.

APPENDIX A

STATE REGULATION

GENERAL LAWS: EARLY TYPE[1]

State	Hours	Nullifying Provision
California Sims' Deering's Code, 1906 Sec. 3244	8 per day	"unless it is otherwise expressly stipulated by the parties to a contract."
Connecticut Gen'l Statutes, 1910 Sec. 5307	8 per day	"unless otherwise agreed."
Florida Revised Gen'l Statutes 1920, Sec. 4016	10 per day	"unless a written contract has been signed."
Illinois Revised Statutes, 1917 Ch. 48	8 per day	"where there is no special contract or agreement to the contrary."
Indiana Burns' Annotated Statutes, 1914 Sec. 7977	8 per day	"overwork for an extra compensation by agreement between employer and employee is hereby permitted." (Exception to 8-hr. provision, agricultural and domestic labor.)
Maine Revised Statutes, 1916 Ch. 87.	10 per day	"unless the contract stipulates for a longer time." (Exception to 10-hr. provision, monthly labor and agricultural employments.)
Michigan Compiled Laws, 1915 Sec. 5587	10 per day	"unless there be an agreement to the contrary."

[1] Data obtained from U. S. Bureau of Labor Statistics *Bulletins* No. 370, 403, 434, 470, 486, 528, 552.

APPENDICES

Minnesota Laws of 1917, Ch. 248	10 per day	"unless a shorter time be agreed upon." (Exception to 10-hr. provision, farm laborers, domestic servants employed by the week or month, persons engaged in the care of live stock.)
Missouri Revised Statutes, 1919 Sec. 6766	8 per day	"nothing in this section to be construed as to prevent parties to any contract for work . . . from agreeing upon a longer or shorter time." (Exception to 8-hr. provision, those employed by the month or farm laborers.)
New Hampshire Public Statutes, 1891, as amended, 1929, Ch. 93.	10 per day	"unless otherwise agreed by the parties."
New York Consolidated Laws, 1909 Chap. 31, Article 5, Sec. 160	8 per day	This section "shall not prevent an agreement for overwork at an increased compensation." (Exception those engaged in farm or domestic work.)
Ohio General Code, 1910 Sec 6241	8 per day	"unless the contract therefor expressly provides otherwise."
Rhode Island Laws of 1928 Ch. 1231, Sec. 37	10 per day	"unless otherwise agreed by the parties to the contract for the same."
Wisconsin Statutes, 1923 Sec. 103.38	8 per day	"where there is no express contract to the contrary."

APPENDICES 263

APPENDIX B

STATE REGULATION
HOURS OF LABOR ON GOVERNMENT WORK[1]

State	Hours	Overtime	General Provisions
Arizona Constitution, Art. XVIII, Sec. 1. Revised Statutes, 1913, Par. 3103.	8 per day	In an emergency as war or the need for protection of property or human life.	All employment by or on behalf of the State or any political subdivision; payment at the current rate of wages in the locality.
California Constitution, Art. 20, Sec. 17. Sims' Deering's Code, 1906, Ch. 257, Sec. 653c.	8 per day	In an emergency as war or the need for protection of life or property.	Stipulated in contract for all public works of the State or any political subdivision.
Colorado Compiled Laws, 1921, Sec. 4175, 6.	8 per day	In an emergency provided that hours in excess of 8 shall constitute part of subsequent day's work and that the work week shall not exceed 48 hours.	On all work undertaken in behalf of the State or any political subdivision.
Delaware Revised Code, 1914, Sec. 2159, 2160, 1.	8 per day	In cases of extraordinary emergency.	All employees of the City of Wilmington; stipulated in all contracts for work for the City of Wilmington; payment at prevailing rate of wages in the locality.
Idaho Constitution,	8 per day	In time of war or for the protection	All employed by or on behalf of the State or

[1] Data obtained from U. S. Bureau of Labor Statistics, *Bulletins* No. 370, 403, 434, 470, 486, 528, 552, and *American Labor Legislation Review*, Dec., 1931, "Labor Legislation of 1931."

APPENDICES

Art. 13, Sec. 2. Laws of 1923, Ch. 93.		of property or human life.	any political subdivision; to be stipulated in all contracts; payment at rate of wages prevailing in the locality. All employed by or on behalf of the State or any of its political subdivisions.
Indiana Burns' Annotated Statutes, 1914, Sec. 7977, 7978.	8 per day		
Kansas Laws of 1923, Ch. 157.	8 per day	In war or for the protection of property or human life.	All employed by or on behalf of State or any political subdivision; all contracts are deemed to be on this basis; payment at current rate of wages of locality. Exceptions: employees of municipal light and water plants in second and third class cities; employees on town or county jobs, grading dirt roads.
Kentucky Statutes 1915, Sec. 2290 B.	8 per day	In extraordinary emergency.	All employed by the State or by any contractor upon any of the public works of the Commonwealth.
Maryland Laws of 1910, Ch. 94.	8 per day	In time of war or to protect property or human life.	All employees of the City of Baltimore; all employees on contracts for work for that City, such employees must be paid the current rate of wages of the locality.
Massachusetts Gen'l Laws, 1921, Ch. 149, Sec. 30, as amended 1926, Ch. 375.	8 per day 48 per week	In extraordinary emergency or in construction of highways or water works when Commissioner of Labor	All employed by the Commonwealth or by any county or town which has adopted this section; all employed on behalf of the Com-

APPENDICES

Minnesota Acts of 1919, Ch. 40.	8 per day	In war or for protection of property or human life.	deems it a public necessity. All employed by or on behalf of the State. Commonwealth or of any county or of any such town; to be stipulated in contracts.
Montana Constitution, Art. 18, Sec. 4, Revised Code, 1921, Sec. 3079, as amended 1929, Ch. 116.	8 per day		All employees on works carried on or aided by the State or any political subdivision.
Nevada Acts of 1919, Ch. 203.	8 per day 56 per week	For protection of life or property.	All employed by or on behalf of State or any political subdivision; to be stipulated in contract. Exceptions: employees of fire departments, hospital nurses, deputy sheriffs or jailers.
New Jersey Acts of 1914, Ch. 253.	8 per day	For protection of property or human life.	All employed by or on behalf of the State or any political subdivision; contracts considered to be on this basis; payment at prevailing rate of wages in the locality.
New Mexico Constitution Art. XX, Sec. 19.	8 per day		All employed by or on behalf of the State or any political subdivision.
New York Consolidated Laws, 1909, Chap. 31, Art. VIII, Sec. 220, as amended 1921, Ch. 642.	8 per day	For protection of life or property.	All employed on contracts to which State or municipal corporation is a party; must be stipulated in the contract; wages must be at rate prevailing in the locality.

APPENDICES

Ohio Constitution, Amendment of 1912, Art. II, Sec. 37. General Code, 1910, Sec. 17-1, as amended, 1919, p. 1286.	8 per day 48 per wk.	In extraordinary emergency.	All employed on any public work carried on or aided by the State or any political subdivision thereof whether done by contract or otherwise.
Oklahoma Constitution, Art. XXIII, Revised Laws, 1910, Sec. 3757, 8.	8 per day	In war or for the protection of property or human life.	All employed by or on behalf of the State or any political subdivision; payment at prevailing rate of wages in locality; all contracts considered to be on this basis.
Oregon Gen'l Laws, 1920. Sec. 6718, 6721, as amended, 1929, Ch. 137, 358.	8 per day 48 per wk.	In an emergency when no other competent labor is available; must be paid double wages.	All employed by or on behalf of the State or any political subdivision; must be stipulated in contracts. Exceptions: State institutions and departments; plants owned by municipality of not more than 1,000 inhabitants may employ labor more than 8 hrs. a day but not more than 56 hrs. a week; foremen, watchmen and timekeepers paid on monthly rate on work funded by public funds; double pay provision shall not apply to any employee of dock commission handling cargo for maritime commerce.
Pennsylvania Statutes, 1920, Sec. 18270, 18271.	8 per day		All employed by or on behalf of the State.

APPENDICES 267

Texas Laws of 1913, Ch. 68, as amended 1921, Ch. 121.	8 per day	In war or for protection of property or human life.	All employed by or on behalf of the State or political subdivision thereof for the construction or repair of r o a d s , buildings or other work of a similar character; all contracts are considered to be made on t h i s basis; payment at prevailing rate of wages in the locality.
Utah Constitution Art. XVI, Sec. 6, Compiled Laws, 1917, Sec. 3667.	8 per day	For protection of life or property.	All employed on works carried on or aided by the State or any political subdivision thereof.
Washington Codes and Statutes, 1910, Sec. 6572, 3.	8 per day	In extraordinary emergency in which it is impossible to get additional laborers; m u s t be paid time a n d a half rate.	All employed on contracts for the State or any political subdivision thereof; must be stipulated in contract.
West Virginia Code of 1913, Sec. 713.	8 per day	In extraordinary emergency.	All employed by or on behalf of the State.
Wisconsin Statutes 1923, Sec. 103. 41.	8 per day	In war or for protection of property or human life.	All employed on contracts for the State. Exception: contracts for construction or maintenance of public highways or bridges.
Wyoming Constitution, Art. XIX; Laws of 1917, Ch. 90.	8 per day	In war or for protection of life or property.	All employed on public works of the State or any political subdivision thereof whether done by contract or otherwise.

APPENDIX C
STATE REGULATION
HOURS OF LABOR OF WOMEN[1]

State	Hours	Overtime	Occupations or Industries Specified
Alabama	None		
Arizona Laws of 1927, Ch. 44.	8 per day 48 per wk.		Manufacturing or mercantile establishment, laundry, place of amusement, restaurant, hotel, telephone or telegraph office or other establishment. Exceptions: canning, domestic work, nurses, telephone or telegraph office employing three or less women.
Arkansas Laws of 1915, Act 191.	9 per day 54 per wk.	90 days a year at time and a half rate, subject to Industrial Welfare Commission's approval (Amendment Laws of 1921, No. 140).	Manufacturing or mercantile establishment, laundry, transportation company. Exception: cotton factory.
California Laws of 1929, Ch. 286. (Amends Act of 1911.)	8 per day 48 per wk.	Subject to limitations by the Industrial Welfare Commission.	Manufacturing or mercantile establishment, laundry, hotel, restaurant, lodging house, apartment house, hospital, place of amusement, transportation company, telephone or telegraph office. Exceptions: graduate nurses in hospitals, canning.
Colorado Laws of 1913, Sec. 4183 (Amends Act of 1903).	8 per day		Manufacturing or mercantile establishment, laundries, hotels, restaurants.

[1] Data obtained from U. S. Dept. of Labor, *Bulletin of the Women's Bureau*, No. 63 and 66; U. S. Bureau of Labor Statistics, *Bulletins* No. 370, 403, 434, 470, 486, 528, 552, *American Labor Legislation Review*, Dec., 1931, " Labor Legislation of 1931."

APPENDICES 269

Connecticut Laws of 1913, Ch. 179.	10 per day 55 per wk.		Manufacturing establishment.
Laws of 1917, Ch. 300. (As amended 1925, Ch. 153.)	58 per wk.		Mercantile establishment, restaurant, cafe, barber shop, beauty parlor, photo gallery.
Delaware Laws of 1917, Ch. 230 (Amends Act of 1913).	10 per day 55 per wk.	2 hrs. on one day a week, if weekly maximum is not exceeded.	Manufacturing or mercantile establishment, laundry, baking or printing establishment, telephone and telegraph office, place of amusement, office. Exception: canning.
District of Columbia 38 U. S. 291 (1914).	8 per day 48 per wk.		Manufacturing or mercantile establishment, laundry, hotel, restaurant, telephone and telegraph office, transportation company.
Georgia [2] Laws of 1910, Sec. 3137.	60 per wk.	To make up time lost, not to exceed 10 days annually.	Cotton or woolen manufacturing establishments. Exception: clerical force.
Idaho Laws of 1913, Ch. 86.	9 per day		Mechanical or mercantile establishment, laundry, hotel, restaurant, telephone or telegraph, transportation company. Exception: canning.
Illinois Laws of 1911, p. 328 (Amends Act of 1909).	10 per day		Mechanical or mercantile establishment, laundry, hotel, restaurant, telegraph or telephone, place of amusement, common carrier, public utility, public institution.
Indiana	None		
Iowa	None		
Kansas Laws of 1915, Ch. 275, created an Industrial	8 (basic) day 48 (basic) wk. 48 per wk. 49½ per wk. 49½ per wk.	4½ hrs. weekly in emergency.	Telephone operators. Public housekeeping occupations. Laundry occupations. Manufacturing occupations.

[2] The provisions of this law include male as well as female operatives. *Cf.* Appendix D.

APPENDICES

Welfare Commission with power to regulate hours.	54 per wk.	1 hr. on 1 day a week.	Mercantile occupations
Kentucky Laws of 1912, Ch. 77.	10 per day 60 per wk.		Manufacturing or mercantile establishment, laundry, hotel, bakery, restaurant, telephone and telegraph office.
Louisiana Laws of 1914, Act 133 (Amends Act of 1908).	10 per day 60 per wk.		Any occupation whatsoever. Exception: store with more than five employees on Saturday night.
Maine Laws of 1915, Ch. 350.	9 per day 54 per wk.	Permitted to make 1 short day per week.	Manufacturing establishment.
	54 per wk.	Permitted at Christmas and Easter to mercantile establishments.	Mercantile establishment, restaurant, telephone or telegraph office, transportation company.
Laws of 1931, Chap. 144.	54 per wk.		Laundries.
Maryland Laws of 1916, Ch. 147 (Amends Act of 1912).	10 per day 60 per wk.	Permitted at Christmas to mercantile establishments outside of Baltimore.	Manufacturing or mercantile establishment, printing, baking, laundry. Exception: canning.
Massachusetts Laws of 1921, Ch. 280 (Amends Act of 1919).	9 per day 48 per wk.	4 hours per week in seasonal work if yearly average is 48 hours per week.	Manufacturing or mercantile establishment, telegraph or telephone office, transportation company, laundry, hotel, beauty parlor, place of amusement, elevator operator.
Michigan Laws of 1929, Act 299 (Amends Act of 1909).	Average 9 per day 54 per wk.		Manufacturing or mercantile establishment, office, hotel, restaurant, place of amusement, laundry, elevator operator, street or electric railways. Exception: canning.

Minnesota	9 per day	Permitted to make 1 short day per week.	Manufacturing establishment, telephone or telegraph office. Exception: canning for 6 wks. annually.
Ch. 349 Laws of 1927, (Amends Act of 1913).	10 per day 54 per wk. 58 per wk.		Mercantile establishment, restaurant.
Laws of 1909, Chap. 490.	10 per day 58 per wk.		Manufacturing establishments outside cities of the first or second class.
Mississippi Laws of 1914, Ch. 165.	10 per day 60 per wk.		Any occupation except domestic servants.
Missouri Laws of 1919, p. 447 (Amends Act of 1913).	9 per day 54 per wk.		Manufacturing or mercantile establishment, laundry, bakery, restaurant, place of amusement, any clerical worker in these industries, common carrier, public utility, public institution. Exceptions: canning in cities of less than 10,000 for 90 days annually; telephone companies; towns having less than 3,000 population.
Montana Laws of 1917, Ch. 70.	8 per day	2 hours per day the week preceding Christmas Day in retail stores.	Manufacturing or mercantile establishment, telephone or telegraph office, hotel or restaurant.
Nebraska Laws of 1919, Ch. 190 (Amends Act of 1913).	9 per day 54 per wk.		Manufacturing or mercantile establishment, laundry, hotel, restaurant, office, public service corporation in metropolitan and first-class cities.
Nevada Laws of 1917, Ch. 14.	8 per day 56 per wk.		Manufacturing or mercantile establishment, laundry, hotel, boarding house, apartment house, place of amusement, transportation company. Exceptions: nurses, canning.

State / Law	Hours	Overtime	Occupations covered
New Hampshire Laws of 1917, Ch. 196.	10½ per day 54 per wk.	Employees in stores for seven days preceding Christmas, provided annual weekly average does not exceed 54 hours.	Manual or mechanical labor in any employment. Exceptions: telephone and telegraph office, hotel, boarding house, nurses, domestic labor, farm labor.
New Jersey Laws of 1921, Ch. 194 (Amends Act of 1912).	10 per day 54 per wk.		Manufacturing or mercantile establishment, bakery, laundry, restaurant. Exceptions: canning; hotels or other continuous business where working hours do not exceed 8 per day.
New Mexico Laws of 1912, Ch. 180.	8 per day	4 hours per week at time and a half rate.	Manufacturing establishment, laundry, hotel, restaurant, cafe, place of amusement. Exceptions: clerical employees, canneries.
	8 per day 48 per wk.		Telephone operators. Exceptions: shift working between 9 P. M. and 7 A. M.; offices where five or less operators are employed.
	9 per day 56 per wk.	2 hours on Saturday in mercantile establishments; 4 hours per week at time and a half rate.	Mercantile establishment, common carrier, public utility. Exception: drug stores.
	10 per day 60 per wk.		Telephone operators on 9 P. M. to 7 A. M. shift, in offices where five or less operators are employed.
New York Laws of 1927, Ch. 453.	8 per day 48 per wk.	9 per day, 49½ per wk., may be worked in	Manufacturing or mercantile establishment, laundry. Exception: canning.

APPENDICES 273

		order to make 1 shorter work day per week. 78 hrs. additional overtime provided that not more than 10 hrs. per day and 54 hrs. or 6 days weekly may be worked. In mercantile establishments, however, 1 day a week may exceed 10 hrs., and from Dec. 18th to Dec. 24th.	
North Carolina Laws of 1931, Ch. 289.	55 per wk.		Manufacturing establishment. Exception: canning.
North Dakota Laws of 1927, Ch. 142 (Amends Act of 1919).	8½ per day 48 per wk.		Manufacturing or mercantile establishment, laundry, hotel, restaurant, telephone or telegraph office, transportation company. Exceptions: villages and towns of less than 500 population; telephone or telegraph operators where special rules are established by the Workmen's Compensation Bureau.
Ohio Laws of 1919, v. 108, pt. 1 (Amends Act of 1917).	9 per day 50 per wk.	Permits mercantile establishment 10 hrs. on Saturday.	Manufacturing or city mercantile establishment, telephone or telegraph office, restaurant, street railway, ticket seller, elevator operator. Exception: canning.

APPENDICES

State / Law	Hours	Overtime	Occupations
Oklahoma Laws of 1919, Ch. 163.	9 per day 54 per wk.	Hotels and restaurants permitted 1 hr. per day if consent of employee is obtained and double time is paid.	All establishments employing women except canning, registered pharmacists, nurses, agricultural or domestic labor, and those outside of towns of 5,000 population and employing less than 5 women.
Oregon Laws of 1913, Ch. 62, created an Industrial Welfare Commission with power to regulate hours.	9 per day 48 per wk.		Manufacturing or mercantile establishment, laundry, personal service occupation, public housekeeping occupation, telephone or telegraph office. Exceptions: canning; rural telephone office may be granted special license by Industrial Welfare Commission.
Pennsylvania Laws of 1913, Act 466.	10 per day 54 per wk.	2 hrs. on not more than 3 days of the wk. if a legal holiday occurs during the week.	Any establishment except nurses in hospitals, work in private homes, farming, canning.
Rhode Island Laws of 1913, Ch. 912.	9 per day 54 per wk.		Manufacturing, mercantile or business establishment.
South Carolina Criminal Code of 1912, Sec. 430.	12 per day 60 per wk.		Mercantile establishments. Street railway employees.
Sec. 431	12 per day	In City of Columbia, provided extra pay for work after eleventh hour; in case of unavoidable delay.	

APPENDICES 275

Sec. 421² as amended 1922, No. 567.	10 per day 55 per wk.	To make up time lost through accident to the extent of 60 hrs. annually.	Cotton and woolen mills. Exception: clerical force.
South Dakota Laws of 1923, Ch. 308.	10 per day 54 per wk.	2 hrs. per day in the 5 days preceding Christmas.	All except farm and domestic laborers, telegraph or telephone operators.
Tennessee Laws of 1913, Ch. 12.	10½ per day 57 per wk.		Any establishment wherein labor is employed except domestic service and agriculture.
Texas Laws of 1929, Ch. 86 (Amends Act of 1915).	9 per day 54 per wk.	2 hrs. per day in laundries at double rate of pay.	Any establishment. Exceptions: stenographers, pharmacists, employees in private charitable institutions, mercantile establishments and telephone or telegraph offices in places of less than 3,000 inhabitants.
Utah Laws of 1919, Ch. 70.	8 per day 48 per wk.		Manufacturing or mercantile establishment, laundry, hotel, restaurant, telephone or telegraph office, hospital, transportation company or office. Exception: canning.
Vermont Laws of 1917, Act 177.	10½ per day 56 per wk.		Manufacturing, mine or quarry. Exception: may be suspended by Commissioner of Industries with the approval of the Governor for not more than two months annually in industries which handle perishable products.
Virginia Laws of 1926, Ch. 538 (Amends Act of 1890).	10 per day³		Manufacturing or mercantile establishments, laundry, restaurant. Exceptions: office workers, canning, mercantile establishments in towns of less than 2,000.

³ Code of 1918, Sec. 4570, prohibits Sunday work.

Washington Laws of 1911, Ch. 37.	8 per day[4]		Manufacturing or mercantile establishments, laundry, hotel or restaurant. Exception: canning.
West Virginia	None		
Wisconsin Laws of 1923, Ch. 185.	9 per day 50 per wk.	1 hr. per day making not more than a total of 55 hrs. per wk. for 4 wks. a year at time and a half rate.	Manufacturing or mercantile establishment, laundry, restaurant, telephone or telegraph office, or transportation company. Exception: canning, subject to regulation by the Industrial Commission.
Wyoming Laws of 1923, Ch. 62.	8½ per day 56 per wk.	Permitted when unusually pressing business demands, at time and a half rate.	Manufacturing or mercantile establishment, laundry, restaurant, hotel, lodging house, apartment house, place of amusement, telephone or telegraph office, or transportation company. Exceptions: canning; nurses in training in hospitals, telephone or telegraph offices employing three or less women.

[4] The Industrial Commission has established a six day week with limited exceptions.

APPENDIX D

STATE REGULATION

HOURS OF LABOR OF MEN IN SPECIAL INDUSTRIES[1]

State	Hours	Overtime	Occupations or Industries Specified
Arizona Penal Code Sec. 713	8 per day	During continuance of emergency in which life or property is in imminent danger.	All employees in underground mines or open pit workings. Exception allowed for changes of shift at stated period.
Revised Statutes 1913, Par. 3108.	8 per day		Hoisting engineers at the mine and furnace men at the smelters.
Par. 3099	8 per day		All employees in or about any electric light or power plant.
Arkansas Digest of 1921, Sec. 7082, 3.	10 per day		All employees engaged in operating or constructing saw and planing mills.
California Laws of 1913, Ch. 186	8 per day	During continuance of emergency in which life or property is in imminent danger.	All employees in underground mines or smelters.
Laws of 1925, Chap. 394	Average of 9 per day; 108 in any 2 consecutive weeks.	In an emergency which is defined as accident, death, sickness or epidemic.	Employees selling drugs at retail or compounding prescriptions.

[1] Data obtained from U. S. Bureau of Labor Statistics *Bulletins* No. 370, 403, 434, 470, 486, 528, 552, and *American Labor Legislation Review*, December, 1931, "Labor Legislation of 1931." State regulation of hours of service on railways has not been included in this table since federal legislation controls absolutely interstate commerce and the separation of this from intrastate commerce is impracticable. State *v.* Missouri Pacific Ry. Co., 212 Mo. 658. Also cf. *supra*, pp. 117-118. Hours regulation of special industries which permits the employee to contract for a longer day, has likewise been excluded.

Colorado Constitution Article 5, Sec. 25a, Compiled Laws 1921, Sec. 4173	8 per day	During continuance of emergency in which life or property is in imminent danger.	All employees in underground or open pit mines or smelters, or reduction processes.
Acts of 1927, Ch. 87.	8 per day	In an emergency in which life or property is endangered.	All employees in cement and plaster manufacturing plants. Exception allowed for semi-monthly or monthly change of shift.
Georgia Code of 1910, Sec. 3137.	10 per day	To make up time lost not to exceed 10 days annually.	All employed in cotton or woolen mills except engineers, firemen, watchmen, mechanics, teamsters, yard employees, clerical force and all help needed to clean up and make necessary repairs.
Idaho Compiled Statutes, 1919, Sec. 2328.	8 per day	During continuance of emergency in which life or property is in imminent danger.	All employees in underground mines, smelters or reduction plants.
Kansas Acts of 1920, Ch. 242.	8 per day	During continuance of emergency in which life or property is in imminent danger.	All employees in lead and zinc mines.
Louisiana Acts of 1902, No. 122.	10 per day within 12 consecutive hours.	In cases of accident or unavoidable delay provided extra compensation is paid and the employee consents.	All employees on street railroads.
Missouri Revised Statutes, 1919, Sec. 6767, 6769.	8 per day		All employees in mines or reduction plants including those engaged in any kind of silica mining or the manufacture of plate glass.

APPENDICES

Montana Constitution, Art. 18, Sec. 4; Revised Codes 1921. Sec. 3079, (as amended 1929), Ch. 116.	8 per day		In underground mines or smelters and in the working, reducing and treatment of coal.
Sec. 3068.	8 per day	To relieve another employee in case of unforeseen cause.	Operators of hoisting engines at or in any mine.
Nevada Revised Laws, 1912, Sec. 6554-9.	8 per day	During continuance of emergency in which life or property is in imminent danger.	All employees in underground mines or open pit mines, smelter and reduction plants, plaster and cement mills.
New Jersey Laws of 1914, Ch. 121, Sec. 10.	1½-8 per day depending on air pressure.		All employees in a tunnel, caisson, compartment or place where the air pressure exceeds normal.
Compiled Statutes, 1910, Sec. 57, p. 5008.	12 hrs. per day to be performed within 12 consecutive hours.		All employees on surface and steam elevated railways.
New York Consolidated Laws, 1909, Ch. 31, Art. V, Sec. 160.	10 hrs. per day within 12 hrs.	In case of accident or unavoidable delay at extra compensation.	All employees of electric surface, subway or elevated railroads where the mileage system is not in use.
Chap. 31, Art. XV, Sec. 430.	1½-8 per day depending on air pressure.		All employees working under compressed air.

280 APPENDICES

Laws of 1914, Ch. 514.	10 per day; 132 in any two consecutive weeks.	6 hrs. per week to make a shorter succeeding week.	All employees in pharmacies or drug stores.
Laws of 1915, Ch. 343.	11 per day 70 per wk.	4 hours on Saturday to eliminate work on Monday.	All employees in grocery or provision stores in first class cities.
North Dakota Laws of 1923, Ch. 246.	8 per day	During continuance of emergency.	All employees in mines and open pit mines.
Oklahoma Laws of 1913, Sec. 4005.	8 per day	Except in cases of emergency.	All employees in underground mines.
Oregon Laws, 1920, Sec. 6716.	8 per day	During continuance of emergency in which life or property is in imminent danger.	All employees in underground mines. Exception: first stages of development, tunnel work to a depth of 200 ft. or shaft work to a depth of 150 ft.
Pennsylvania Statutes, 1920, Sec. 5433.	1½-8 per day		All employees in any tunnel, caisson, compartment or place in which air pressure exceeds normal.
Rhode Island Gen'l Laws, 1923, Ch. 252.	10 per day within 12 consecutive hours.	In case of unavoidable delay or an unexpected contingency at increased compensation.	All employees on street railways.
South Carolina Criminal Code of 1912, Sec. 431.	12 per day		All employees of street railways.
Sec. 421 (as amended 1922, No. 567).	10 per day 55 per wk.	To make up time lost through accident to the extent of 60 hours annually.	All employees of cotton and woolen manufacturing establishments. Exceptions: mechanics, engineers, watchmen, firemen, teamsters, yard employees and clerical force.

APPENDICES

Acts of 1916, No. 544.	10 per day	In case of unavoidable delay.	All employees of interurban electric railways not over 40 miles in length.
Utah Constitution, Art. XVI, Compiled Laws, 1917, Sec. 3667.	8 per day	During continuance of an emergency in which life or property is in imminent danger.	All employees in underground mines or smelters or reduction plants.
Washington Code and Statutes, 1910, Sec. 6578,	10 per day		All employees on street railways.
Sec. 6583.	8 per day		All underground employees in coal mines.
Wyoming Constitution, Art. XIX, Compiled Statutes, 1910, Sec. 3499, 3500.	8 per day	During continuance of emergency in which life or property is in imminent danger.	All employees in underground mines, smelters or reduction plants.

APPENDIX E

STATE REGULATION
GENERAL LAWS: LATE TYPE[1]

State	Hours	Overtime	Occupations or Industries Specified
Mississippi Laws of 1912, Ch. 239.	10 per day	In cases of emergency; or to make 1 short day a week.	All employed in manufacturing or repairing. Exceptions: public service employees.
Oregon Laws of 1920, Sec. 6708, as amended 1923, Ch. 122.	10 per day in factories; 8 per day, 48 per wk. in sawmills, shingle mills, planing mills, and logging camps.	3 hours per day at time and a half rate.	Exceptions: logging, train crews, firemen, watchmen, repair men, those employed in care of quarters or live stock, conducting mess halls, superintending and direction of work, or the loading and removal of forest product.

[1] Data obtained from U. S. Bureau of Labor Statistics, *Bulletins*, Nos. 370, 403, 434, 470, 486, 528, 552, and *American Labor Legislation Review*, Dec., 1931, "Labor Legislation of 1931."

APPENDIX F

AVERAGE HOURS ESTABLISHED BY PRINCIPAL UNIONS, 1930 [1]

Organization	Membership	Per day	Per week	No. on 5-day week
Bricklayers, Masons and Plasterers, I. U. of A.	90,000	8	44	24,300
Bakery and Confectionery Workers, I. U. of A.	20,100	8-14	48, 49	
Carpenters and Joiners	302,000	8	42	125,000
Electrical Workers of A., International Brotherhood	142,000	8	40-44	40,000
Garment Workers, United	46,300	8	40-44	7,500
Granite Cutters	8,500	8	40	6,000
Hodcarriers, Building and Common Laborers, I. U. of A.	115,000	8	40-44	9,500
Ladies' Garment Workers, International	47,500	8	40	45,000
Machinists, International Association	77,600	8	44	15,000
Maintenance of Way, Brotherhood of	32,200	8	48	
Mine Workers of America	400,000	8	48	
Molders Union of North America, International	15,200	8	48	
Painters, Decorators and Paperhangers of A., Broth.	96,400	8	40	76,543
Photo Engravers Union of N. A., International	9,000	8	8 mo. 44 4 mo. 40	7,200
Plasterers, International Association of U. S. and Canada	37,700	8	40	26,448

[1] Data obtained from American Federation of Labor, *Proceedings*, 1931, pp. 29, 30, 100-103. The comparative accuracy of this table is supported by the Bureau of Labor Statistics' study of hours of trade union members in nine trade groups as of May 15, 1930. *Bulletin* No. 540, p. 3. The hours of the principal non-Federation unions, i. e.: the Railroad Brotherhoods and the Amalgamated Clothing Workers, have been given. *Cf. supra*, pp. 82-91, 200.

Plumbers and Steamfitters of U. S. and Canada, United Association	45,000	8	40	41,076
Printing Pressmen and Assistants Union of N. A., International	40,000	8 com'l 7½ news	44 com'l 45 news, day 40 news, night	
Sheet Metal Workers, International Assn.	25,000	8	44	
Stonecutters Assn. of N. A., Journeymen	5,800	8	40-44	
Teamsters, Chauffeurs, etc., International Brotherhood of	92,000	9	54	
Textile Workers, United	30,000	9	50	
Typographical Union, International	77,500	8	44	5,000
Upholsterers' International Union of N. America	10,100	8	44	4,404

APPENDIX G

Average Hours in Predominantly Unorganized Industries [1]

Industries	Hours
Boot and Shoe, 1930	48.9
Cane Sugar Refining, 1930	58.7
Cigarette Manufacturing, 1930	49.9
Cotton Goods Manufacturing, 1930	53.4
Dyeing and Finishing of Textiles, 1930	50.9
Furniture Workers, 1931	51.8
Lumber, 1930	56.5
Motor Vehicle Workers, 1930	48.8
Portland Cement, 1929	60.8
Rayon and other Synthetic Yarns Mfg., 1930	50.2
Slaughtering and Meat Packing, 1929	49.2
Woolen and Worsted Goods Mfg., 1930	49.3

[1] Data obtained from U. S. Bureau of Labor Statistics, *Bulletins* No. 502, 525, 526, 532, 533, 535, 537, 539, 540, 546, 547, 551. *Monthly Labor Review*, May, 1931, Mar., 1932.

APPENDIX H
FULL-TIME HOURS PER WEEK

Year	Douglas [a] (standard hours per week)	United States [b] Census of Manufacturers	National [b] Industrial Conference Board	Bureau of Labor [b] Statistics— Union Labor
1890	58.4			
1894	57.8			
1899	57.5			
1904	55.7			
1909	54.9	57.3		
1914	53.5	55.6	55.0	48.9
1919	51.3	51.2	50.0	
1920	50.4			45.8
1921	50.3	50.7	49.7	45.9
1922	50.5		50.0	46.1
1923	50.4	51.1	50.0	46.1
1924	50.0		49.8	45.9
1925	49.9		49.9	45.5
1926	49.8		49.8	45.4
1927			49.6	45.2

[a] Douglas, P. H., *Real Wages in the United States*, Boston, 1930.
[b] National Bureau of Economic Research, *Recent Economic Changes*, vol. ii, p. 444.

APPENDICES

APPENDIX I

DATA FOR ESTIMATE OF THE PER CENT OF WAGE EARNERS WHOSE HOURS ARE REGULATED BY LAW [1]

Federal Government [2]	848,349
State, County and City [3]	898,661
Public Construction [4]	1,000,000
Women [5]	4,372,942
Railroads [6]	1,300,000
Extraction of Minerals [7]	254,441
Oregon and Mississippi [8]	180,419
	8,854,812

Wage Earners (excluding Agriculture),[9] 27,565,193, i. e., 31%.

[1] In the absence of an estimate by a statistical expert, such as Dr. Wolman's of the percent of organized wage earners, the writer has made this rough approximation of the number of wage earners whose hours are affected by legislation.

[2] *National Municipal Review*, January 1932, p. 54.

[3] *Ibid.*, pp. 57, 62, 67.

[4] Wolman, Leo, *Planning and Control of Public Works*, New York, 1930, p. 115. This estimate includes employees in States which do not regulate the hours of work on public contracts. Since more than half the States, including most of the densely populated areas, have some regulation, the error cannot be large.

[5] Census of 1930 (Population Bulletin, 2nd Series) gives 4,580,402 female wage earners in manufacturing, trade and transportation, the three fields in which laws generally establish the hours of labor for women. From this total has been substracted the number of women employed in these fields in the States which have no regulation of hours for women workers.

[6] Senate Hearings on Establishment of a National Economic Council, p. 24.

[7] Census of 1930 (Population Bulletin, 2nd Series) gives 1,147,770 employees in this field. The number used here includes only those employed in States which regulate the hours of miners and smelters. An error is introduced by the fact that these laws apply in some States to underground miners, only. This error, however, is more than offset by the impossibility of including in this estimate figures of the number

employed in such fields as plaster and cement mills, street car operations, etc., in the various States which regulate hours in these lines of work.

[8] Census of 1930 (Population Bulletin, 2nd Series). A very slight error is introduced here because it is impossible to separate the number employed in forestry from those engaged in fishing in Oregon.

[9] Estimated as same percent of total gainfully employed as in 1920. Dr. Wolman's estimate of 23,480,077 wage earners, excluding agriculture, has been used to obtain this figure. The possibility of error is introduced here by the fact that the ten-year period may have changed the proportion of self-employed and salaried classes to wage earners.

BIBLIOGRAPHY

BOOKS AND ARTICLES

Albrecht, A. E., *International Seamen's Union of America*. Washington, 1923.
American Federation of Labor, *Proceedings of the Annual Conventions*.
Barnett, G. E., "The Printers," *American Economic Association Quarterly, October, 1909*.
Bonnett, C., *Employers' Associations of the United States*. New York, 1922.
Bridge, J. H., *The Inside History of the Carnegie Steel Company*. New York, 1903.
Brown, E. C., *Book and Job Printing in Chicago*. Chicago, 1931.
Carter, W. S., "The Workers' View," *Proceedings of the Academy of Political Science, 1917*.
Chase, Stuart, *Nemesis of American Business*. New York, 1931.
Committee on Work Periods in Continuous Industries of the Federated American Engineering Societies, *The Twelve-Hour Shift in Industry*. New York, 1922.
Commons, J. R., and Associates, *History of Labor in the United States*, New York, 1918. 2 vols.
Commons, J. R., ed., *A Documentary History of American Industrial Society*. Cleveland, 1910-11. 10 vols.
Dahlberg, Arthur, *Jobs, Machines and Capitalism*. New York, 1932.
Documentary History of the Amalgamated Clothing Workers: *Reports of the General Executive Board and Proceedings of the Biennial Conventions*.
Douglas, P. H., and Director, A., *Problem of Unemployment*. New York, 1931.
Drury, H. B., "Three-Shift System in the Steel Industry," *Bulletin of the Taylor Society*, February, 1921.
Dumas, C. J., "When the Linotype Came," *Typographical Journal*, September, 1931.
Eaves, L., *History of California Labor Legislation*. Berkeley, 1910.
Ely, R. T., *The Labor Movement*. New York, 1886.
Feldman, Herman, *The Regularization of Employment*. New York, 1925.
Fitch, J. A., *The Steel Workers*. New York, 1910.

Ford, Henry, in collaboration with Samuel Crowther, *My Life and Work*. Garden City, 1923.
Frankfurter, Felix, "Hours of Labor and Realism in Constitutional Law," *Harvard Law Review*, 1916.
Frankfurter, Felix, and Goldmark, Josephine, *The Case for the Shorter Work Day*. New York, n.d. 2 vols.
Freund, E., *The Police Power*. Chicago, 1904.
Goldmark, Josephine, "Standard Working Hours," *Human Engineering*, Vol. 1, No. 3, 1911.
Gompers, Samuel, *Seventy Years of Life and Labor*. New York, 1925. 2 vols.
Illinois Centennial Commission, *Centennial History of Illinois*. Springfield, 1918-20. 5 vols.
Interchurch World Movement, Commission of Inquiry, *Report on the Steel Strike of 1919*. New York, 1920.
International Seamen's Union, *Proceedings of the Annual Convention*.
Keynes, J. M., *Essays in Persuasion*. London, 1931.
Knights of Labor, *Proceedings of the Annual Conventions*.
Lauck, W. S., and Watts, C. S., *The Industrial Code*. New York, 1922.
Leitch, J., *Man to Man*. New York, 1919.
Lippman, Otto, "Hours of Work and Output," *International Labor Review*, April, 1924.
McNeill, G. E., *The Labor Movement*. Boston, 1887.
Miller, E. J., *Workmen's Representation in Industrial Government*. Urbana, 1924.
National Bureau of Economic Research, *Recent Economic Changes*. New York, 1929. 2 vols.
National Industrial Conference Board, *The Growth of Works' Councils in the United States*. New York, 1925.
————, *The Five Day Week in Manufacturing Industries*. New York, 1929.
Olmstead, V. H., "Betterment of Industrial Conditions," *Bulletin of the United States Department of Labor*, November, 1900.
Pearlman, S., *A History of Trade Unionism in the United States*. New York, 1922.
Peters, J. P., ed., *Symposium: Labor and Capital*. New York, 1902.
Phillips, Wendell, *Speeches, Lectures and Letters*. Boston, 1894.
Powderly, T. V., *Thirty Years of Labor*. Columbus, c, 1889.
Powell, L. M., *History of the United Typothetae of America*. Chicago, 1926.
Powell, T. R., "The Supreme Court and the Adamson Law," *Pennsylvania Law Review*, 1916-17.
Pound, Roscoe, "Liberty of Contract," *Yale Law Journal*, 1908-1909.

BIBLIOGRAPHY

Price, C. W., and others, *Working Conditions, Wages and Profits.* Chicago, 1920.
Robinson, J. S., *The Amalgamated Association of Iron, Steel and Tin Workers.* Baltimore, 1920.
Selekman, B. M., *Employees' Representation in Steel Works.* New York, 1924.
"Six Hour Day," *Locomotive Engineers Journal,* November, 1930.
Staley, E., *History of the Illinois Federation of Labor.* Chicago, 1930.
Stevens, G. A., *New York Typographical Union No. 6,* Albany, 1913.
Stockton, F. T., *International Molders' Union of North America.* Baltimore, 1921.
Sylvis, W. H., *Life, Speeches, Labors and Essays,* edited by J. C. Sylvis. Philadelphia, 1872.
Tarbell, Ida, *Life of Elbert H. Gary.* New York, 1925.
Taylor, A. G., *Labor Policies of the National Association of Manufacturers.* Urbana, 1928.
Tolman, W. H., *Industrial Betterment.* New York, 1900.
———, *Social Engineering.* New York, 1909.
Tracy, G. A., *History of the Typographical Union.* Indianapolis, 1913.
Walker, C. R., *Steel, The Diary of a Furnace Worker.* Boston, 1922.
Ware, N. J., *The Labor Movement in the United States,* 1860-1895. New York, 1929.
Weyl, Walter, "Street Railway Employment in the United States," *Bulletin of the United States Department of Labor,* March, 1905.
Wolman, Leo, *The Clothing Workers of Chicago.* Chicago, 1922
Wright, C. D., *The Battles of Labor.* Philadelphia, 1906.

Government Documents

Colorado Bureau of Labor Statistics, *Report,* 1899-1900.
Illinois Bureau of Labor Statistics, *Report,* 1886.
Kansas Bureau of Labor, *Report,* 1899.
Maryland Bureau of Industrial Statistics, *Report,* 1886-87.
Massachusetts Bureau of Statistics of Labor, *Reports,* 1870-1886.
New Jersey Bureau of Statistics of Labor and Industries, *Reports,* 1886-1905.
New York Bureau of Statistics of Labor, *Reports,* 1886, 1890, 1892, 1895.
New York Governor's Committee on Unemployment, *Report,* 1930.
Ohio Bureau of Labor Statistics, *Reports,* 1886, 1890.
Pennsylvania Bureau of Statistics of Labor and Agriculture, *Report,* 1872-73.
U. S. Bureau of Labor Statistics, *Bulletins* in series, "Labor Laws of the United States" and "Wages and Hours."

————, *Bulletin* No. 198, "Collective Agreements in the Men's Clothing Industry," 1916.
————, *Bulletin* No. 287, "National War Labor Board," 1921.
U. S. Commissioner of Labor, *Report,* 1886.
U. S. Commission on Industrial Relations, *Report,* Washington, 1916. 11 vols.
U. S. *Congressional Record.*
U. S. Eight Hour Commission, *Report,* Washington, 1918.
U. S. House of Representatives, *Hearings on Bills to Establish Eight Hours for Laborers on Government Work,* Washington, 1900, 1902, 1904, 1906, 1908.
U. S. Industrial Commission, *Report,* "Relations of Capital and Labor," Washington, 1900-1902. 19 vols.
U. S. National War Labor Board, *Memorandum on the Eight Hour Working Day,* Washington, 1918.
U. S. Senate, *Hearings on Bills to Establish Eight Hours for Laborers on Government Work,* held by Committee on Education and Labor, Washington, 1903, 1904, 1912.
————, *Hearings on Bill to Establish a National Economic Council,* held by a Subcommittee of the Committee on Manufactures, Washington, 1932.
————, *Report,* "Conditions of Employment in the Iron and Steel Industry," Washington, 1911. 4 vols.
————, *Report,* "Investigation of Strike in Steel Industries," Washington, 1919.
————, *Report,* "Relations Between Capital and Labor and Testimony Taken by the Committee," Washington, 1885. 5 vols.
————, *Report,* "Strike at the Bethlehem Steel Works," Washington, 1910.
U. S. Women's Bureau, *Bulletin* No. 63, "State Laws Affecting Women Workers," 1927.
————, *Bulletin* No. 66, "History of Labor Legislation for Women in Three States," 1929.
Wisconsin Bureau of Labor and Industrial Statistics, *Report,* 1885-86.

PAMPHLETS

Brown, L. J., *What of the Six Hour Day?* 1931.
Cameron, A. S., *Eight Hour Question.* New York, 1872.
Citizens' Industrial Association, *Bulletin* No. 1. Indianapolis, 1903.
Danryid, L., *History and Philosophy of the Eight Hour Movement.* Washington, 1899.
Druggists' League for Shorter Hours, *A Plea for Shorter Hours.* New York, 1897.

BIBLIOGRAPHY

Fabian Syllabus, London, 1931.
Furniture Workers' Union, *Normal Work Day of Eight Hours*. New York, 1879.
Gompers, Samuel, *Eight Hour Work Day*, Washington, n.d.
————, *Workers and the Eight Hour Work Day*. Washington, n.d.
Gray, Wm., *Argument on Petitions for Ten Hour Law*. Boston, 1873.
Green, Wm., *The Five Day Week Inevitable*. Washington, 1932.
Gunton, G., *Economic and Social Importance of the Eight Hour Movement*. Washington, 1889.
McNeill, G. E., *Eight Hour Primer*. Washington, 1899.
National Association of Manufacturers, *Eight Hours by Act of Congress: Arbitrary, Needless, Destructive, Dangerous*. New York, 1904.
National Industrial Conference Board, *Industrial Relations Activities at Cheney Bros*. New York, 1929.
————, *Research Reports*, No. 4, 7, 12, 16, 18, Hours of Work as Related to Output and Health of Workers in Cotton Manufacturing, Boot and Shoe Industry, Wool Manufacturing, Silk Manufacturing and Metal Manufacturing Industries. Boston, 1918, 1919.
————, *Research Report* No. 32, Practical Experience with the Work Week of Forty-Eight Hours or Less. New York, 1920.
Parry, D. M., *Disastrous Effects of a National Eight Hour Law*. Indianapolis, n.d.
Steward, Ira, *Poverty*, Boston, 1873.
Typographical Union No. 6, *Referendums*, February 10, and 25, 1932.
U. S. Chamber of Commerce, *Referendum* No. 31, 1920.

NEWSPAPERS AND PERIODICALS

American Federationist.
American Labor Legislation Review.
Bulletin of the Bureau of Labor Statistics of New York. (After 1901, *Bulletin of the Department of Labor of New York.*)
Monthly Labor Review.
Nation.
New Republic.
New York Times.
New York Tribune.
Survey.
Typographical Journal.
Workingman's Advocate (Incomplete file 1866-1872 in New York Public Library).

INDEX

Adamson Eight Hour Law; 57, 87-89, 165
Amalgamated Clothing Workers: 171, 189-206, 217
American Federation of Labor: 11, 16, 17, 19n, 22, 24, 26, 31, 46, 48-58, 66, 75, 81, 137n, 138, 152-169, 170, 171, 174, 175, 180, 181, 185, 187, 205n, 211, 212, 217, 252; local Federations: 51, 52, 56, 101, 119, 120, 122, 133, 189
Arguments for and against shorter hours: employers: 13-20, 61, 225, 226, 252-254, 256, 257; employees: 13-20, 28, 39, 40, 44, 137, 167, 173, 196, 257
Attorney General: Federal: 69, 70, 74, 76-78; State: 101, 105, 120

Bakers: *see* Lochner
Bill of Grievances: 51, 76
Black International: 156
Bolshevism: 212
Boycott: 42, 45, 47, 182, 185
Brewster Carriage Company: 145, 148, 230
Building trades: 142-146, 148, 150, 155-158, 253

Cabot Fund: 214, 216
Capital: 15, 64, 137n, 212, 233, 250. *See also* Relations between Labor and Capital
Carpenters: 150, 160-162
Central Labor Union: 156
Cities, growth of: 14, 31
Closed shop: 178, 181-184
Collective bargaining: 26, 85, 90, 91, 138, 151, 154, 171, 177, 183, 184, 187, 188, 192, 195, 199-201, 204, 207, 208, 211, 212, 217
Commerce: 88, foreign: 21, 68, 85, 93; interstate: 21, 22, 67, 68, 82, 84, 85, 93, 118
Communism: 147, 212

Congress: 21, 36, 41, 51, 58, 63, 65, 67, 69, 70, 73, 75-77, 82, 84-88, 90-93, 118, 232
Constitution: Federal: 21, 23, 66, 82, 93, 102, 114, 120; State: 23, 119, 122, 124, 130. *See also* Fourteenth Amendment
Constitutional amendment: Federal: 21, 51, 58, 67, 68; State: 123, 133
Constitutional powers: 67, 91
Constitutional provision: 22, 106
Constitutionality of hour legislation: 23, 51, 56, 68, 85, 88, 97, 99, 103-105, 111-115, 117-119, 122, 124-126, 128, 133. *See also* Contract, freedom of
Consumption: mass: 17; and leisure: 16, 17; and production: 13, 17, 20, 167
Consumer: 15, 17, 196, 215, 252
Contract: 39, 58, 107n; freedom of: 23, 61, 69, 98, 103, 108, 113, 114, 121, 126, 130, 132; government, federal: 50, 61, 63, 64, 69, 77-81, 195; city and state: 39, 94, 98-106; for overtime: 25, 95-97, 133. *See* Appendices A, B
Court decisions: 23; on general hour legislation: 97, 98, 129, 130-133; on legislation to regulate hours on government work: 70, 72, 74, 75, 99, 101-106; hazardous or unhealthy work: 23, 116n, 118, 119, 122-124, 128; *see also* Holden *v.* Hardy *and* Lochner; for railroad employees: 85, 88, 118; for women: 23, 108, 111-115
Cost: of living: 64, 252, 256; of operation and production: 15, 86, 100, 203, 210, 213, 215, 216, 226, 229, 238, 239, 243, 246, 247, 250, 253, 256; of strikes: 26, 27, 140, 150, 180, 184, 185, 217

295

INDEX

Danryid, L: 16, 17, 160
Depression: 19, 20, 170, 255; of 1873: 139, 148, 149, 173; of 1893: 162, 175, 206; of 1921: 20, 167, 183, 185, 201, 244; of 1929: 5, 16, 20, 58, 89, 188, 217, 254, 255, 257, 258
Direct action: 5, 21, 22, 26-28, 32, 41-44, 48-50, 52-58, 97, 132, 222, 223, 241, 258. See Part II and Appendix F
Distribution: 17, 243
Drury, Horace: 213

Economists: 18, 19, 160, 227, 237, 257
Eight Hour Commission: 87-89
Eight hour label: see Trade Union Label
Eight Hour Laws, Federal: 21, 22, 35-38, 50, 60-62, 64-67, 86, 93, 107, 173, 248; of 1868: 22, 69-73; of 1888: 72; of 1892: 22, 51, 60, 63, 72-78, 101; of 1912: 22, 52, 77-81; of 1912, amended: 78. See also Adamson Law.
Eight Hour Laws, State: 24, 25, 34, 36, 37, 39, 45, 47, 50, 52-54, 59, 61, 62, 94-107, 111-116, 119-128, 133, 140-143, 234; California, for women, 1911: 113-115; Colorado, for miners and smelters, 1899: 122, 123, 126, 128; Kansas, for government employees, 1891: 104-106; New York, for government employees, 1899: 100-103; Utah, for miners and smelters, 1896; 51, 119-122, 124. See Appendices A-F
Eight Hour Leagues: 33-35, 39, 67, 95, 144, 146, 148, 153
Eight Hour Ordinance, City: 47, 99, 157
Emergency: 73-75, 81, 83, 84, 100, 104, 119, 129. See Appendices B, D, E
Employees: 39, 42, 47, 57, 69, 80, 81, 97, 120, 146, 155, 177, 189, 190, 221, 227-231, 235, 236, 239, 242, 251, 252, 255-257; government: 26, 53, 55, 58, 67, 222; federal: 21, 22, 36, 47-49, 68-82, 93; state and city: 23-25, 39, 94, 95, 98-106, 157; Jewish: 253; in hazardous or unhealthy work: 22-26, 51, 55, 57, 58, 94, 95, 116-128, 130; of the steel industry: 206-216, 233, 245, 246, 253; railroad: 22, 57, 82-91, 119. See also Minors; Seamen; Women; Works' Councils; Unions, company
Employers: 6, 18, 20-22, 42, 47, 48, 54, 58-65, 69, 80, 81, 96, 97, 108, 116, 121, 124, 126, 142, 144, 152, 154, 155, 158, 161, 162, 166, 172, 174, 177, 180, 182, 184, 186, 189, 190, 194, 196-199, 206, 208, 213; model: 22, 68, 82, 100, 195; organized: 77, 147. See also Arguments, Voluntary action
Employers' Associations: 27, 60-65, 79, 171, 172, 174, 177, 178, 181, 194, 195, 201, 202, 221, 240, 253. See Manufacturers' Associations, United Typothetae
Enforcement of hour legislation: federal: 22, 32, 34, 37, 38, 41, 44, 48, 49, 51, 64, 68, 71-73, 75-77, 79, 84, 93; state: 96, 99-101, 104, 105, 108-111, 115, 124, 130. See also Strikes to enforce.
Executive Department: Federal: 49, 69, 70; see President; State: 96, 100, 107, 108, 113, 138, 141, 147, 158; City. 158
Executive Order: 32, 76, 79

Federation of Organized Trades and Labor Unions: 43-45, 48, 153, 159n
Fels & Company: 234, 235
Fitch, John A.: 208
Ford, Henry: 17, 27, 241, 248, 250, 252-256
Fourteenth Amendment: 103, 104, 111, 118, 125, 127, 129
Frankfurter, F.: 23, 79, 104n, 108, 112, 131, 238n

Gary, Elbert H.: 211-213, 253
George, Henry: 155, 160
Government regulation of hours: 41, 59, 60, 170, 221-223, 255; federal: 21, 22, 32, 53, 57, 58, 62, 64-93; state: 11, 23-25, 32, 53, 62, 82, 94-133, 239; foreign: 15, 32, 50, 92, 131. See Appendices A-E, I. See also Eight Hour, Ten Hour Laws
Greeley, Horace: 140
Gunton, George: 17, 160

INDEX

Hart, Schaffner & Marx: 189-191, 194, 198
Haymarket disaster: 156, 159
Health: 14, 113; and hours: 13-15, 196, 209, 215, 226, 236, 237, 249, 256; *see also* Output; and legislation; 57, 106, 108, 111, 119-121, 123, 127-131; public: 103, 116, 121, 123, 125
Hearst papers: 235, 256, 257
Holden *v.* Hardy: 118, 120-125, 127, 128
Homestead Strike: 207
Hours: *see* Government regulation, Uniformity, Work-day, Work-week
Hours of Service Act, 1907; 84-86, 117, 118

Industrial Brotherhood: 39
Industrial leaders: 5, 16, 17, 160
Industrial unrest: 80, 127, 223, 251
Industrial Welfare Commission: 115, 116. *See* Appendix C.
Industries: continuous: 14, 209, 214, 238, 239; unorganized: 171. *See also* Steel Industry. *See* Appendix G
Intellectuals: 5, 28, 224, 237
Inter-Church World Movement: 211-213
International Working People's Association: 156
International Workmen's Congress: 161
Interstate Commerce Commission: 84, 85n, 86, 90, 91
Interpretation of hour legislation: federal: 47, 68-73, 75, 77-79, 85; state: 100, 108. *See also* Court decisions.
Iron Moulders' Union: 32, 35, 53n, 141, 150

Jewish Sabbath Alliance: 253

Knights of Labor: 31, 39-48, 149, 150, 153-155, 160; local assemblies: 102, 155, 156, 158

Labor: 5, 11, 21, 70, 79, 81, 97, 109, 120, 121, 129, 133, 232, 234, 237, 248, 250, 251, 256; leaders: 127, 137; opposition to shorter hours: 206, 210, 215, 226; organized: 7, 12, 22, 23, 26, 27, 54-56, 66, 71, 77, 81, 113, 120, 137, 166, 169, 170, 217, 225, 242, 251, 254; unorganized: 22, 27, 31, 54, 55, 56, 58, 107, 137, 168, 172, 217, 221, 242. *See also* Arguments, Direct Action
Labor Departments: Federal: 32n, 81n, 92, 106, 171n, 189n, 208, 209, 234n, 235n, 254; State: 19n, 75, 99-101, 103-105, 110, 115, 122, 125, 139, 143, 148, 155-159, 161, 229n, 239, 240n. *See also* Massachusetts Bureau of Statistics of Labor
Labor organizations: 31-40, 60, 67, 93, 140, 150, 154, 192; local: 24, 95, 105, 139; national: 11, 62, 72, 149. *See* names of *individual organizations.*
Labor Party: 36-39, 66, 145, 146
LaFollette Bill: 92, 93
Laissez-faire: 24, 59, 60, 126
League for Industrial Rights: 64, 65
Legislative Action: 5, 6, 21-28, 138, 139, 141, 150, 153, 165, 168, 217, 221, 222, 258. *See* Part I.
Legislative hearings: 60-63, 77, 238
Legislatures, State: 36, 37, 39, 47, 61, 67, 82, 95-97, 99, 100, 106-111, 113, 119, 121-123, 126-128, 130, 133, 141, 228
Leisure: 6, 13, 14, 16, 17, 39, 40, 137, 162, 223, 250, 252, 254, 256
Lochner: People *v.*: 125; *v.* New York: 126-129, 131, 132
Lockout: 152, 192, 198, 200, 201

McNeill, George: 33, 39, 143, 150, 160
Machinists: 12, 53n, 54, 155, 156, 163, 232, 235, 241
Management, increased efficiency in: 6, 15, 223
Manufacturers' Associations: 45, 178, 182, 191, 192, 194, 197-199, 202, 204, 248, 256. *See also* National Association of Manufacturers.
Massachusetts Bureau of Statistics of Labor: 59, 107, 109, 139n, 224-229
May Day: 161
Miners and smelters: *see* Holden *v.* Hardy

Minors: 39, 50, 52, 55, 58, 108, 112, 133

National Association of Manufacturers: 62-64, 80, 249, 250, 253, 254
National Cash Register Company: 234, 235
National Consumers League: 131n, 195
National Industrial Conference Board: 242n, 248, 249, 254
National Labor Union: 11, 36-40, 66, 95, 96, 139n
"Natural evolution": 27, 221, 238, 241, 254

Open shop: 175, 178, 182, 184, 201
Output: 5, 20, 252n; in relation to hours: 13, 15, 228, 231, 233, 236, 240, 243, 248-250, 256. See also Production
Overtime. 7, 47, 85, 109, 208; punitive: 18, 21, 25, 79, 82, 85-90, 97, 130, 131, 166, 180, 246, 247n. See also Contract. See Appendices B-E

Panama Canal: 76
Parry, D. M.: 62, 63
Patent Laws: 39, 67
Phillips, Wendell: 33, 34, 39, 139
Pioneer: 11, 27, 28, 95, 106, 110, 223, 233n, 258
Pittsburgh Survey: 208
Police Power: 98, 103, 108, 120, 121, 123, 125, 128, 129
Powderly, T. V.: 40, 41, 43-47, 155
Precedent judicial: 23, 85, 95, 98, 105, 106, 114, 118, 122-125, 129
President of the United States: 48, 51, 57, 70, 71, 76, 78, 84, 86, 87, 91, 92, 212, 214, 215
Production: 109, 242; and consumption: 13, 17, 20, 167; and hours: 16, 18, 21, 186, 206, 226, 227, 231, 240, 243-246; *see also* Output; increases in: 5, 12, 16, 17, 167, 196; mass: 17, 252; war: 81, 197, 210
Productive capacity per worker: 252
Profits: 13, 15, 19, 226, 230, 232, 251; war: 81

Prosperity: 6, 11, 17, 20, 38, 167, 170, 223, 255
Public opinion: 14, 34, 43, 92, 97, 132, 167, 168, 172, 190, 208, 210, 212, 216, 221, 231
"Public works": 73, 74, 101, 105, 106

Railroad Brotherhoods: 57, 82-84, 86-90, 165
Railroad executives: 83, 86, 87, 90
Railroads: 12, 82, 84-86, 89, 90, 149, 257; intrastate: 118
Relations between Labor and Capital: 232, 236, 237; Senate Committee Report: 149, 229-231. See also United States Industrial Commission
Rest period: 82, 84, 91, 117, 118, 235

Saturday half-holiday: 7, 82, 181, 243
Seamen: 22, 91-93
Secret circular: 44, 155
Senate Investigation: 209, 212. See also Relations between Capital and Labor.
Socialism: 54, 56, 63, 157; state: 117
Standard of living: 17, 259
Steel Industry: 27, 172, 206-217, 229, 232, 233, 238, 240, 244-247, 253
Steward, Ira: 16, 17, 33, 34, 39, 137, 139, 250
Stockholders' Investigating Committee: 209, 214
Strike: assessment: 172, 175, 176, 179-183, 217; benefit: 147, 180, 184; breakers: 156, 184, 198, 212
Strikes: 12, 48, 86, 87, 91, 138-140, 149, 150, 153, 163, 189-191, 217, 226, 233, 235; general, of May 1, 1886; 43-46, 49, 138, 154-159, 164, 174, 229; of May 1, 1890: 160-162, 164; Amalgamated Clothing Workers': 192-195, 197-200; Granite Cutters, 1900: 163, 164; Typographical Union: 174, 175, 179, 183-187; steel workers: 27, 207, 208, 211-214, 246; to enforce Eight Hour Laws: 26, 37, 97, 101, 122, 138, 140-148, 151, 152, 230

INDEX 299

Sylvis, William: 32, 33, 35n, 37, 150

Technological Improvement: 6, 12, 13, 15, 40, 41, 169, 208, 223
Ten Hour Laws: 23, 25, 32, 83, 111, 112, 113, 116, 131n; Massachusetts, for women, 1874: 107-110, 228; New York, for bakers, 1895: 124-128. *See* Appendices, A, C, E
Trade Union Action: *see* Direct Action
Trade Union label: 144, 152n, 191
Trade unions: *see* Unions
Trades: organized: 21, 26, 157, 164, 185, 189, 196, 236, 254; seasonal: 18, 21; unhealthy or dangerous: 55, 58, 125-128; unorganized: 6, 189, 190
Typographical Union, International: 152, 165, 171-188, 204, 217, 240n

Unemployment: 6, 12, 13, 17, 38, 44, 61, 66, 68, 91, 137, 148, 167, 169, 204, 213, 224, 255-258; cyclical: 18-20, 89, 175, 188, 258; seasonal: 18, 20, 196; technological: 18-20, 89, 162, 168, 175, 188, 191, 196, 203, 205
Unemployment: assessment: 188; insurance: 205
Uniformity of hours: 24, 51, 68, 94, 116
Union: 54, 83, 159, 170, 194, 195, 200, 202, 203, 206, 211, 235, 238, 254; non-union: 54, 171, 179, 180, 185, 194, 203, 204
Unions: 18, 20, 26, 27, 32, 50, 55, 122, 140, 141, 145, 149-151, 154, 162, 166, 171, 207, 216, 233, 239n, 240, 247; company; 167, 221, 230, 241; craft: 44, 171, 212, 217; German-speaking: 158; industrial: 171, 212; local: 142, 150-152, 155, 164, 172-174, 176, 177, 179, 180, 182, 183, 186-188, 191, 194, 203; national: 31, 35, 125, 150-153, 165, 170; trade: 6, 27, 34, 38, 54, 115, 144, 146, 164, 167, 170, 221, 222, 241, 255. *See also* Labor organizations, *and individual unions*. *See* Appendix F.

Unionize: 91, 200, 235; non-unionize: 239
Unionism: 27, 139, 171, 207, 217
United Garment Workers: 171, 189-192
United Mine Workers: 53n, 54, 56, 122, 162
United States Industrial Commission, 1901: 83, 84, 124, 137n, 232, 233, 235
United States Steel Corporation: 209-215, 246, 247
United Typothetae of America: 174, 176-178, 181-183

Voluntary Action: 5, 11, 16, 21, 27, 28, 32, 47, 59, 170, 195, 199; classic examples of: 237, 239, 242. *See* Part III

Wages: and hours: 15-17, 61, 69, 70, 90, 100-102, 104, 106, 137, 142, 151, 154, 157, 162, 167, 173, 174, 182, 183, 188, 196, 198, 203, 226, 232, 240, 244, 246, 250, 252, 255, 257; and overtime: 80. *See also* Overtime
War: 78; Civil: 6, 11, 13, 21, 31, 94, 107, 138, 171, 173, 197, 224, 248; World: 24, 26, 57, 79-81, 89, 165, 166, 197, 210, 224, 239, 241-243, 251. *See* Appendix B
War Department: 76, 79, 195
War Labor Board: 80, 81, 197
Washington Hours' Convention: 67
Williams, J. H., Company: 232, 233
Women: 23-25, 50, 52, 55, 58, 61, 62, 67, 94, 95, 106-116, 130, 133, 222, 234-236
Work-day: 6, 7, 12, 21, 27, 31, 86, 91, 167, 168, 208, 226, 228, 237, 258; elastic: 257, 258; fifteen hour: 42, 91, 119; thirteen: 139, 228, 238; twelve: 14, 25, 91, 207-211, 213-215, 228, 229, 231, 232, 239n, 240, 245, 247; eleven: 119, 139, 208, 227, 228, 231, 232, 235, 237, 238, 257; ten: 7, 25, 32, 44, 45, 59, 61, 63, 70, 84, 85, 107, 114, 120, 124, 128, 139-141, 143, 144, 148, 150, 152, 157, 173, 216n, 225, 227, 228, 230-232, 235-237, 239, 240, 242-244, 257; ten, basic: 82, 83; nine and a half: 45, 46, 176, 234; nine: 25, 46, 49, 62, 92, 150,

151, 154, 155, 158, 161, 162, 174-177, 179, 232, 233, 235, 239-244; eight: 7, 11, 16, 21, 25, 31-40, 42-47, 49, 50, 52, 54-57, 61, 63-67, 85, 86, 90, 93, 95, 124, 129, 133, 139, 140, 142-146, 148-166, 168, 173, 174, 177-181, 184, 191, 195, 206-210, 213-216, 225-227, 229, 234, 236-241, 243-246, 248, 251, 255; eight, basic: 79, 80, 81, 86-88, 166, 246; six: 66, 89, 90, 169, 255-257. *See* Appendices A-F
Work-week: 6, 7, 12, 16, 20, 91, 117, 192, 199, 209, 211, 216, 226, 244, 247n, 252, 255; seven day: 91, 210, 213, 253; five day; 7, 19n, 66, 90, 99, 166-169, 185-188, 205, 244, 252-256; three day: 244; one hundred to one hundred and thirty two hour: 125; sixty hour: 108, 116, 126, 129n, 209, 216, 226, 229, 231, 257; fifty eight: 110, 231, 249; fifty six: 110, 229, 249, 251; fifty five: 129n, 247 n, 249; fifty four: 110, 114, 178, 190, 193, 200, 247n, 248, 249, 251; fifty two: 190, 191, 247n, 248; fifty one: 191, 193, 195, 247n; fifty: 119, 191, 193, 248; forty eight: 25, 58, 111, 113, 114, 182, 190, 193-197, 199-202, 233n, 247n, 249, 257; forty four: 81, 82, 166, 181-183, 185, 196-203, 205, 251; forty four, basic; 247n; forty: 188, 201-205, 244. *See* Appendices B-H
Works' Councils: 241-247